Just MARRIED

Mark D. Ogletree, PhD

Covenant Communications, Inc.

Cover image: *Holding Hands* © BenDower, iStockphotography.com

Cover design copyright © 2015 by Covenant Communications, Inc.

Published by Covenant Communications, Inc.
American Fork, Utah

Printed in the United States of America
First Printing: May 2015

21 20 19 18 17 16 15   10 9 8 7 6 5 4 3 2 1

ISBN: 978-1-62108-903-2

Just MARRIED

To Janie, the love of my life and the wife of my youth. Your faith and devotion to the gospel have been a constant source of inspiration to me. I have learned more about being a great husband, father, and grandfather by watching your selfless example. Thank you for always believing in me.

Acknowledgments

I express my thanks to Covenant Communications for inviting me to pursue this work. I am particularly grateful for Phil Reschke and his encouragement with the manuscript, and Stacey Owen, whose editing made this volume more readable and user friendly.

I am thankful to my wife, Janie, and her unfailing support and wonderful insight. Reliving some of our early marriage experiences as I worked on this manuscript was an incredible journey down memory lane.

I also express thanks to my married children and their spouses—Brittany and Tyler, Brandon and Amanda, and Bethany and Will—for the practical suggestions and humorous experiences they shared with me.

I am also indebted to my students at Brigham Young University. Their thirst for knowledge and desire for practical marriage tools were the inspiration behind this endeavor.

I, alone, am responsible for the content in this book.

Mark D. Ogletree
January 2015

CONTENTS

Introduction xiii

Chapter 1: Understanding Marital Expectations 1

Chapter 2: Effective Communication in Marriage 15

Chapter 3: Expressions of Dating, Love, and Affection 29

Chapter 4: Financial Preparation for Newlyweds 43

Chapter 5: Learning to Deal with Differences in Marriage 53

Chapter 6: Managing Individual Differences in Marriage 73

Chapter 7: Personality Issues in Marriage 83

Chapter 8: Resolving Conflict in Marriage 99

Chapter 9: Meekness in Marriage 115

Chapter 10: Making Marital Adjustments 133

Chapter 11: Sexual Intimacy in Marriage 151

Chapter 12: The Transition to Parenthood 177

Chapter 13: Dealing with Parents and In-Laws 197

Chapter 14: Applying Christlike Virtues in Marriage 211

Chapter 15: Keeping Your Marriage Strong 227

Conclusion 241

INTRODUCTION

"It is often said that being happily and successfully married is generally not so much a matter of marrying the right person as it is *being the right person.*"
-President Howard W. Hunter[1]

YEARS AGO, PRESIDENT SPENCER W. Kimball prophesied that the "time will come when only those who believe deeply and actively in the family will be able to preserve their families in the midst of the gathering evil around us."[2] That day has come. We live in a time when the forces of evil have concentrated their attack on marriage and family life. Social media, news outlets, the Internet, and prime-time television programming are no longer family friendly institutions. Moreover, many of us live in communities where divorce, single-parenthood, cohabitation, and same-gender influences are prevalent. Face it—we now live in an anti-family culture. To be happily married and raise a righteous family may be more difficult now than ever before.

The late LDS family therapist and scholar Carlfred Broderick called marriage "the most popular—and the roughest—contact sport in the country."[3] There is ample evidence that Dr. Broderick was spot on. Today, entering the marriage arena can be a risky proposition, which could explain why fewer and fewer people are willing to give it a shot. Recently, the Pew Research Center reported that 40 percent of Americans believe that marriage is becoming obsolete.[4] Another study documented that among adults between the ages of 25–34, 45 percent are married, but 46 percent have *never* tied the knot. Therefore, the proportion of young adults who have never been married now exceeds the number of those who are.

Not only are fewer people marrying, but for those individuals who choose to wed, they are waiting much longer to tie the knot. In a recent publication entitled *Knot Yet*, researchers reported that in 1960, the average age to marry was 20 for women and 23 for men. Today, the average woman is 27 when she marries, while the average man is 29—historic highs for both genders.[5]

Nevertheless, the probability of an adult marrying at some point still hovers around 90 percent.[6] Therefore, most people will marry at some point in their lives, but almost one-half of those marriages will fail and end in divorce. Incidentally, for the one-half of people who stay married, I do not wish to imply that their marriages are completely full of bliss, excitement, and satisfaction. For too many, marriage is not always synonymous with happiness.

Perhaps for this reason, and for many others, instead of marrying, many couples in America are electing to cohabitate. The Centers for Disease Control and Prevention reported that between 2006 and 2010, almost 50 percent of women cohabited with a partner, compared with 34 percent in 1995. Fifty years ago, hardly anyone lived together prior to marriage; today, practically everyone does. However, contrary to what many people believe, cohabitation does not necessarily lead to marriage. In one recent study, 40 percent of first-time premarital cohabitations transitioned to marriage within 3 years, which means 60 percent did not.[7] Unfortunately, where cohabitation does not necessarily lead to marriage, it often leads to parenthood. In our country, 40 percent of all births are out of wedlock.[8] Many of these children will be raised in adverse conditions by a single mother or relative.

Soul-Mate Marriage

The Millennial Generation is different from previous generations; many of these individuals do not want to take on the responsibilities and obligations that accompany marriage and parenthood. Instead, they seek for "soul-mate marriages," where all of their personal needs and fantasies can be met by an ideal spouse. Soul-mate marriages are characterized by a lack of responsibility, commitment, and children. Such couples want an eternal honeymoon, complete with constant intimacy, romance, and deep emotional connection. Couples in soul-mate marriages would rather read poetry to each other while they walk their poodle down the street than raise children or create strong families. In their minds, children would interfere with their beauty sleep and time at the spa.

Time magazine recently ran a cover photograph of a young married couple lying on a beach together, wearing matching swimsuits and sunglasses. The caption was "The Childfree Life: When having it all means not having children." *Time* reported that from 2007 to 2011, the fertility rate in America decreased 9 percent. Today, 20 percent of American women end their childbearing years child-free, compared to 10 percent of women in the 1970s.[9] Incidentally, to sustain a population, there should be a replacement rate of 2.1. The American fertility rate was once the envy of the world; however, in 2013 this rate dropped to 1.88—the lowest since 1987.[10] Not only will this trend have a significant impact on the American economy, but it also speaks of a self-absorbed society that seems to have little interest in the future of our country.

Divorce in the LDS Culture

How do these trends impact newly married Latter-day Saints? Mormons are not immune to divorce or marital challenges. LDS scholars Alan Hawkins and Tamara Fackrell recently reported that 25 to 30 percent of LDS couples who regularly attend church experience a divorce. "Other researchers estimate that the lifetime divorce rate for returned missionary men was about 12 percent and for women about 16 percent."[11] Latter-day Saints report higher-quality marriages and fewer divorces when compared to those not of our faith. Several years ago, the *Los Angeles Times* reported that Mormon temple marriages are built to last, citing a 6-percent divorce rate among temple marriages. *Demography Magazine* concluded that members of The Church of Jesus Christ of Latter-day Saints who marry in one of the Church's temples are the least likely of all Americans to divorce.[12] That doesn't mean that we, as Latter-day Saints, do not have challenges in our marriages. However, with an eternal perspective, we strive to work through our marriage problems rather than simply throw in the towel.

Stress-Filled Marriages

Overall, Latter-day Saints marry at a younger age when compared to national averages. In fact, there is a good chance that if you are reading this book, you are married and in college at the same time. Many of you may be working full-time or at least part-time as you navigate your first years of marriage and your final years of college. There are many roles and responsibilities to juggle as newlyweds. Beware of biting off more than you can chew in the early years of your marriage.

Dr. James Dobson once warned young married couples to be aware and concerned about a marriage filled with busyness and stress. "Beware of this danger [over-commitment and physical exhaustion]. It is especially insidious [treacherous] for young couples who are trying to get started in a profession or school. Do not try to go to college, work full-time, have a baby, manage a toddler, fix up a house, and start a business all at once."[13] Funny, that is exactly what many Latter-day Saints do! We often marry while we are relatively young, in school, working, and starting our families. Despite all of these challenges, there is no reason *not* to marry and expect a life of happiness ahead. However, we should also be wise enough to know that if we do not make time for our spouse and nurture the relationship, then our marriage will lose momentum and strength, and both partners will be frustrated and unfulfilled.

More than 60 percent of the population of the state of Utah report being Latter-day Saints.[14] Therefore, by analyzing marriage and divorce statistics from Utah, we can make some general inferences about Latter-day Saint marriages. Consider the following statistics that show the percentage of divorces in Utah and when they occur during the marriage.

Duration of Marriage	Percentage of Divorces	Cumulative Percentage
Less than 1 year	6.5	6.5
1 Year	8	14.5
2 Years	8.4	22.9
3 Years	8	30.9
4 Years	7.2	38.1
5 Years	6.1	44.2
6 Years	5.5	49.7[15]

According to this table, of all the divorces that occur in Utah, 6.5 percent take place before the couple has been married one year, and 8 percent happen during the first year. Half of all divorces in Utah occur within the first six years of marriage. The question is why. Why do so many divorces occur early in the marriage? Perhaps some couples are not mature enough to marry. Maybe others are selfish or difficult to deal with. I am sure addictions also play a role in some of these divorces. Or possibly some of the couples were not equipped to deal with the stress of balancing school, work, pregnancy, new careers, in-laws, and relocating to a new city.

Another question is, "Could some of those divorces have been prevented?" Sure they could have. Most divorces could be prevented if couples kept the commandments and their covenants, worked at practicing Christlike attributes, and focused on meeting each other's needs. When challenges occur in marriage, the best option isn't to divorce but to seek forgiveness and change behaviors. As Latter-day Saints, we should be committed for the long haul. We don't pull the plug when we have difficulties; we find out what's wrong and fix the problems!

The Richly Rewarding Life

Being married and having children can be one of the richest experiences life has to offer. Yes, it takes effort, work, and sacrifice to be happily married and raise a righteous family, but isn't that the purpose of our mortality? The greatest, richest, deepest, and most significant experiences in my life have been with my wife and children. I cannot imagine an existence without them. President Ezra Taft Benson taught that "marriage, home, and family are established by God as part of His divine plan for the blessing of His children. The richest blessings and deepest joys of this life and the life to come are tied up with the performance with these sacred duties. In fact, our very exaltation in the celestial kingdom is directly related to the family and the eternity of the marriage covenant."[16] I wholeheartedly agree.

For those couples who choose to marry and raise families, you may feel you are swimming in a tumultuous sea, with the winds, waves, and storms brought on by the anti-marriage culture. Thank goodness, we are navigating those seas in the good ship *Zion*. For our compass, we have the scriptures, the words of the living prophets, and the Holy Ghost to guide and direct us. Our first mate is the prophet—God's mouthpiece on the earth—and of course, our captain is the Savior himself. With that team, we won't fail, no matter how turbulent the conditions become. If we follow the directives of our captain and first mate, we will be successful.

This book is to help you navigate through the first years of marriage. In the anti-marriage culture we live in, creating a happy and fulfilling marriage is not an easy task. Back in the days when your grandparents lived, it seemed like everyone was married and had families. The tenor of the country was pro-family and pro-religion. It was much easier to create a happy marriage in a culture that endorsed and supported the family. Today, those of us who are married and have children are swimming upstream against an extremely strong current.

This does not mean you cannot be successful in your marriage or in raising children. What it does imply is that you may not get much support from the government, the community, your neighbors, and friends. Thank goodness we have the Church and wonderful Saints who surround us, sustain us, and support us. If you want to be successful in this endeavor, you will not only need ideals and beliefs, but you will also need skills. The purpose of this book is to help you identify the values you believe in, to help you become converted to some of the gospel principles that will make your marriage stronger, and to acquire some of the skills you need to be successful in marriage.

Although this is the first book I have written alone, I do not believe writing is something that is ever done in isolation. There were many times during the course of this writing process that I felt the guidance of heaven as I thought, prayed, and wrote. I am also thankful for my wife, Janie, who has been such a wonderful source of inspiration and motivation in my life. As I wrote about many of these experiences from our first years of marriage, I often had a lump in my throat. Since those early married days in the mid-1980s, our love has continued to grow and deepen. We both love each other, our children, their spouses, and our grandchildren. The psalmist wrote, "Lo, children are an heritage of the Lord: and the fruit of the womb is his reward. As arrows are in the hand of a mighty man; so are children of the youth. Happy is the man that hath his quiver full of them: they shall not be ashamed, but they shall speak with the enemies in the gate" (Psalms 127:3–5). For Janie and me, our quiver is full, and our cup "runneth over" (Psalms 23:5) with blessings we never imagined from our children, their spouses, and our grandchildren.

I also wish to thank so many of the students I have taught at Brigham Young University. I teach a course in the religion department on marriage and the Latter-day Saint family. Many of my students have shaped my thinking through the experiences they have shared in the classroom and in the "one-on-one" visits in my office. It is such a privilege to teach at BYU and be surrounded by the greatest colleagues and students our country has to offer.

I hope this book will be helpful as you begin the greatest journey of your life—that of marriage and family life. My desire is that the doctrines, principles, and practices in this book will help you to have a happy and successful marriage. I also pray that our Heavenly Father will give you the love, guidance, and direction you need as your forge your journey together.

He will if you ask Him; He wants you to be happy and successful. May God bless you!

References

1 Howard W. Hunter, *The Teachings of Howard W. Hunter,* ed. Clyde J. Williams, (Salt Lake City: Deseret Book, 1997), 130.

2 Spencer W. Kimball, "Families Can Be Eternal," *Ensign*, November 1980, 4.

3 Dr. Carlfred Broderick, *Couples* (New York: Simon & Schuster, 1979), 13.

4 D. Cohn, J. Passel, G. Livingstone, W. Wang & E. Patten, "Barely Half of U.S. Adults Are Married—A Record Low," *Pew Research Center*, 14 December 2011, 2.

5 K. Hymowitz, J. Carroll, W. B. Wilcox & K. Kaye, *Knot Yet: The Benefits and Costs of Delayed Marriage in America* (The National Marriage Project at the University of Virginia, 2013), 3.

6 "In U.S., Proportion Married at Lowest Recorded Levels," Mark Mather & Diana Lavery, *Population Reference Bureau*, accessed 27 October 2014, http://www.prb.org/Publications/Articles/2010/usmarriagedecline.aspx.

7 C. Copen, K. Daniels & W. Mosher, "First Premarital Cohabitation in the United States: 2006–2010 National Survey of Family Growth," *National Health Statistics Reports*, Number 64, 4 April 2013, 1–3.

8 J. Martin, B. Hamilton, M. Osterman, S. Curtin & T. Matthews, "Births: Final Data for 2012," *National Vital Statistics Reports,* Volume 62, Number 9, 30 December 2013, 1.

9 "Having It All Without Having Children," Lauren Sandler, *Time*, 12 August 2013; http://time.com/241/having-it-all-without-having-children/.

10 "America's Fertility Rate Falling, Now Lower Than France's," Lois Collins, *Deseret News*, 17 August 2012, http://www.deseretnews.com/article/865560796/Americas-fertility-rate-falling-now-lower-than-Frances.html?pg=all.

11 Alan J. Hawkins & Tamara A. Fackrell, "Should I Keep Trying to Work It Out? Sacred and Secular Perspectives on the Crossroads of Divorce," *BYU Studies*, 50, 2, (2011), 143–144.

12 See "Temple Marriage," Newsroom, *The Church of Jesus Christ of Latter-day Saints*, http://www.mormonnewsroom.org/article/temple-marriage.

13 Dr. James Dobson, *Love for a Lifetime: Building a Marriage that Will Go the Distance* (Sisters, Oregon: Multnomah Publishers, 2003), 95.

14 "Census: Share of Utah's Mormon Residents Holds Steady," Matt Canham, *The Salt Lake Tribune*, 17 April 2012, http://www.sltrib.com/sltrib/home3/53909710-200/population-lds-county-utah.html.csp.

15 Utah's Vital Statistics: *Marriages and Divorces, 2009–2010*; Table R16: Dissolutions of marriage by duration of marriage in years and type of decree: Utah, 2010, R10-22.

16 Ezra Taft Benson, *Teachings of President Ezra Taft Benson*, (Salt Lake City: Deseret Book, 1988), 490–491.

CHAPTER 1
Understanding Marital Expectations

"Two people coming from different backgrounds learn soon after the ceremony is performed that stark reality must be faced. There is no longer a life of fantasy or of make-believe; we must come out of the clouds and put our feet firmly on the earth. Responsibility must be assumed and new duties must be accepted. Some personal freedoms must be relinquished, and many adjustments, unselfish adjustments, must be made."
-President Spencer W. Kimball[17]

I OFTEN ASK NEWLY MARRIED students in my classes, "What has surprised you most about marriage?" Of course, their responses vary. I have had women say, "I had no idea he was going to be on the computer as much as he is." Men have told me, "I didn't understand how long it would take her to get ready for church. She starts two hours before our services begin, and we're still late."

Once couples are married, idealistic expectations can begin to take their toll on the relationship. If couples want to have a successful marriage, they will need to learn to identify and work through their expectations—especially the ones that are *not* so practical. Before marriage, each couple has expectations of what their future would soon be like. Most of us had dreams of the perfect spouse, and we hoped our future marriage would be characterized by complete marital harmony, romance, love, and, of course, intimacy. For example, there are men who assume they will come home each night to a perfectly clean home and eat a succulent steak dinner while their wife rubs their shoulders and talks to them about their day. For women, many hope that their marriage will be akin to a romance novel, or maybe at least a vampire movie. I am sure there are women who go into marriage expecting poetry, music, song, love notes, roses, and sharing deep feelings late into the night.

Janie and I have learned that the older we get, the more diverse we are in terms of our expectations regarding fun and entertainment. Janie is an introvert, and I am a full-fledged extrovert. For a day of entertainment, Janie would love to watch a movie at home, sip some hot chocolate, play a board game, or put together a 5,000-piece puzzle. Unfortunately, those activities don't do much for me. Instead, I would like to get my kids or some friends, rent some WaveRunners, get on the lake early in the morning, and try my hardest to end up in the emergency room by the end of the day. For me, there isn't anything much better than going about forty miles an hour on a WaveRunner, cutting the handlebars as sharp as you can, and seeing how far you can fly. Janie thinks that's just plain stupid. So did the doctor in the ER.

I understand that these examples are "lighter" in nature. However, I know that many couples expect much more from each other when it comes to sexual intimacy or affection or support or appreciation or even spirituality. In these areas, deeper problems can emerge if such expectations are not addressed. A husband who needs affection and doesn't get it will live in constant frustration. A wife who needs time or deeper communication with her husband yet is neglected will be miserable in her marriage.

The Origin of Our Expectations

Where do our marital expectations come from? Many of them emerge from the family we were raised in. Whether you like it or not, your parents served as role models for your future marriage. Perhaps you will try to emulate what you saw in their marriage or, in some cases, do the complete opposite! Perhaps as you were growing up, you noticed a certain couple in your ward or community who seemed to have marriage figured out. Conceivably, their portrayal of marriage is what you hope for in your own relationship. However, what you may never realize or comprehend is the serious trouble a couple may be experiencing when their marriage is not on public display.

I remember practically idolizing a couple and their relationship when I was a teenager. Both the husband and wife were sharp looking, "cool," and talked to all the teenagers in the neighborhood. Both were models of fitness and could often be seen jogging together through our subdivision. They had cute little kids that often played in the front yard. This couple seemed to have it all together. I thought, *This is what I hope my future marriage is like.* Then, one day, I noticed their house was for sale. My mom explained to me that this incredible couple was getting divorced because the husband had been engaged in an affair with a woman at his office for many years. I was shocked and wondered if anyone could have a happy marriage.

Others gain their marital expectations from the books they read or the movies they watch. Unfortunately, the way marriage is depicted in romance novels is that couples cannot keep their hands off each other as they ride horses together on the beach in Costa Rica. Then later in the evening they eat shish kebabs by the fire—of course, on the beach, next to the horses. In the movies we watch in awe as couples ride together on a Harley Davidson and then stop at a quaint Italian restaurant on the California coast where they feed each other spaghetti and laugh hysterically at their inside jokes. What the media never exposes in marriage are the real-life scenarios, such as who is going to change the baby's diaper or unclog the toilet?

The Role of Marital Expectations

LDS marriage and family therapist Charles C. Beckert taught, "A major cause of marital dissatisfaction is the unwillingness and/or ability of one partner in a marriage relationship to behave in the manner expected by the spouse."[18] When expectations aren't met, spouses become frustrated. Eventually, frustration turns into anger and resentment, and the marriage quickly becomes unsatisfying, unhealthy, and unhappy.

For example, when Janie and I first started dating, we jogged often and played racquetball at least weekly. I remembered thinking how great life would be once we were married. In my fantasy world, our married life would consist of waking up together at 6:00 a.m., reading our scriptures, jogging with each other down the tree-lined streets of Provo, eating a wonderful breakfast together, and leaving for work or school by 8:00. I had every reason to believe that after about fifteen years of marriage, we would instill this same pattern into the lives of all our able-bodied children. Not only would Janie and I be jogging together, but our eight children would be jogging behind us, single file. I imagined we would all be wearing matching jogging suits and whistling hymns as we made our way down the lane of our beautiful neighborhood.

However, that is not what happened. Shortly after our honeymoon, we returned to Provo in April to begin our summer jobs and hopefully save enough money for our fall tuition. The day after we moved into our basement apartment just south of the Brigham Young University campus, I suggested to Janie that we wake up early and go jogging. Dutifully, Janie accompanied me on our morning run, but I could tell she wasn't really into it. After about a mile, we stopped, and she confessed her major transgression. She said, "There is something I need to tell you."[a]

I braced myself for the worst and said, "Go ahead."

Janie admitted, "I actually hate jogging. I simply don't like it at all. Never have, and never will."

I was confused because we had jogged so often during our engagement. So I asked the obvious question, "Janie, why have you jogged with me almost daily the past six months?"

She said, "Because I wanted to be with you, and I knew you liked it when I jogged with you. But now that we're married, I need to come out of the closet. I abhor jogging, and worse than that, I don't like waking up at 6:00 a.m. either."

Wow, I was stunned. My whole plan of having a jogging family with matching sweatpants was just flushed down the toilet. However, I loved Janie very much, and I realized this issue would not be a deal breaker. After all, it wasn't that she was throwing *all* exercise out the window. She explained to me that she still wanted to do aerobics and dance classes, but she simply didn't like running. I had to lower my expectations in this area and realize that my new bride was different from me. The more I thought about it, I knew I needed to relax my expectation and find other activities we could do together.

Similarly, before we were married, Janie gave me a list she had created a few years earlier in her Laurel class. The list consisted of all the key attributes that her future husband would possess. One of the attributes read: *My future husband will love politics and keep informed of current events.* At the time, I wasn't really into politics, news, or current events. However, in order to make her happy, I began reading the newspaper and watching the news. In fact, for many years, I listened to several radio programs daily that were political in nature, and Janie and I religiously watched the late night news together each night before bed. However, after about fifteen years of these activities, I realized that the news stressed me out and politics was quite frustrating—at least for me. As I became older, and my life became much more demanding both with Church responsibilities and professionally, the last thing I needed before going to bed was to view acts of war, violence, and terror. So several years ago, *I* came clean and told

---

a   Since I'm a worry wart, I thought this is where she would drop the bombshell and tell me that she really didn't like me that much and it took her a full week of marriage to figure that out.

Janie I was done with the news and politics. I explained to her that it was much better for my mental health to watch something funny before going to bed instead of something nerve-wracking and stressful. I still casually read the paper each day, but that's about all. I know Janie is disappointed because she is passionate about politics and civic affairs; nevertheless, she still loves me and has been willing to let go of this marital expectation.

Several months ago, Janie and I were riding with our daughter-in-law, Amanda, on a road trip. Since we had plenty of free time, I asked Amanda how my son was treating her in their marriage. She reported that things were going well but that married life was very different from what she expected. Amanda then related to me that before she and my son, Brandon, were married, she imagined they would go hand in hand to the grocery store. Amanda fantasized that they would meander up and down each aisle, holding hands, pushing their shopping cart, sharing jokes, flirting it up, and acting the same way many newlywed couples in Provo, Utah, act in grocery stores. Instead, something very different happened.

About a week after their wedding, Amanda said to Brandon, "Hey, we need to go to the grocery store to get some food. What time would you like to go?"

Brandon replied, "Never. I don't go to grocery stores. In fact, I hate shopping."

And that was it. Amanda reported that she went to the store alone, wiping tears from her eyes. She was so disappointed. Her expectation of romance in the produce aisle was ruined right off the bat. Without proper preparation, many spouses are surprised when their partner isn't as ambitious or romantic or happy as they thought they were during the engagement. Every couple should discuss their expectations long before the wedding day.

The Marital Expectation Quiz

I would recommend that you and your spouse respond to the following questions. If possible, have a civilized discussion where your answers differ.

1. How will you keep track of finances? Will you have a budget? Will you have two checking accounts or one? How will you invest your money? How much will you save each month? What do you need or expect from each other?

2. How will you deal with your parents/in-laws? How often will you visit them? How involved will they be in your personal decisions

and affairs? What do you expect from each other in terms of your relationships with your parents?

3. How will you demonstrate romance and physical affection in your marriage? How do you want each other to show love and affection? What do you need and expect from each other?

4. What role will the gospel play in your married lives? Will you read and study the scriptures together? When will you pray? How will you serve in the Church? How devoted will you be to your covenants? How can the doctrines of the gospel strengthen your relationship? What do you expect from each other in terms of spirituality? How will you keep the Sabbath day holy?

5. What will your roles be in the home? Who will be responsible for the yard work, home repairs, painting, fixing things up, and remodeling the home? Who will clean the garage? Who will make dinner and do the dishes? What do you think are important roles for a husband? What are important roles for a wife? How can you compromise? What do you expect from each other in terms of marital roles?

6. How will you communicate with each other in positive ways? Should you talk to each other when one of you is mad or let some steam off first? When is a good time for you to communicate? How can each of you become better listeners? What do you expect from each other in this area?

7. What kind of parents do you hope you will be? How do you see each other as future parents? How could you be a better parent? What are your expectations here?

8. What do you hope you will do for recreation and entertainment? How often should you go on dates or get away? What do you like to do for entertainment? What do you enjoy for recreation? What do you expect from each other?

9. What do you like to do on weekends? What would an ideal weekend be like for you? What could you see yourselves doing together? What household chores should be done on weekends? What do you expect from each other in this area?

10. What traditions did you have in your family? What traditions would you like to keep? What is your favorite Christmas tradition? What

traditions helped your family live the gospel? What do you expect from each other regarding traditions?

11. How will you resolve conflict in your marriage? How would you prefer that conflict is handled? How do you feel about marital conflict? What do you expect from each other when it comes to resolving your problems?

12. How do you feel about your spouse's career/work? Do you feel that they put their career over your family? How do you feel career and family should be balanced? What do you expect from each other?

13. How do you feel about your sexual relationship? Is there anything you could do to make things better? How do you feel about your sexual frequency? What do you expect from each other in terms of sexual intimacy?

14. How will you share in your parenting duties? Who will be responsible for what? Who will give primary care to the baby? What about a teenager? What do good fathers do? What do good mothers do? What do you expect from each other?

Negotiating Marital Expectations
So what do you expect from your spouse? What are some of your marriage ideals? Write down your marital expectations in the following areas. Feel free to jot down the expectation for your spouse and yourself.

	Your Expectations	Your Spouse's Expectations
Spirituality		
Education		
Career		
Fitness/ Exercise		

Financial Management		
Social Life		
Recreation		
Continued Courtship/ Dating/ Romance		
Child Rearing/ Discipline		
Following Prophets/ Keeping Commandments		
Household Duties/ Chores		
Sexual Intimacy		
Media Time/ Television/ Social Media		
Health/ Diet		
Appearance of Home/ Yard		

Several years ago, the Association of Mormon Counselors and Psychotherapists reported on the most common problems facing Latter-day Saint couples in marriage. According to the study, the number one issue facing LDS couples was *unrealistic expectations*.[19] Therefore, as a newlywed, you should understand that there is an extremely good chance you will have to navigate your way through swamps of unrealistic expectations throughout your marriage. Elder Russell M. Nelson's wife, Dantzel, was often asked how she managed with such a large family and a husband who was rarely home.[b] With a twinkle in her eye, she responded, "When I married him, I didn't expect much, so I was never disappointed."[20]

Perhaps some of us have set our expectations too high, and we must lower them so that they are much more realistic. Women, your husband most likely isn't going to write poetry each night and rub your feet in front of the fireplace while you watch *The Notebook*. Men, your wife is not going to laugh at every joke you tell and will probably not want to engage in sexual intimacy as much as you will. Both husbands and wives need to discuss their expectations and then strive to meet each other's needs.

Dr. David T. Seamons, an LDS marriage and family therapist, taught:

> So many of our expectations regarding what we think is "right" or "wrong" behavior, or "normal" to us, do not surface until our lives become more complicated by earning a living; a variety of homemaking tasks; car insurance, loans, and maintenance; debt; intimacy; pregnancy; colicky babies; how we reconcile after a spat; and myriad other potential trouble spots. Marital satisfaction— how well marriage satisfies our own personal goals—is influenced in important ways by how well our known and yet-to-be-discovered expectations mesh around as married partners.[21]

Meeting Expectations

How will you discover your spouse's expectations? How will they become aware of yours? How will you meet such expectations? You will have several steps.

First, you must be willing to discuss your expectations with each other.

Second, you must be prepared to compromise and work with each other. I recently talked to a newly married young woman who told me of a small dilemma she and her husband had to reconcile the first month of their marriage. They recently moved into a new home, and the wife was anxious to get to know the members of their ward. There was a Relief Society meeting that evening, and she hoped to attend and meet some new friends. On the other hand, her husband would be coming home from work and "expected" that they would have couple time together.

---

b   Elder Nelson was a busy heart surgeon and a stake president.

As this couple discussed their dilemma, the husband said, "Well, I'm not happy that you're going." To that, the wife responded, "Well, happy or not, I am going." This argument was fueled by unmet expectations. The husband thought that every night his wife would sit next to him on the couch while he watched television. The wife, on the other hand, was anxious to establish the tradition that they would be active in the Church and do their duties. So who is right, and who is wrong? There is no right or wrong. Both activities can be justified. The husband wanted to spend time with his wife, and the wife wanted to meet new members of her ward. However, this is something the couple will have to work out.

Third, after you have discussed each other's needs and expectations, you must strive to make your spouse happy.

Finally, you will periodically need to review your expectations and periodically adjust them.

I recommend that every couple have a weekly meeting to discuss their marriage and family relationship. In our health-conscience culture, many people work out at fitness centers, take vitamins, make regular visits to the doctor, and participate in triathlons. People who care about their health are passionate about taking care of their bodies. Likewise, individuals who hope that their cars will last a long time get regular tune-ups and oil changes. They even occasionally rotate their tires. Why don't we have the same passion for preserving and fortifying our marriages? After all, in the next life, all we will take with us is our knowledge, our memories and experiences, and our family relationships. Yet, what types of preventative maintenance measures do we take to preserve and strengthen our marriages? The couple's meeting provides a great opportunity for husbands and wives to solve problems before they begin and to create a happy and fulfilling relationship.

This meeting should *not* be an "inventory" or "grueling" session. This is a chance for couples to come together, coordinate, plan, and strengthen the marriage. It is an opportunity to review finances, goals, plans, and dreams. Of course, it would be a bonus if couples could discuss their marital needs and find out how they can best make their spouse happy. This is a very productive meeting if couples do it regularly.

I recommend the following agenda for a couple's meeting:

1. **Prayer:** No matter how you feel toward each other, a prayer is always an opportunity to bring the Spirit into your marriage. With the Lord directing you, you cannot go wrong.

2. **Spiritual thought or scripture:** Sharing scriptures and gospel principles with each other strengthens emotional bonds and creates a spiritual intimacy so that gospel ideas and feelings can be shared often.

3. **Reviewing the weekly calendar:** This is one of the greatest benefits to the couple's meeting. You can plan your week together, share your meetings and obligations with each other, and coordinate your lives so they will meld together—not apart. Early in our marriage, I would often walk out the door for a meeting, and Janie would ask, "Where are you going?" In my mind, I thought I had told her, but according to her, she knew nothing of it. Reviewing the calendar together can help reduce marital tension.

4. **Reviewing the budget:** It is a healthy practice for couples to get on the same page financially. I continue to meet with spouses in my counseling practice who have ruined their marriage with errant spending practices. Reviewing the budget, the income, and the bills together is a practice that will help you stay out of debt.

5. **Review family and parenting issues or issues a child is dealing with:** Proactively discussing problems is much better than trying to deal with them after the damage has been done. The couple meeting provides each of you with an opportunity to discuss family and parenting issues with calm, rational minds. This is more effective than trying to resolve such problems in the heat of the moment.

6. **Planning dates for the week or month:** Once again, taking a proactive approach to dating demonstrates how strongly you feel about the marriage. If a husband tells a wife on a Friday night to hop in the car, and they drive around town with no plan, the date is often unfulfilling. However, a well-planned, well-prepared date speaks volumes to a spouse. I believe husbands and wives should take turns planning dates each month. Husbands, when it's your turn, you have the "whole ball of wax," which includes getting a babysitter!

   Several years ago, our life became so hectic with children, work, and Church responsibilities that Janie and I discovered we hardly had any time for each other. Our only opportunity to date each other—Friday or Saturday evening—was filled with children's games and activities. We both discussed our expectation to continue to keep a spark in the romantic part of our relationship. At the time, I was a full-time marriage and family therapist and had my own practice. Since it was my business, I was in control of my schedule. Therefore, Janie and I started a fun tradition of going on lunch dates. The kids were in school, and I could often get away for a couple hours in the middle of the day so that we could be together. By thinking outside the box, we were able to find time for us and meet our marital expectations. You will be able to do the same as you discuss with each other your expectations and try to meet them.

7. **Reviewing couple's needs, goals, and expectations:** When you become frustrated with your marriage partner, you can often prevent emotional damage by saving your issue for the couple's meeting rather than spewing your venom all over your spouse in the heat of the moment. As you discuss needs and expectations, limit your issues to only one per week. Women, if you tell your husband twelve things you need from him, he's going to crash and burn. Husbands, if you overwhelm your wife with demanding needs, she may not be able to deliver any of them. This is a great opportunity for a wife to simply say, "I need to spend more time with you this week, is there something we could do together?" Or for a husband to say, "I think I could use more affection this week. I feel we're beginning to take each other for granted, and affection always helps me to feel connected to you." That's all. Keep it simple and don't overwhelm each other.

Couples should also review goals together. In my years as a marriage and family therapist, I have been amazed how many people I have met who have goals to run marathons and become millionaires by the age of forty. They seem to have a plethora of personal and business goals. I have met very few people who have goals as a couple, yet their marriage should be the most important priority in their lives. Goals move us; goals help us progress; goals give us a forum to improve as individuals and as a team. If you don't have goals as a couple, I give you the assignment to go to a fun place, take some time, and come up with five to ten significant goals—things you want to accomplish and become *as a couple*. To work as a team on the same dreams is a surefire way to make a good marriage great. Such goals could include your spiritual desires for your family, your financial dreams, how you will serve others and spread the gospel, the kind of home environment you wish to create, what kind of neighbors you hope to be, what projects you would like to work on as a couple, what books you hope to read, your health and fitness goals, and perhaps places to visit or travel to. There is no limit to what you can accomplish as a team—with the Lord's help.

8. **Planning fun activities, trips, or vacations:** Some men and women have fallen into the trap of going through life just assuming that fun, relaxation, and pleasure will simply happen automatically. Well, it doesn't. If you want to have a fun and adventurous life, you must plan for that to happen. Everyone needs something exciting to look forward to. Plan fun trips and vacations together. Dream, plan, and save together. This process can be exciting for your entire family, and it's a wonderful way to make memories together.

Homework:
- Find a time when you can talk about your marital expectations. Put it on your schedule.
- List your expectations on a sheet of paper and visit with each other about what you expect from each other. Go somewhere you can have a positive, healthy discussion.
- Find ways to meet your spouse's needs and expectations. Keep your spouse's expectations somewhere you can review them weekly.
- Try to meet one expectation each week. Remember, keep it simple.

Additional Reading:
- Elder Hugh W. Pinnock, "Ten Keys to Successful Dating and Marriage Relationships," *Brigham Young University Speeches 1981*, 3 May 1981.
- Brent A. Barlow, "The Highs and Lows of Marriage," *Ensign*, October 1983, 43–47.
- Jeffrey & Patricia Holland, "Some Things We Have Learned—Together," *Brigham Young University Speeches 1984–85*, 15 January 1985.
- Brent A. Barlow, *Just for Newlyweds* (Salt Lake City: Deseret Book, 1992).

References
17 Spencer W. Kimball, "Oneness in Marriage," *Ensign*, March 1977, 3.

18 Charles B. Beckert, "Well, What Do You Expect?" in *Eternal Companions*, eds. D.E. Brinley & D.K. Judd (Salt Lake City: Bookcraft, 1995), 102.

19 As cited in T.B. Holman, J.H. Larson & R.F. Stahmann, "Preparing for an Eternal Marriage," in *Strengthening Our Families: An In-Depth Look at the Proclamation on the Family*, ed. D.C. Dollahite (Salt Lake City: Bookcraft, 2000), 39.

20 Russell M. Nelson, "Identity, Priority, and Blessings," *Brigham Young University 2000–2001 Speeches* (Brigham Young University Publications and Graphics: Provo, Utah, 2001), 89.

21 David T. Seamons, "Ready or Not—Here We Are," D.E. Brinley & D.K. Judd (eds.) *Eternal Companions* (Salt Lake City: Bookcraft, 1995), 118.

CHAPTER 2
Effective Communication in Marriage

"If we would know true love and understanding one for another, we must realize that communication is more than a sharing of words. It is the *wise* sharing of emotions, feelings, and concerns. It is the sharing of oneself totally."
-Elder Marvin J. Ashton[22]

JUST BEFORE OUR FIRST CHILD was to be born, Janie and I lived in a triplex with two other married couples just south of BYU campus. Since we needed to make room for a baby crib, one particular Saturday we spent the afternoon rearranging the furniture in our home. Back in those days, waterbeds were much more common than they are now. You could purchase a waterbed the size of your driveway for about a hundred dollars. They were quite affordable—especially for poor college students. However, moving a waterbed was a cumbersome chore. First, you had to drain all the water out of the "bladder" of the bed. Next, you had to disassemble the bed and move it to where you wanted it. Then, you had to put the bed back together again. Finally, once the bed was where you wanted it, you had to fill the bladder with water again. If I remember correctly, the entire process took most of the day.

After I had moved the bed to its new location and put it back together, I was working on the final step—filling the bladder up with water. However, I glanced at my watch and realized that I had home teaching appointments beginning in about fifteen minutes. I quickly jumped into the shower and got dressed. On my way out the door, I said to Janie, "As soon as the bladder gets full, turn the water off."

I ran to my appointments and came home about an hour later. As I approached the front door, I noticed that the water from the outside faucet was still running. I ran into the house, and to my dismay—and amazement—the bladder of the waterbed was so full that it had expanded and stretched three feet above the height of the bed. The bladder was on the verge of bursting! How a bed that heavy didn't fall through the wooden floor of a fifty-year-old-home, I'll never know. As soon as I shut the water off, I went to Janie and asked the obvious question: "Why didn't you turn the water off like I asked you to do?"

She responded, "I was just following your instructions. When you left, you said, 'Whatever you do, *do not* turn the water off.'" Janie explained that even though the water bed looked unusually large, she trusted that I knew what I was doing.

After I shut the water off and began draining the excess water, we talked about communication and about how my message became so mangled. I was insistent that I told her to turn the water off, and she was just as confident that I had said the very opposite. We were at an impasse. Thankfully, we worked through that issue and learned to laugh about it later.

Communication is one of the most essential skills necessary to maintain a strong marriage. Couples who struggle in their communication will find it difficult to have a strong marriage relationship. Stephen R. Covey called communication the most "fundamental and necessary skill in life."[23] In my opinion, one of the most critical skills you can develop during marriage is to learn how to communicate effectively with each other.

For example, I like to talk to Janie about issues immediately when they occur. If there is a dispute we need to settle or an issue we need to work through, I want to talk about it right then and there. Janie, on the other hand, is a thinker. She likes to process her thoughts and mull them over for a day or two before she discusses anything with me. Janie likes to think about what she is going to say before she opens her mouth. I, on the other hand, learn how I feel and what I think while I'm flapping my gums—what a crazy concept. Therefore, in our marriage, we have had to learn to meet each other's needs when it comes to communicating around conflict because we are both so different when it comes to how we process our feelings.[a] On the other hand, when it comes to talking in general,

---

a Although we don't have it totally figured out. For the past two years, I have had my friend's bright-orange canoe stored in our backyard. Every time Janie saw that canoe, she would say, "Isn't there some other place we could put that canoe?" After several complaints, I got the distinct impression that she really didn't like having the canoe in our backyard. So I sold the canoe, and my friend and I split the money. When I told Janie the good news—she was upset. She said, "I really liked that canoe. Now how will we ever go canoeing?" I just shrugged my shoulders, scratched my head, counted the money, and moved on to my next harebrained idea.

we both like to share our ideas and opinions and have had many great discussions over the years because we enjoy that part of our marriage.

Gender Differences in Communication

What men and women need from each other when it comes to communication is often quite different. For women, communicating is an emotional experience. Women connect with others through talking—that's how they build relationships. Women enjoy talking about people, family, health, weight, food, and a variety of other personal things.

In Relief Society meetings, women can share their deepest, darkest secrets, along with struggles and challenges. Together, the women cry, they hug, and they lift and heal each other. Could you imagine if men engaged in the deep sharing of feelings and emotions during a priesthood quorum meeting? If a good brother in an elders quorum said, "Before the lesson begins, I just need to share with all of you how I am struggling this week. My wife is being mean to me, my boss chewed me out three times this month, and I have no idea how I'm going to pay my electric bill. I just need a hug." Most of the other men in the room would begin to slide their chairs away and some may even run for the hills. Men often have a difficult time sharing their emotions—especially in public. This tendency may explain why women live longer than men—they don't keep all of their problems bottled up inside of them. Most experts would agree that sharing emotions is healthy and cathartic.

Women tend to be wonderful at expressing their problems with each other because, remember, they connect through talking. It would be common for a group of women to sit around a table at a restaurant and share their issues and challenges with each other. For them, it's wonderful to know that others are going through some of the same struggles. Women don't necessarily solve each other's problems—they simply listen and connect.

For me, a common practice for years was to come home from work and ask Janie how her day went. Occasionally, she would share some her frustrations and challenges. I was always good at giving practical advice, so I would share with Janie some ideas about how to fix the problem. If she was concerned that the children weren't doing their chores, I would say, "Well, then create a chore chart." If she wasn't happy the way one of the children was acting, I would respond, "Well, here's what you need to do to discipline that child."

One day, after about ten years of marriage—and after I had provided an incredibly insightful solution to a problem—my wife looked at me and said, "Can I share something with you?" Janie then explained, "I really don't need you to solve my problems. I'm a big girl—I can do that. I just need you to listen and show some empathy."

That was a revelation for me. I never understood that when Janie was sharing her problems *she didn't need my help to solve them*. The sooner husbands can learn that most wives do not necessarily want help solving their problems (men just need to listen, to show empathy, and to validate their wives' feelings), then they will build stronger emotional bonds with their spouses. Since women connect by talking, men should try to engage their wives in conversations and practice empathic listening.

Men, on the other hand, prefer to discuss things outside themselves. Therefore, men enjoy talking about news, sports, computer programs, mutual funds, home repairs, hunting, and a slew of other things. Men do not usually talk to other men about relationships, marriage, or family. Unlike women, men most often do not connect by simply talking—instead, men bond and connect by doing things with each other. For example, if I want to connect with my son, Brandon, we shoot guns, we play golf, we rent some WaveRunners and tear Bear Lake to shreds, or we watch a football game on television while eating a hunk of meat. Sometimes, when I come home from these excursions, Janie will say, "So how is Brandon doing?"

I have to say with all sincerity, "I have no idea, but I'm sure he's doing fine."

Janie will reply, "Wait a minute. You mean you spent the entire day with him, and you have no idea how he's doing?"

I will then respond, "I'm sure he's doing great—if he wasn't—he would have told me."

Women can't understand this concept because if they spent three hours with a female friend, they would come back knowing the amount of their tax return, the names of each of their children, what child takes medication, why a child returned prematurely from a mission, where the husband works, what their Church callings are, and that the lump on the back of their neck is benign.

Not all relationships are this stereotypical. In some marriages, the husband is more emotional than his wife or communicates more. The point is, even though one spouse may or may not communicate well, communication is the key to building loving, lasting relationships. Effective communication is what builds friendships and binds couples together during dating, courting, engagement, and marriage. Communication is vital in moving relationships from more superficial levels to deeper realms.

Two years ago, I interviewed ten newly married couples at Brigham Young University. The couples were different in personality, how they met, what their engagement was like, and a host of other variables, but there was one common thread that these couples shared. Each couple told me that one of the fundamental ingredients to the success of their relationships was that they could talk freely, openly, and about anything. In fact, each couple also told me that this free and open communication was present from the moment they met.

As these couples related their experiences to me, I was taken back to my own courtship with Janie. I remembered how easy Janie and I could talk together when we first met. It wasn't uncommon to talk on the phone or on dates for hours. Talking to Janie came so easy, and I believe she would say the same thing about me. I believe most newly married couples could share that same quality or they wouldn't be married to each other. However, once couples are married, it is easy to become distracted, busy, or apathetic and neglect your martial communication. Be on guard, and never let this happen. If you do, your marriage will suffer, and so will you.

Three Levels of Communication in Marriage
There are three levels of communication in marriage that are worth considering. The first level is *superficial*. Every married couple spends a significant amount of time at this level. Superficial communication is safe, non-argumentative, and information processing. Superficial topics are easy to discuss and involve a low level of risk. In my own marriage, superficial communication usually takes the form of coordination and planning. I call home and ask my wife, "So what's for dinner tonight?" or "Do any of the children have a game or performance?" In the early stages of marriage, you will most likely be coordinating your busy schedules and trying to find avenues to be with each other.

As I teach couples about superficial communication during counseling sessions, usually a husband or wife will say, "So superficial communication is bad, right?" But, no, superficial communication is good, and it's vitally important. However, I then ask couples to tell me how much time they spend in superficial communication. I try to have them attach a percentage to it. It is my personal feeling that couples should spend no more than 25 percent of their time in superficial communication. The couples I worry about are those who spend 50 percent or more of their time engaged in this type of communication.

The second level of communication in marriage is *personal*. Personal communication is when you share your ideas, beliefs, opinions, and feelings with each other. This kind of communication is more risky as we are putting our ideas and opinions "out there" for scrutiny. Examples of personal communication can range from expressing feelings about neighbors, ward members, or Church leaders; sharing ideas about religion, politics, or societal issues; sharing opinions about how things should be done; the choices your friends make; or the last gospel doctrine lesson you sat through. The personal level of communication is where couples begin to bond and grow emotionally together—it's where you fall in love. It's when you realize that another person has the same passions you have in certain areas. For couples who are married, this level of communication can keep the love fires burning. This is where you say, "Wow, we feel the same way about so many things." For married couples, personal communication strengthens emotional bonds and strongly contributes to emotional intimacy. Couples who can spend 40 to 50 percent of their communication time in personal areas will report high levels of marital satisfaction.

Marriage experts, Judith Wallerstein and Sandra Blakeslee commented on why personal communication is crucial for nurturing and healing marriages:

> Our needs for comforting and encouragement are deep and lasting. A main task of every marriage from the early days of the relationship to its end is for each partner to nurture the other. The loneliness of life in the cities, the long commutes, the absence of meaningful contact with people in so many jobs, the anonymity of suburban life, and the distances that separate close friends and family have all sharpened our emotional hungers. . . . We feel tired, driven, and needy. More than ever before we need someone special who understands how we feel and responds with tenderness. Love begins with paying attention. . . . A marriage that does not provide nurturance and restorative comfort can die of emotional malnutrition.[24]

This statement leads to the third level of communication in marriage, *validation*. This type of communication is edifying, healing, nurturing, and complimentary. In this level of communication, husbands and wives freely express praise to their spouse. Couples who can do this on a regular basis will witness their relationship flourish. In order to distinguish validation from "cheerleading" or simply blowing smoke, there are two key rules. First, the validation must be specific. If Janie said to me, "You are just awesome," that really means nothing. In fact, for the past twenty years, parents have been giving their children these kinds of compliments in the name of self-esteem, and they don't work. Research shows that these kids have grown up, looked around, and realized that they really aren't "awesome." Generic praise, such as, "You are so wonderful," and "You're the best," are hollow, fake, and pointless.

However, if a compliment can be specific, it will be valued and treasured. For example, if Janie says to me, "You know what I love about you? You are one of the hardest working people I've ever met. You get up early every morning, and you work until six or seven each night, and every weekend you work on the house from sun up to sun down. I don't know many people who can do that." Wow! I will now run through a brick wall for her, head first. That compliment means something.

If I say to Janie, "You know, what I love about you is the incredible relationship you have with all of our kids—especially our girls. I often see you all sitting at the kitchen table late at night, laughing and talking as if you are old college roommates. I admire that quality so much. I know our children look up to you and admire you, and so do I." That compliment is extremely meaningful to my wife and would inspire her to continue her practice of connecting with our children. Remember—*rewarded behavior continues.* The rule applies to both children and adults.

Next, for validation to be meaningful, the spouse expressing the compliment must share how that trait impacts them. For example, after my wife compliments me on how hard I may work, she could say, "And I love that because I know that no matter how hard times may become, I believe you will always find a way to provide for our family." Or, to Janie, I may say, "And I love that you spend time with our children and talk and laugh with them because I know they look up to you, and if they ever had a problem in their lives, they would feel comfortable talking to you about it. And I know that they admire you as a mother and will treat their children the way you have treated them. I know my grandchildren will be in good hands." When couples can enter into this level of communication and express these kinds of compliments, you can actually feel love in the room. It's powerful. Couples who can spend 30 percent of their communication time validating will enjoy a rich exchange with each other. Their words will not fall on deaf ears but will heal the wounded soul, recharge the heart of a tired and exhausted spouse, and rekindle love almost instantaneously. If you don't believe me, try it.

I imagine that the Savior would validate those around Him. He would freely give compliments and praise, and He would smile as He spoke kind words to his followers. Our quest is to become like Him, including in the way we communicate with each other. Once you feel comfortable with this level of communication, your relationship will thrive and blossom.

Christlike Communication

When couples come to visit me in counseling, they often believe that poor communication is the root of their marriage problems. In fact, on the first visit with every couple, I always ask, "What are the three most significant problems in your marriage?" In almost every case, the husband and wife will tell me that communication is one of their core problems. I rarely believe that communication is a root problem, unless a husband or wife has been through some torture where their tongue has been cut off. Instead, I teach couples that their lack of communication is a symptom of a more significant problem.

After all, most men and women are pretty good communicators. If a wife tells me her husband is a terrible communicator, I will often scratch my head and wonder how she could say such a thing. I have often talked to the husband one-on-one and noticed that he can communicate very effectively. In fact, sometimes I learn that he has great relationships at work and everyone in his ward and neighborhood love him. As it turns out, he's an extremely good communicator—*just not with his wife.*

And when husbands tell me their wives cannot communicate, I am often bewildered. I have met with the wife, and she communicated their marriage problems with clarity and pinpoint accuracy. I often come to learn that as the Primary president or volunteer coach or leader in the community, the wife is an excellent communicator. *She just doesn't communicate well with her husband.* If someone can communicate well with everyone but their spouse, it's not a communication problem—it goes deeper than that.

Several years ago, Elder Russell M. Nelson shared the following experience in general conference:

> As we Brethren travel about the world, sometimes we see worrisome scenes. On a recent flight, I sat behind a husband and wife. She obviously loved her husband. As she stroked the back of his neck, I could see her wedding ring. She would nestle close to him and rest her head upon his shoulder, seeking his companionship.
>
> In contrast, he seemed totally oblivious to her presence. He was focused solely upon an electronic game player. During the entire flight, his attention was riveted upon that device. Not once did he look at her, speak to her, or acknowledge her yearning for affection.
>
> His inattention made me feel like shouting: "Open your eyes, man! Can't you see? Pay attention! Your wife loves you! She needs you!"
>
> I don't know more about them. I haven't seen them since. Perhaps I was alarmed unduly. And very possibly, if this man knew of my concern for them, he might feel sorry for me in not knowing how to use such an exciting toy.[25]

Do you believe this man on the airplane lacked communication skills? Or was he just a selfish individual? Personally, I would explain that the root of his problem was selfishness. In fact, his selfishness impeded his ability to communicate affection to his wife. From this experience and many others, I have come to believe that pride and selfishness are the roots of almost all communication problems in marriage.

If communication is such a problem in LDS marriages, why isn't it addressed more in our general conferences? For example, we know that pornography is a huge problem, and you can count on at least several talks every general conference to address it. If communication, or the lack of it, is such an issue, why aren't there more talks addressing the subject?

Recently, I collaborated with a student to search every general conference talk given since 1970, looking for ones that addressed communication in marriage. We could only find nine talks on that subject during the past 40 years. There have been 80 conferences in the past 40 years, and there have only been nine talks on communication. Therefore, there have been .11 talks on communication every general conference since 1970. Communication talks in general conference are about as rare as Halley's Comet.

In contrast, during the past 40 years, there have been 363 talks either on pornography or that have mentioned pornography. Therefore, since 1970 there have been 4.5 talks on pornography every general conference. There is quite a difference when it comes to these two topics.

So why don't our General Authorities spend their time discussing communication problems in marriage? I personally believe that the Brethren recognize that communication isn't the root problem. Instead, our leaders hit right at the core—they teach us about pride and selfishness. They also discuss kindness and charity. Since 1970, pride has been mentioned 571 times in general conferences, a ratio of 7.1 times per general conference, and selfishness has been discussed or mentioned 460 times, for a ratio of 5.8 times per general conference. Do you see my point? From the perspective of those who lead our Church, communication isn't the core problem in marriage. When we examine the root of marital problems, we come to learn that what actually happens is that couples lose the Spirit and communicate in non-Christlike ways.

Therefore, if you want to be a good communicator, learn to become more like Christ. Talk the way He does; say the things He would say. Learn to speak "with the tongue of angels" (2 Nephi 32:2). Brigham Young taught that in family relationships, we should treat each others "as an angel"[26] would treat a husband or wife. The Apostle Paul taught the Ephesians, "Let no corrupt communication proceed out of your mouth, but that which is good to the use of edifying, that it may minister grace unto the hearers" (Ephesians 4:29). Husbands and wives should practice only speaking things to each other that are edifying and healing. The surest way to keep your love growing is to see your spouse the way our Savior does and communicate those wonderful thoughts and expressions that the Savior would.

My mission president, L. Dale Hanks, was the most kind, compassionate man I have ever known. He radiated goodness, kindness, and Christlike love. Make no mistake, President Hanks was not a lightweight—he was also the most powerful and commanding man I have ever known. When he walked into a room, he was the unquestioned leader. However, he had a wonderful way to express faith, trust, and confidence in all of his missionaries. What I remember most about him is that whenever I was in his presence, whether it was a formal interview or an informal exchange, I always left feeling about ten feet taller, happier, and frankly, healed and renewed. My mission president had a great gift to lift and build everyone around him. There was nothing pretend or fake about his praise and love. It was so real and genuine you could actually feel it. I often imagined that my mission president treated us just as the Savior would have. In fact, it wasn't difficult to feel the Savior's influence when President Hanks was nearby. I have always wanted to be the type of husband, father, and priesthood leader that my mission president was. I have fallen short on many occasions but am determined to keep trying.

If I want to be successful in my marriage and family relationships, I need to speak kind and healing words to my wife and children. All of us do. President David O. McKay taught, "No member of this Church—husband—father—has the right to utter an oath in his home or ever to express a cross word to his wife or to his children. . . . Never must there be expressed in a Latter-day Saint home an oath, a condemnatory term, an expression of anger or jealousy or hatred. Control it! Do not express it!"[27]

Several years ago, Elder Jeffrey R. Holland declared,

> Think of how many arguments could be avoided, how many hurt feelings could be spared, and, in a worst-case scenario, how many breakups and divorces could be avoided if we were not so easily provoked, if we thought no evil of one another, and if we not only did not rejoice in iniquity but didn't rejoice even in little mistakes.
>
> Think the best of each other, especially of those you say you love. Assume the good and doubt the bad.[28]

Kindness and charity begin in the home and, specifically, in the marriage relationship. A husband and wife who speak kind words to each other will notice the "trickle down" effect upon their own children. For those preparing for marriage, develop the habit now of finding the good in others. Learn to not be judgmental and critical but to be building and edifying. No one likes to be around someone who is mean, grumpy, negative, or constantly pessimistic. Learn to cultivate a spirit of optimism and faith. Look for the good in others, and express it often.

Finding negative qualities in others requires no talent or skill whatsoever. Besides, very few people have ever changed as a result of being criticized. Remember the last time someone really "nailed" you with some criticism? Did you respond by saying, "You know, you're right. I really do need to improve in that area. In fact, I'll get right on that." No, if you are human, you probably thought, "You little punk. Who do you think you are talking to me that way?"

President Hinckley spoke of Elder Joseph Anderson, who lived longer than any other General Authority of the Church—he died at age 102. Elder Anderson was the private secretary to Heber J. Grant for many years. Toward the very end of his life, President Grant had a stroke and was seriously ill. His secretary, Joseph Anderson, went to pay him a visit. President Grant asked, "Joseph, have I ever been unkind to you?"

And Joseph said, "No, President Grant, you have never been unkind to me."

And then President Grant, with tears rolling down his cheeks, said, "Joseph, I am grateful that I have never been unkind to you."

President Grant died the very next day. President Hinckley concluded with this expression: "But what a marvelous thing that a man who had worked with him for so very many years could say that the man who directed his efforts had never been unkind to him."[29] I find this story amazing, but imagine how powerful it would be to look at our spouse, while on our death bed and say, "Have I ever been unkind to you?" And then to have them respond, "No, you have never been unkind to me." What a powerful moment that would be.

I conclude with a story shared by former BYU family science professor Dr. Brent Barlow:

> During times of sickness, life-threatening situations often arise. It was so for an elderly LDS man in California. I was in his stake to deliver a Know Your Religion speech. After I finished, he came up with his walker and shared with me an event that had happened with him and his now-deceased wife. She had gone to the doctor one day, concerned about some growths on her cheek. The lab report informed them that she had cancer.
>
> The aging husband described for me what their marriage was like as the cancer gradually began to eat away at her face. Because of the chemotherapy treatment, all her hair fell out. She had been a beautiful woman, but now she was ashamed of her appearance. The husband told me that little else mattered to him in the marriage from that point on except helping her through the difficult situation and an imminent death.
>
> As the cancer progressed, she didn't want him or anyone else to see her. She just wanted to be alone. The husband told me,

however, that as her condition grew worse, a light began to radiate from her face. He believed it was her spirit. The worse the cancer got, the brighter the light grew. He said he fell in love with the radiance about her face. He kept telling her how beautiful she was. At first she wouldn't believe him, but finally he convinced her of his love and concern.

"She died," he said, holding back his tears, "believing she was the most beautiful woman on earth."[30]

Although there are many skills that will help us become better communicators, becoming like the Savior and expressing the words He would say is the most crucial communication skill there is. I would encourage you to learn to speak with the tongue of angels. If you can incorporate that trait into your life, you will bless your spouse, your family, and all of those around you.

Homework:
- Write down in your journal or a notebook how you need to improve as a communicator.
- Practice validation with your spouse. If you would like, begin with small steps, such as writing a note or an e-mail. Express a specific compliment, and then tell your spouse how the trait you're complimenting has impacted you.
- Practice being more positive and optimistic in your communication in every aspect of your life.

Additional Reading:
- Elder Marvin J. Ashton, "The Tongue Can Be a Sharp Sword," *Ensign*, May 1992.
- Elder Jeffrey R. Holland, "The Tongue of Angels," *Ensign*, May 2007.
- Mark D. Ogletree, "Speak, Listen, and Love," *Ensign*, February 2014.
- Lola Walters, "The Grapefruit Syndrome," *Ensign,* April 1993, 13.

References
22 Marvin J. Ashton, "Family Communication," *Ensign*, May 1976, 52.

23 Stephen R. Covey, *Marriage and Family: Gospel Insights*, (Salt Lake City: Bookcraft, 1983), 198.

24 Judith S. Wallerstein & Sandra Blakeslee, *The Good Marriage: How and Why Love Lasts*, (Boston: Houghton Mifflin Company, 1995), 239–240.

25 Russell M. Nelson, "Nurturing Marriage," *Ensign*, May 2006, 36.

26 Brigham Young, *Discourses of Brigham Young*, ed. John A. Widtsoe, (Salt Lake City: Deseret Book, 1954), 197–198.

27 David O. McKay, as cited in Stephen R. Covey, *Spiritual Roots of Human Relations*, (Salt Lake City: Deseret Book, 1993), 190–191.

28 Jeffrey R. Holland, "How Do I Love Thee?" *BYU Speeches 1999–2000*, (Brigham Young University Publications and Graphics: Provo, Utah, 2000), 160–161.

29 Gordon B. Hinckley, *Regional Conference, Priesthood Leadership Meeting*, Port Harcourt, Nigeria, 14 February 1998; as cited in *LDS Church News*, "Messages of Inspiration," June 6, 1998.

30 Brent A. Barlow, *Dealing with Differences in Marriage*, (Salt Lake City: Deseret Book, 1993), 137–139.

CHAPTER 3
Expressions of Dating, Love, and Affection

"Pray for the love which allows you to see the good in your companion.
Pray for the love that makes weaknesses and mistakes seem small. Pray
for the love to make your companion's joy your own. Pray for the love to
want to lessen the load and soften the sorrows of your companion."
-Henry B. Eyring[31]

MANY HUSBANDS AND WIVES WOULD die for their spouse if they had to.
In their minds, they love their spouse with all of their heart, might, mind,
and strength. However, sometimes they forget to demonstrate this love.
Some marriage partners rarely express sentiments of love or affection.
What good is love if it isn't expressed? Husbands and wives, how often do
you openly express feelings of love and affection to your spouse?

Do not ever assume that your spouse simply knows you love them.
Love must be renewed and rekindled daily. If you don't share such
expressions of affection, you are guilty of neglect. Elder Richard G. Scott
related some of the ways he and his wife, Jeanene, demonstrated affection
to each other:

> Early in our marriage, often I would open my scriptures to
> give a message in a meeting, and I would find an affectionate,
> supportive note Jeanene had slipped into the pages. Sometimes
> they were so tender that I could hardly talk. Those precious notes
> from a loving wife were and continue to be a priceless treasure of
> comfort and inspiration.
>
> I began to do the same thing with her, not realizing how much it
> truly meant to her. I remember one year we didn't have the resources
> for me to give her a valentine, so I decided to paint a watercolor on
> the front of the refrigerator. I did the best I could; only I made one
> mistake. It was enamel paint, not watercolor. She never let me try
> to remove that permanent paint from the refrigerator.

I remember one day I took some of those little round paper circles that form when you punch holes in paper, and I wrote on them the numbers 1 to 100. I turned each over and wrote her a message, one word on each circle. Then I scooped them up and put them in an envelope. I thought she would get a good laugh.

When she passed away, I found in her private things how much she appreciated the simple messages that we shared with each other. I noted that she had carefully pasted every one of those circles on a piece of paper. She not only kept my notes to her, but she protected them with plastic coverings as if they were a valuable treasure. There is only one that she didn't put with the others. It is still behind the glass in our kitchen clock. It reads, "Jeanene, it is time to tell you I love you." It remains there and reminds me of that exceptional daughter of Father in Heaven.[32]

When we hear Elder Scott speak with passion and emotion about his marriage, we understand the powerful feelings of love he and Jeanene had for each other. Hopefully, all of us are seeking for the kind of marriage relationship enjoyed by Elder and Sister Scott. I believe that such a relationship is within reach for all of us if we will put into practice the gospel of Jesus Christ.

The Power of Love

We learn in the Doctrine and Covenants that "thou shalt love thy wife with all thy heart, and shalt cleave unto her and none else" (D&C 42:22). In this verse, we are commanded to love our spouses with all of our hearts—that is with all the energy of our souls—with all our minds, and with all our strength. There is one law higher than this. In the New Testament, we learn, "Thou shalt love the Lord thy God with all thy heart, and with all thy soul, and with all thy mind" (Matthew 22:37). We should love our Heavenly Father with every fiber of our being—with every ounce of energy we have. We should love our God more than any other person or possession.

Now, here is the miracle. When we put God at the center of our lives and love Him more than we love anyone else, our capacity to love others increases drastically. Thus, you can love your spouse with more power and more energy and more intensity if you simply go *through* God rather than *around* Him.

Many would argue that this principle is illogical. It would seem that if you bypassed God, you would have more love in store for others. Such individuals seem to believe that love is akin to a pitcher of water, and every person we love has a cup. They falsely assume that we divide our love by pouring water in the cup of each person we have a relationship with. However, this model is faulty because it stipulates that we only have a certain amount of love (water) and we must share it equally. Thus, we must be miserly when it comes to "pouring out" our love. Under this premise, if we love a spouse too much, then we will have little love (water) to share with our children or other family members. Or, if we give one child a large dose of love, other children or a spouse may go thirsty.

The Lord's model of love is much different. Instead of viewing love as a pitcher of water, the Lord teaches that love is like a continuous fountain; hence, there is an endless supply for all with whom we have relationships. God is the source of all love; His love fills the immensity of space. There is no shortage of love! As long as we love the Lord and put Him first, we have unlimited access to His fountain, and we can share as much as we want with whomever we want. The more we love the Lord and put Him first, the deeper we can draw from the fountain.

With the Lord's plan, I can love my spouse and children with an unlimited supply of water—so to speak. No one will ever go thirsty. If we are filled with the Lord's love, we can endure any problem, overcome any obstacle, confront any fear, forgive any mistake, and love more deeply than we ever imagined. Just think of how powerfully we can love our spouse or children if we link ourselves to our Heavenly Father and our Savior by covenants.

I have had well-intending ward members question Janie and me on how many children we have. Because we have eight children, some have assumed that not all of the kids could possibly feel loved—especially compared to smaller families. These individuals assume there is only "x amount" of love that parents can dole out. They don't understand the principle that the Lord's love comes from an endless fountain and that I can love each of my children with 100 percent capacity! It's not like I only have 100 units of love that I must divide between a wife and eight children. If I tap into the Lord's love, I can love each person with 100 units or more!

Moreover, Joseph Smith taught, "A man filled with the love of God, is not content with blessing his family alone, but ranges through the whole world, anxious to bless the whole human race."[33] Therefore, the more I become like my Father in Heaven, the greater my desire will become to love my spouse, children, ward members, neighbors, and others. As I come to know my Heavenly Father and understand His nature, my capacity to love will be strengthened.

Furthermore, "God is love" (1 John 4:8), and when we love Him and our Savior, we are able to tap into the power of the Atonement. A fruit of the Atonement is charity—the love our Heavenly Father and Savior possess. Charity is Christlike love. When we love our God first, he blesses us with the gift of charity; we access that gift through the power of the Atonement. Through this process, our Heavenly Father gives us the ability to love others. We begin to see others as He sees them—as children of God who are trying their very best. We can overlook faults, weakness, issues, blemishes, and warts. Instead, with our Heavenly Father's help, we learn to see the good—the best—in each other and to see potential.

Without our Heavenly Father's endowment of love, most of us are too judgmental, too critical, too opinionated, too irritable, too mean, and too proud to love others unconditionally. His love is a gift to us—His children. Our power to love is linked to our obedience to commandments and covenants; as we obey God's commandments, our desire to help and bless those around us increases. Conversely, when we disobey God's commandments, the more selfish we become and the less we care about our fellowmen.

Orson Pratt applied this concept to marriage when he taught:

> The more righteous a people become the more they are qualified for loving others and rendering them happy. A wicked man can have but little love for his wife; while a righteous man, being filled with the love of God, is sure to manifest this heavenly attribute in every thought and feeling of his heart, and in every word and deed. Love, joy, and innocence will radiate from his very countenance, and be expressed in every look. This will beget confidence in the wife of his bosom, and she will love him in return; for love begets love; happiness imparts happiness; and these heaven-born emotions will continue to increase more and more, until they are perfected and glorified in all the fullness of eternal love itself.[34]

A former colleague related to me the following experience. He explained that at one point of his life, he was being stretched to the limits; he was busy with his family, with his Church calling, and especially with his new job. My friend wasn't wicked at all—in fact, he was quite righteous, in my opinion. But his life was about like yours and mine, and he felt he was burning the candle at both ends. Consequently, he didn't feel the companionship of the Spirit like he wanted to. He recognized that he needed his spiritual batteries recharged.

One morning, he decided to journey to the wilderness to pray, to ponder, and to receive answers from a loving Heavenly Father. He had made up his mind beforehand that he would attempt to spend most of the day in prayer and contemplation. For him, this proved to be a taxing day physically, emotionally, and spiritually. Throughout the day, he continued to persist in prayer, even though he didn't feel he was gaining much spiritual strength in the process. In fact, he began to question in the middle of his experience if his idea was ridiculous. Nevertheless, he persevered in prayer, meditation, reading, and thought. Before he knew it, he realized he had been gone most of the day.

Since he was so engaged in communing with God, you would assume that this was one of the most spiritual days of his life. Instead, he reported that by the time he walked to the car and began the drive home, he actually felt more exhausted than anything else. My friend expected to feel a divine spiritual outpouring; instead, he felt nothing other than fatigue and perhaps the feeling that he had wasted his day.

However, after a good night's sleep, my friend noticed that some interesting things began to occur in his life. The day after his experience in the wilderness, when he put his arms around his wife and held her close and then held his small children one by one, he felt a greater intensity of love for his family than he ever had. As he engaged in his professional and priesthood duties, he felt the convincing power of God stronger than he had ever felt it. When he opened up the scriptures and began reading, he saw the majesty of the Savior on every page. For weeks, my friend felt a greater outpouring of the Spirit and of love than he ever had in his life.[35]

This was rooted in the experience of putting the Lord first in his life and seeking His will by spending a day on a mountain in prayer and thought. Consequently, his power to love those around him was enhanced. This blessing is available for all of us who put the Lord first in our lives. However, we don't have to pray on a mountainside all day to demonstrate our love for the Lord or to receive His love. There are many things we can do to offer our whole souls unto Him (see Omni 1:26).

Love Languages
Often when I speak at marital workshops, I will ask the audience if there is anyone present who speaks a foreign language. Of course, in Mormon audiences, there are usually many participants to choose from. Once two individuals who speak two completely different languages are identified, I invite them to come to the front of the room and greet each other in their other language. After their initial exchange, I then invite the pair to briefly plan a lunch meeting in their different languages, and I give them two minutes to accomplish their assignment. Often, if the languages are rather obscure, most people in the audience don't understand a word of what was spoken, and neither do the participants. The two participants are then asked to explain to the audience what they were talking about.

Afterwards, I ask the audience how this exercise applies to husbands and wives and their expressions of love. If the crowd is with me, they will provide several good examples. For instance, a husband may enjoy more physical touch than his wife. If so, he will find himself often giving love the way he wants to receive it—in a physical way. Thus, he will often touch and massage his wife's back and neck, or hold her hand. The problem is that this may not be interpreted by the wife as love—especially if she is not a *physical* lover. She may prefer verbal compliments. Therefore, she will often praise and speak kind words to her husband because that is her love language. Both end up frustrated and feeling that their spouse doesn't love them.

Do you see the problem? Like the pair speaking a foreign language, the husband has shot a "love arrow" that has completely missed the target. Unfortunately, this problem is all too common. Because spouses do not understand the concept of love languages, they speak a foreign tongue to each other, often resulting in one or both being frustrated. Some men and women have told me in counseling that they have tried everything to show love in their marriage but their spouse doesn't seem to care. I have tried to help them understand that most likely, they are showing their spouse love in their own love language, not necessarily in the language of their spouse. So I encourage them to discover their spouse's love language and learn how to speak it. That's when their spouse will feel the most loved.

Several years ago, a colleague of mine shared an experience that illustrates this principle. Mike and a few of us were talking in the hallway at our workplace. The conversation turned to marriage, and Mike told us, "You know what is weird about my wife? Every day she sends me off to work with this mega-lunch. Then, when I go home each evening, the very first words from her lips are, 'Hi, honey. How was your lunch?'" Mike mentioned that sometimes in the afternoon, his wife would call and ask him how his lunch was. He seemed quite perturbed about the situation. Mike couldn't understand why his wife was obsessing over his lunch. She really didn't seem to care much about his day, other than his mega-lunch. By the way, for those of us who were lunch deprived, Mike's lunch looked awesome! He usually had a couple of sandwiches, a nice apple, some tasty chips, cookies, pudding, and always, a nice fruit pie.

At the same time, Mike complained that his wife was more concerned about his lunch than their romantic life. He felt the intimate part of their marriage was lacking and could use a little spark—well, more like a bonfire. Anyway, as Mike explained this situation, I said, "Mike, your wife is a task/service-oriented lover. You, on the other hand, are probably a physical touch–oriented lover."

Of course, by now everyone was tuned into the conversation. I then asked Mike if the way his wife showed her love to him was through service or doing things for him. As Mike thought about this, it was as if a switch was triggered. Instantly, he began to piece together how his wife would often serve him and do nice things for him. He began to realize that his wife showed her love by doing things for him, like making him a big lunch every day. The mega-lunch, to his wife, was equivalent to him wanting to spend a romantic evening.

This phenomenon is described by Gary Chapman in his book *The Five Love Languages*. Chapman contends that there are five major love languages: (1) words of affirmation, (2) quality time, (3) receiving gifts, (4) acts of service, and (5) physical touch. And it is typical for individuals to give love the way they like to receive it. For instance, if you like to receive words of affirmation from others, that is likely the way you will show love to your spouse. If you like physical contact, then that form of expression is most likely what you will dish out to your sweetheart. The point is *a good indicator of your love language can be found in how you demonstrate your love to your wife and children.*

Love Language #1: Words of Affirmation

Verbal lovers need compliments; they need praise; they need encouragement. Mark Twain said he could live for two months on a good compliment. I often tell Janie that after I paint a room, if she will just walk in and say, "Wow, this looks amazing," then I will run through a brick wall for her. Over time, she has learned to speak the language of praise to me. Likewise, every couple needs to learn each other's love language. Showing love to your spouse in his or her language is one of the greatest ways to strengthen a relationship.

Elder Hugh W. Pinnock shared the following story about what a middle-aged woman told him: "Somebody has to keep my husband humble. He gets so much attention from others that he needs to be brought down a peg or two. He gets too big for his britches." Elder Pinnock then commented: "How sad! Every husband needs a wife who will build him up. Every wife needs a husband who honors and respects her. Building each other with sincere compliments is never a sign of weakness; *it is the right thing to do*."[36]

Verbal-oriented lovers want to hear expressions such as "You look beautiful in that dress," "You are such an incredible leader," "I love the way you take your church calling seriously," "You are a wonderful mom. I am so grateful that my children have you for their mother."

When verbal lovers hear such words, they are pleased and feel a sense of accomplishment and recognition. It makes their day. If your spouse seems to speak this language, be aware of the need to compliment them. Find ways to inspire your spouse with kind, sincere praise.

Love Language #2: Quality Time

Careers, church responsibilities, children's activities, household duties, and community involvement often interfere with maintaining a close connection with one's spouse. For many contemporary couples, marriage is still a high priority, but not necessarily where couples spend a high degree of quality time. In fact, research documents that the longer people are married, the less time they spend together. Yet the amount of time couples spend together in face-to-face interaction is critically important to marital happiness and satisfaction. Many contemporary marriage experts and scholars believe that the most significant contributor to the breakdown in marriages today is the *lack of time together*.

Couples who experience a high degree of stress and little time together report lower levels of marital satisfaction. Conversely, couples who invest in each other, make time for each other, and prioritize their marriages report high levels of marital happiness. If successful marriages take work, time, and effort, what can be said, then, of marriages in which couples have little time to devote to nurturing their relationship? Such marriages will struggle to thrive in our time-starved environment.

One of the most significant ways to strengthen a marriage is to spend meaningful moments together—which is the language of time. For such lovers, time is measured when you participate in deliberate and mindful activities together. It is taking a walk, going out to eat, sitting on a park bench together, sharing an ice cream cone, getting away for the weekend. Love is spelled T-I-M-E. Those who speak this love language simply love being together—regardless of what they are doing.

I remember a few years ago, I was trying to get some things done around the house on a Saturday afternoon. My daughter Bethany decided to come with me as I hauled a trailer full of junk to the landfill. As I unloaded the trailer with my daughter, I wondered how many high school cheerleaders would be at the dump that day helping their dads unload a trailer full of junk. I concluded there were probably very few, and my daughter was one of those. I also knew that Bethany expressed her love the same way her mother did—by spending time together. I am grateful I understood that my teenage daughter being with me at the dump was her way of saying, "Dad, you're a good guy; I like hanging out with you."

Incidentally, back in the early days of our marriage, Janie would often invite me to go to the grocery store with her to shop. I would often decline, finding extremely important reasons why I could not—such as "I need to iron the dog" or "the man on television told me to stay tuned." However, ultimately I learned that this was Janie's love language—she just wanted to hang out with me while she shopped. Once I discovered this, I started viewing our trips to the grocery store as dates, and both of us were happier.[a]

If you find yourself being critical about the lack of time you and your significant other have to spend together, you are probably a quality time lover. Here is another indicator: if you're craving time with your spouse and find yourself willing to do things you normally wouldn't do, just so you can have some time together, you are probably a quality time lover. For example, if all of the sudden you decide you love racquetball or classic movies in a foreign language, you might be a quality-time lover! I knew Janie fell into this category when I suggested we go camping and she took me up on it.

---

a Well, going to the grocery store technically isn't a date. I learned that the hard way too.

Love Language #3: Receiving Gifts

In many marriages, certain spouses love to receive gifts—that is their love language. A gift is tangible evidence you can actually hold in your hand and say, "Look, he was thinking of me," or "She remembered me." There is no way to give a gift to someone unless you were thinking about them. The actual gift is simply a symbol of the care and concern. I once had a lady in my counseling office turn to her husband and say, "I would love it if you just stopped off at a convenience store in your way home from work and bought me a Slurpee." That woman was certainly a gift-oriented lover!

The good news is that giving gifts is one of the easiest languages to learn. Instead of ignoring your spouse's hints, pick up on them! Go out and spend some money on them; or, better yet, don't spend much money at all. Gift-oriented lovers would be the first to attest that "it's the little things that count." As you attempt to speak this love language, write a surprise note, or make something by hand for your spouse. Don't wait for a special occasion. Gift-oriented lovers also enjoy surprises, so keep them guessing!

Love Language #4: Acts of Service

Some individuals choose to express their love by doing things for their spouse. These task-oriented lovers express love by completing the chore list, running errands, cleaning, organizing, fixing, repairing, serving, and doing things for those they love. Just as the Savior washed the feet of His Apostles, so husbands can serve their wives and wives can serve and help their husbands with this task orientation.

Furthermore, these task-oriented lovers need to be loved by being served. You can express your love by doing things for them. Such tasks include vacuuming, cleaning cars, painting rooms, weeding gardens, taking out garbage, cleaning up baby spills, changing diapers, cleaning the garage, and a host of other activities.

When Jesus Christ washed the feet of His disciples, He was expressing love by the service He rendered. During that time, people wore sandals and walked on dirty and dusty trails and paths. It was customary for servants to wash the feet of arriving guests. Jesus had taught His disciples to love one another, and what better way to demonstrate that than by taking a basin of water and a towel and washing their feet?

In a marriage relationship, this story has profound implications. A husband can, in effect, wash his wife's feet by helping with the household tasks, fixing a leaky faucet, helping with the laundry, picking up his clothes. A wife can wash her husband's feet by having the house look neat and clean when he comes home from work, by making his favorite meal for dinner, or by helping him clean the garage or wash the car.

Task- or service-oriented lovers express love by what they do for their spouse. This is the way they wish to receive love from their spouse. Verbal compliments or physical affection do not fill the tank of a task-oriented lover. For these people, spouses need to discover what their needs are and do all in their power to meet them. Often it is simple. "Would you mind just vacuuming the family room?" Or, "Could you help me with the dishes?"

Love Language # 5: Physical Touch

Physical touch is one of the most powerful mediums for expressing marital love. Holding hands, kissing, embracing, and sexual relations are all ways of communicating love to one's spouse. Can you imagine what marriage would be like without physical affection? For the physical-touch lover, a touch of the hand, a kiss, or a back rub are all equivalent to saying, "I love you."

Speaking Your Partner's Love Language

In most marriage relationships, husbands and wives speak different love languages. Sometimes, a wife will do things for her spouse, like make him elaborate meals or keep the house clean (acts of service). However, what if a husband doesn't like gourmet meals; instead, he wants physical affection? This tendency is very common. Remember, we tend to demonstrate love in the way we want to receive it. This is why a wife may say, "I show my husband love all of the time, and he never seems to care." A husband may bemoan, "I try everything to impress my wife and do things for her, and she doesn't seem to notice." The reason couples express these concerns is that they are often speaking their *own* love language to their spouse—they are not speaking their spouses' love language. For example, if a husband wants gifts, you can't give him praise. If a wife wants physical affection, then compliments won't always work. Pull the arrow back, and shoot for a bull's-eye by speaking your spouse's love language—not yours! For the physical touch lover, holding hands, kissing, backrubs, and sexual intimacy are all equivalent to saying, "I love you."

At this point in the chapter, you have probably discovered your primary love language. Perhaps as you have read a little bit about each language, you have though to yourself, "That sounds just like me." Maybe a few of you are bilingual, as you seem to be characterized by one or two love languages. Even if you speak several love languages, you still will have a dominant language. If you're still not sure what language you are, I recommend you read *The Five Love Languages* by Gary Chapman or visit Chapman's website to take the love language test.

The key is to learn to speak your spouse's love language. If their language is words of affirmation, then give them compliments and praise; if they are time oriented, then do a fun activity together; if they are task oriented, then gear your love toward serving and doing things for them. Visualize Cupid pulling back his arrows of love, letting them fly, and hitting absolutely nothing. This is what happens constantly in relationships when love languages are not understood or spoken.

For example, Janie and I had been married for several years when we realized I was speaking German to her and she was speaking Chinese to me. I am more verbal and physical, so, of course, I was trying to love her in my own love languages—not necessarily hers. Meanwhile, Janie is more time and gift oriented, and I was missing that completely. Happiness in marriage comes when we learn to speak our spouses' love language and nurture them in that language. Otherwise, there is little traction gained when a verbally oriented male continues to try to give praise and compliments to a time- or task-oriented female. In my own marriage, if I want to hit the bull's-eye, I need to pull my arrow back and shoot it right toward spending time with Janie and doing things with her. Discovering how to speak your spouse's love language is a crucial exercise that can point you to the goal of marital satisfaction and happiness.

However, it should be stated that the ultimate goal in marriage isn't to speak a certain love language. The highest objective is to learn to love the way the Savior loves. Our Savior was kind and compassionate, and He loved others more than He loved Himself. He loved by serving, by touching, by giving, and by expressing words and kindness and love. His love was unconditional, and He accepted people the way they were—He required no one to change before offering His love.

Finally, I would advise you to be careful in comparing your feelings and demonstrations of love to the way other couples show their love for each other—especially in public. For example, many couples demonstrate their love outwardly, while others are more private in the way they show their affection. Don't worry so much about what other couples do.

Case and point: A young man, whom I will call Tyler, determined that his parents were very different from couples in the movies. After all, Tyler's parents didn't seem to say sweet things to each other, and he never ever saw his mom and dad kiss. Tyler felt unhappy about the lack of love his parents seemed to have for each other.

However, Tyler's feelings changed one day when the dam in their community broke and his family's farm was flooded. His parents put him in the attic for safety. Tyler lay in the attic, alone, shivering while rising water lapped at the foundations of the house. In his fear for himself and his parents, he looked out the attic window. A bolt of lightning split the dark night and illuminated the surrounding farm. For a brief moment, Tyler saw something he would never forget. He saw his parents up to their thighs in swirling water, walking shoulder to shoulder against the wind. His mother had an armful of frightened chicks she had rescued from the henhouse. His father was carrying a newborn lamb. Although Tyler only saw his parents for a brief moment, he never again worried about whether they acted like loving couples in the movies. In fact, he was convinced that his parents had something far stronger than what Hollywood depicted on the silver screen.[37]

Be cautious of comparing the way you demonstrate love with other couples. Each couple will demonstrate love differently. The key is that you discover how your partner wants to be loved, and then you can help meet those needs.

Homework:
- Based on what you have read, what is your primary love language? What is your secondary love language?
- What is the love language of your spouse?
- What makes you feel most loved by your spouse?
- How do you express love to your spouse? Do they recognize your expressions of love?

Additional Readings:
- Gary Chapman, *The Five Love Languages*, Northfield Press, 2010.
- The Five Love Languages Quiz, http://www.5lovelanguages.com/assessments/love/.
- Jeffrey Holland, "How Do I Love Thee?" *Brigham Young University 1999–2000 Speeches*, 15 February 2000.

References

31 Henry B. Eyring, "Our Perfect Example," *Ensign*, November 2009, 71.

32 Richard G. Scott, "The Eternal Blessings of Marriage," *Ensign*, May 2011, 96.

33 Joseph Fielding Smith, Joseph Smith, *Teachings of the Prophet Joseph Smith* (Salt Lake City: Deseret Book, 1938), 174.

34 Orson Pratt, as cited in *Eternal Marriage Student Manual* (Salt Lake City: Intellectual Reserve, 2003), 157.

35 George W. Pace, *Our Search to Know the Lord* (Salt Lake City: Deseret Book, 1988), 39–40.

36 Hugh W. Pinnock, "Making a Marriage Work," *Ensign*, September 1981, 33.

37 Adapted from Blaine J. Fowers, *Beyond the Myth of Marital Happiness* (San Francisco: Jossey-Bass, 2000), 155–156.

CHAPTER 4
Financial Preparation for Newlyweds

"Members of the Church [are] to use their own gifts and abilities, their
financial and personal resources in becoming temporally self-reliant
and then reaching out to help others to gain that same capacity for
self-reliance. We should strive for self-reliance physically, emotionally,
financially, and most important of all, spiritually."
-Elder J. Thomas Fyans[38]

ONE OF THE MOST SIGNIFICANT practices young married couples must
learn is to live within their means. Some couples get into financial trouble
early in their marriages, and consequently, some struggle for years with
money issues. If you want a happy family life, avoid debt, and live frugally.
Doctrine and Covenants 38:30 states that "if ye are prepared ye shall not
fear." This counsel has just as much to do with temporal preparation as it
does spiritual preparation.

The Principle of Self-Reliance
Simply stated, to be self-reliant is to take responsibility for our own needs—
physical, emotional, spiritual, social, and financial. Therefore, instead
of being a drain on the Church, our family, or the community, we can
actually be a strength and resource for those around us. President Spencer
W. Kimball taught that "no true Latter-day Saint, while physically or
emotionally able will voluntarily shift the burden of his own or his family's
well-being to someone else. So long as he can, under the inspiration of the
Lord and with his own labors, he will supply himself and his family with
the spiritual and temporal necessities of life."[39] The Apostle Paul taught
the Saints, "But if any provide not for his own, and specially for those of
his own house, he hath denied the faith, and is worse than an infidel"[a]
(1 Timothy 5:8). In Doctrine and Covenants 75:28, the Lord taught,

---

a   Most translations I have read regarding this verse change the word "infidel" to
"unbeliever."

"Every man who is obliged to provide for his own family, let him provide, and he shall in nowise lose his crown."

It is clearly taught in the scriptures and from living prophets that husbands and fathers have an unmistakable responsibility to provide for their families. Most individuals I meet have a strong desire to become self-reliant and uphold that sacred obligation. However, occasionally I have met Latter-day Saints, especially when I was a bishop, who actually believed it was the Church's responsibility to provide for them or teach the gospel to their children or solve all of their problems. Such thinking is certainly off course. The Lord has given us the strength, His Spirit, our own intellect, and good people around us to resolve these problems on our own.

To become self-reliant and better prepared for marriage, we should
- have money set aside for emergencies
- avoid debt and live within our means
- use the earth's resources wisely
- learn to prepare meals
- manage time wisely
- learn to maintain living quarters by keeping our apartments or homes clean
- understand basic homemaking skills
- practice principles of health and fitness
- learn to work hard
- learn to perform basic home repairs
- prepare for the future by making spending and savings plans
- practice wise spending habits and being frugal
- obtain the fullness of education
- find gainful employment
- grow gardens and store food
- help those around us become self-reliant

Finances in Marriage
Nothing can wreck a marriage quicker than out-of-control spending and intense financial pressure. President Gordon B. Hinckley declared,

> I urge you, brethren, to look to the condition of your finances.
> I urge you to be modest in your expenditures; discipline yourselves
> in your purchases to avoid debt to the extent possible. Pay off debt
> as quickly as you can, and free yourselves from bondage.

This is a part of the temporal gospel in which we believe. May the Lord bless you, my beloved brethren, to set your houses in order. If you have paid your debts, if you have a reserve, even though it be small, then should storms howl about your head, you will have shelter for your wives and children and peace in your hearts.[40]

Peace comes to those who avoid debt and manage their finances prudently. Presently, it is easy for college students to acquire debt quickly. As a newly married couple, you may receive ten to twenty "invitations" to sign up for a credit card every month via the US mail. Everywhere you turn, people seem to really like you—they all want to give you borrowed money.

I am aware of a college student who applied for a credit card after he received an application in the mail. Initially, he decided he would only use the credit card for emergencies. However, one weekend he was a little short on cash, so he decided to pull out his credit card to purchase some food and gas. He learned how easy it was to use his new piece of plastic. Soon, he was going out to eat more often and purchasing items he rationalized he needed. After one year of college, he had racked up almost $5,000 of charges. When he reviewed his monthly bill, he was shocked to see that most of his purchases were for ridiculous things, like snacks and entertainment. Since credit card payment plans are designed so that you will pay on them for years, it literally took this young man five years after graduation to pay off his debt. The saddest part of this story was that he was paying for *borrowed* burritos, tacos, and soda years after he had devoured them—not a new car, a nice computer, or an appliance for his new home. He began his marriage in a difficult financial position.

In the Old Testament, a great financial truth is taught in Proverbs: "The rich ruleth over the poor, and the borrower is servant to the lender" (Proverbs 22:7). In the Doctrine and Covenants, we read, "Pay the debt . . . Release thyself from bondage" (D&C 19:35; see also D&C 104:78). To be in debt is to live daily with a huge weight on your shoulders. President Heber J. Grant declared, "From my earliest recollections, from the days of Brigham Young until now, I have listened to men standing in the pulpit . . . urging the people not to run into debt; and I believe that the great majority of all our troubles today is caused through the failure to carry out that counsel."[41] Perhaps the most famous statement on debt came from J. Reuben Clark Jr., when he taught: "[Debt] never sleeps nor sickens nor dies; it never goes to the hospital; it works on Sundays and holidays; it never takes a vacation; . . . it is never laid off work. . . . Once in debt, [it] is your companion every minute of the day and night. . . ."[42]

From my own personal experience, I would urge you to avoid debt at all costs—especially credit cards. Janie and I cut up our credit cards about five years ago—a much cheaper form of *plastic surgery*—and haven't used one since. People have asked me, "How do you book airplane tickets or hotels without a credit card?" Easy, I use my debit card, and it's not a big deal. Today, you can make almost any purchase with a debit card. Our leaders have urged us to avoid debt with few exceptions, such as a home, a modest vehicle, and education.

The summer before my freshman year of college, I worked in the oil fields of west Texas. I worked daily with a man named Odell, who was well into his sixties. Knowing that I would be going to college in the fall, Odell would often tell me, "It's not how much you make; it's how much you save." This older man had built up a small fortune by saving his money and living frugally for years. He was not a corporate executive—he was an oil field worker—but he had learned and put into practice a vital principle for happiness: *Live on less than you make!*

How many professional athletes are you aware of that have made millions of dollars a year, and two years after their retirement (at age thirty-two) are completely broke? I know of several individuals who have made large sums of money throughout their lives, but they have also partied hard and played well. Even years after making close to half a million dollars each year, they still have massive amounts of credit card debt, and their homes are not paid off.

Part of the problem is that many of us spend *everything* we make— and then some more. Most individuals believe that if they just made an extra $100 or $1,000 a month, all of their financial issues would be solved. More money isn't the answer; instead, the *discipline* of spending less than we make is where happiness can be found. If you make $100 a week, you will spend it; and if you make $10,000 a week, you will spend that too. Being financially wise and spending less than you earn takes self-discipline.

I often tell my students that I presently make 5 or 6 times more than I did when I first graduated from college. However, my current house payment is also three times more than the house payment on our first home, and I could say the same for our cars. Moreover, we eat out a lot more than we did twenty-five years ago, and we certainly take more expensive vacations. Therefore, we haven't gained much in terms of "saved money." I only share that example because I know I am not alone in this tendency. It's human nature to want bigger and nicer things.

Years ago, Elder Marvin J. Ashton was interviewing a couple just prior to their marriage. This couple was well prepared for marriage in practically every way. However, when Elder Ashton asked the couple, "Who is going to manage your money?" they admitted they had never discussed financial matters with each other.[43] Elder Ashton was shocked this couple had neglected such a key aspect of marital preparation: money management. The response of this couple probably wasn't unusual. I would assume from my counseling experiences that in marriage, financial matters are often neglected, or rarely discussed, unless there is a problem. Then those discussions often become heated, and often the relationship is damaged emotionally. All couples need to be proactive when it comes to money matters.

I would also advise you to beware of lusting after material possessions. Most of us would like nice homes, expensive cars, designer clothes, plasma screen televisions, computers, iPods, iPads, iPhones, boats, WaveRunners, and a cabin in the canyon. However, the desire for these possessions can get us into trouble—especially if we cannot afford them. Moreover, what will some families ever look forward to when they have everything? What do second graders have to look forward to when they own smart phones and iPads?

Early in our marriage, Janie took our two young children to visit her family for a couple of weeks while I painted our first home and landscaped the yard. I wanted to have a big surprise waiting for our children when they came home, so I purchased our first trampoline and had it all set up when they arrived home. I thought Janie would be happy, but she was actually upset. I asked her what was wrong. Why didn't she like the trampoline? I'll never forget her words. She said, "If our kids have a trampoline now, what will they have to look forward to when they are older?" I had never thought about that before. Janie and her siblings were given their first trampoline for Christmas when they were all teenagers, and I think Janie wanted that for our kids. On the other hand, my family never had a trampoline, so I wanted one—and I wanted it immediately.[b]

---

b Look, let me just confess something here. At the time I bought the trampoline, our oldest kid was a year and a half and our second kid was six months old. The trampoline was for me. I freely admit that. And I completely enjoyed it.

I have watched many couples get into financial trouble because they simply were living beyond their means. I have seen young couples purchase homes so large that they could not afford to furnish them. I have seen middle-aged couples purchase cabins and boats, only to sell them a year later—realizing they had bit off more than they could financially chew. I have seen older couples have their cars repossessed or have garage sales to raise enough money to pay the mortgage in a country club neighborhood. Financial trouble equates to marriage trouble. President Gordon B. Hinckley observed, "I am satisfied that money is the root of more trouble in marriage than all other causes combined."[44] In a similar vein, family scholar Dr. Jeffrey Dew recently reported,

> Consumer debt is also an equal-opportunity marriage destroyer. It does not matter if couples are rich or poor, working class or middle class. If they accrue substantial debt, it puts a strain on their marriage.
>
> Assets, on the other hand, sweeten and solidify the ties between spouses. Assets minimize any sense of financial unease that couples feel, with the result that they experience less conflict.
>
> Assets also decrease the likelihood of divorce. Interestingly, the protective power of assets only works for wives, and for two reasons. First, wives with more marital assets are happier in their marriages and, as a consequence, are less likely to seek a divorce.
>
> Second, assets make wives more reluctant to pursue a divorce because they realize that their standard of living would fall markedly after a divorce.
>
> Perceptions of how well one's spouse handles money also play a role in shaping the quality and stability of family life in the U.S. When individuals feel that their spouse does not handle money well, they report lower levels of marital happiness. They are also more likely to head for divorce court.[45]

Dr. Dew concluded, "Not surprisingly, new research that I have done indicates that conflict over money matters predicts divorce better than other types of disagreement."[46] There is no question that poor money management, greed, over-indulgence, and debt all negatively impact marital quality and satisfaction.

Financial Principles and Practices

I would like to share with you ten financial rules that have blessed my marriage and those of many other couples that I know.

1. *Meet current Church expenditures first.* This means pay your tithing and fast offerings before you pay anything else. If you wait to see if there is any money left over, you will never have enough. Pay the Lord first, and he will open to you and your spouse the windows of heaven. But the blessings are not always financial. My own personal belief is that the blessings that come from tithing include the health and well-being of our families. However, if you need financial blessings, pay a generous fast offering and then stand back and watch the Lord perform miracles. I have seen it over and over again in my life.

2. *Meet your current expenses and bills next.* Latter-day Saints should have a reputation for meeting their obligations in a timely manner. If your bills exceed your income, then you need to take a hard look at making some drastic changes. Perhaps your home costs too much or some of your leisure and recreational activities need to be scaled back. When I was a bishop, I was surprised at how many families wanted financial assistance but were unwilling to eliminate their satellite dishes and health club memberships.

3. *Create an emergency fund.* A short-term savings account is essential to meet life's little surprises. The car breaks down, the computer gets a virus, the washing machine leaks, or the air conditioner in your home malfunctions. All of this will happen, and if your life is anything like ours, sometimes they happen all at the same time! If couples don't have an emergency fund, they most often place these repairs on a credit card that will take a long time to pay off. We have been greatly blessed by having a thousand-dollar emergency fund for such repairs and other needs. College students may be able to get by with a few hundred dollars in such a fund.

4. *Put money into savings each month.* I am not a financial wizard, so I cannot recommend whether you should invest in an IRA or a mutual fund. You can find an expert who can help you with that. However, compound interest is practically magical, and it is amazing how much you can save over time. Remember what President Gordon B. Hinckley taught: "Set your houses in order. If you have paid your debts, if you

have a reserve, even though it be small, then should the storms howl about your head, you will have shelter for your wives and children and peace in your hearts."[47] Shortly after we moved to Texas in 1999, a major recession hit the Dallas area hard, and many members of our ward and stake lost their jobs. I was surprised how many members of the Church were able to live for a year, and sometimes two, on their savings. At that point in our lives, we could have lived on our savings for about three hours. It was a vivid reminder of how crucial a savings plan is.

5. *Have adequate insurance.* The purpose of insurance is to protect you, your spouse, and your family against major catastrophes. Every married couple should have health insurance, life insurance, car insurance, and home or renter's insurance. I know of several newly married couples who never purchased any health insurance. A few had babies born with major complications. Instead of having to pay a few hundred dollars when leaving the hospital, they owed over $50,000. Most college students—or even well-established adults—do not have that kind of money sitting in a jar at home. A $100 premium for health insurance is much easier to deal with than a lump sum of $50,000 to $100,000 for medical expenses.

6. *Learn self-control.* Too many young couples get themselves into financial trouble because they purchase material goods they really can't afford. Often, newly married couples want to furnish their apartments with all the luxuries their parents have: big-screen televisions, MP3 players, computers, laptops, furniture, and cell phones. Married couples demonstrate maturity when they can discipline themselves as well as their impulses. Learn that the best things in life are worth waiting for. Start off slow.

7. *Avoid debt at all costs.* Debt is easy to incur and extremely difficult to pay back. Avoid the practice of borrowing money and using credit cards. Debt is a major marriage stressor. Credit cards are set up so that if you only pay the minimum payment, it will take thirty to forty years to pay off. The price of debt is burdensome.

8. *Pay in cash for most purchases.* You can purchase almost anything with cash or a debit card. If you cannot pay cash for something, then you should not purchase it—it's that simple. Trust me; you will enjoy something much more if you pay for it with a debit card instead of

a credit card. Life is much more rewarding when you do not have to borrow money for your pleasure and enjoyment.

9. *Live on a budget.* One of the most "freeing" experiences in our marriage came when we began to live on a budget. Soon, we had discretionary funds that we never knew were available. I am convinced that couples with an average income can become wealthy simply by implementing a budget. We can follow the model of the Church and budget each month for our expenditures. Budgets do not rob us of freedom; instead, they provide economic freedom and flexibility.

10. *Read the book* The Total Money Makeover *by Dave Ramsey.* Janie and I read this book together about five years ago, and it changed our financial life, reduced our debt drastically, strengthened our marriage, and set us on a healthy financial course. We were able to climb out of a deep financial hole we had been in for about twenty years. Now when our children get married, we tell them we will not pay for a wedding until they read this book, and then we quiz them. Janie and I wish we would have had this book as a resource when we were first married— it would have saved us years of financial heartache and stress.

Homework:
- Sit down together, and create a budget. There is free software out there that will provide you with some wonderful financial tools.
- Plan a way to save a $500 to $1,000 emergency fund.
- Set financial goals as a couple. Look at short-term, medium-, and long-range financial goals.
- If you don't have life, health, home or renter's, or auto insurance, get going!
- If you are in debt, read Dave Ramsey's *The Total Money Makeover*, and then create a debt elimination plan.

Additional Readings:
- President Dieter F. Uchtdorf, "Two Principles for Any Economy," *Ensign*, November 2009.
- Elder D. Todd Christofferson, "Come to Zion," *Ensign*, November 2008.
- Self-Reliance and Provident Living, http://www.lds.org/service/serving-in-the-church/relief-society/messages-from-leaders/

additional-relief-society-meetings/self-reliance-provident-living?l
ang=eng&query=food+storage.

- *Gospel Solutions for Families*: "Family Finances, Part 1," Episode
77, Matt Richardson, Mark Ogletree, and Craig Israelsen. http://
www.mormonchannel.org/gospel-solutions-for-families/77.

- *Gospel Solutions for Families*: "Family Finances, Part 2," Episode
78, Matt Richardson, Mark Ogletree, and Craig Israelsen. http://
www.mormonchannel.org/gospel-solutions-for-families/78.

References

38 J. Thomas Fyans, "Individual and Family Self-Reliance Featured in Leadership Session," *Ensign*, May 1983, 84.

39 Spencer W. Kimball, "Welfare Services: The Gospel in Action," *Ensign*, November 1977, 77–79.

40 Gordon B. Hinckley, "To the Boys and to the Men," *Ensign*, November 1998, 52–54.

41 Heber J. Grant, *Conference Report*, October 1921, 3.

42 J. Reuben Clark Jr., *Conference Report*, April 1938, 103.

43 Marvin J. Ashton, *One for the Money: Guide to Family Finance* (Salt Lake City: Intellectual Reserve, 1992), 1.

44 Gordon B. Hinckley, *Cornerstones of a Happy Home* (Salt Lake City: Intellectual Reserve, 1984), 8.

45 Jeffrey Dew, *Bank on It: Thrifty Couples are the Happiest* (National Marriage Project's 2009 State of our Unions), 25–26.

46 Ibid, 27–28.

47 Gordon B. Hinckley, "To the Boys and to the Men," *Ensign*, November 1998, 54.

CHAPTER 5
Learning to Deal with Differences in Marriage

"Men mistakenly expect women to think, communicate, and react the
way men do. . . . We have forgotten that men and women are supposed
to be different. As a result our relationships are filled with unnecessary
friction and conflict."
-John Gray[48]

ACCORDING TO PRESIDENT GORDON B. Hinckley, differences in marriage
"make the companionship more interesting."[49] For couples preparing
for marriage, learning to understand some of the differences between
the genders is an essential quest. Those who are slow to learn about such
differences will find their marriage relationship becoming frustrating.

When Janie and I began dating, I began to notice some of our
differences. For example, in our spare time she liked to read or watch
chick flicks; I liked to engage in outdoor activities. I also noticed that
Janie loved to talk and relax, while I loved going about 100 miles per hour.
However, I had no real reason to believe that any of our differences were
gender driven. I simply assumed our personalities were different. It wasn't
until we had children that I began to discover how gender differences can
drive behavior.

For example, Brittany, our firstborn, was all girl. She didn't like to
have dirt on her hands and would figuratively walk a mile to have us
remove a speck of dust from her finger. For her first birthday, she received
a baby doll and a stroller. A baby herself, she would push that little dolly
around in the stroller and take care of it for half the day. As other children
were born into our family, Brittany practically became a second mother—
helping Janie to feed our younger children and even change diapers. Each
year, presents for her birthday and Christmas seemed to center on future
motherhood: a kitchen set, complete with refrigerator and oven; more
dolls; and a white board with markers.

When Brittany was in elementary school, she would come home each day, gather her younger sisters, and play "school" until dinnertime. When they weren't playing school, they played "church." The girls had converted our garage into a chapel. They had set up a row of chairs, and one of the girls would say, "I would like to bear my testimony," as they talked into the screwdriver they were using for a microphone at a podium made out of milk carton crates. All of my girls were under the age of seven, yet they were pushing strollers around, pretending to feed their babies, and taking their dolls to church. Indeed, many parents do an incredible job of socializing their children into their divinely appointed roles. By the time Brittany was a teenager, Janie and I joked that she could probably run our household better than us—which I believe she could. Today, she is a wonderful mother to her two little girls.

A year after Brittany was born, our only son, Brandon, came into the world. It didn't take long to see that Brandon "beat to a different drum." Instead of being afraid of dirt, he wallowed in it like a pig. Instead of playing with dolls, Brandon loved to play sports. I would come home from work, and from 4:30 to 6:30 every evening until his later elementary years, we were playing football, soccer, or basketball. Brandon was also extremely competitive.

Unlike Brittany, when Brandon was four, he couldn't change his siblings' diapers or vacuum the house. In fact, he could barely walk because he had three Ninja Turtle swords shoved down each pant leg. And he didn't play "primary" or "house" or "school." Instead, he had the entire Phoenix Suns roster memorized and could tell you which brand of shoe each player wore. Oh yeah, I almost forgot, and he could terrorize his sisters extremely well!

One day, I had come home from work during lunchtime, and all four of our daughters were standing on our sidewalk in front of our home. They were each crying and pointing their fingers down the street. I had no idea what was happening but knew it must have been something tragic—maybe a puppy got run over in the street, a tree fell on the mailman, or a house was on fire. However, in the minds of my girls, the tragedy was much more serious than any of the possibilities *I* imagined. I turned my head down the street and saw Brandon riding toward our house on his bike. He had "kidnapped" all of the girls' dolls and had tied a rope around the neck of each one. Then, he had tied the other end of the rope to his bike and was dragging these dolls around the street. He would ride up to the girls and ask them if they wanted their dollies back, and they would all cry,

"Yes." Then he would laugh and drive his bike off. I guess this little game had been going on for some time. I could share a hundred more examples of this kind of behavior, but I'll save that for another book. Needless to say, the way Brandon was socialized, as well as other young men in his cohort, would not make him necessarily a candidate for "Future Father of the Year," but he certainly would be prepared to be a Navy Seal, a rodeo clown, or something else along those lines.

As our children became teenagers, we continued to notice many gender-based differences between our son and his seven sisters. Our girls were much more emotional and verbal. Brandon was always more physical and logical. Often before bedtime, our daughters would visit with Janie and me for hours about their lives, their friends, and their activities. Conversely, when Brandon came home after a week of EFY or football camp and we asked him how everything went, he would say, "Fine," as he cracked open a box of cereal.

I believe we actually learn more from our own children than from anything our parents taught us. I have certainly learned more about gender roles by observing my own children than from any book I have read on the topic. After thirty years of marriage and eight children, I have come to know that our Heavenly Father has made men and women different for many reasons. By divine design, we have distinct roles and responsibilities. I believe our Father in Heaven has created us differently in order to bless our children and help build God's kingdom here on the earth. Knowing you are preparing for a wonderful marriage, several key differences are worth mentioning.

Physical Differences

Obviously, men and women are different physically. After all, physical attraction is what caused you and your significant other to notice each other in the first place. However, there are other differences that many people are not aware of. Dr. Paul Popenoe, founder of the American Institute of Family Relations in Los Angeles, has uncovered some significant data on the physical differences between the sexes.

1. Men and women differ in every cell of their bodies due to the chromosome combinations that make up males and females.

2. Women have a greater constitutional vitality, perhaps because of their chromosome make-up. Females outlive males four to eight years in the United States.

3. Women have a lower metabolism than men.

4. Women differ in skeletal structure. For instance, a woman's first finger is usually longer than her third. Also, girls' teeth do not last as long as boys' teeth.

5. Women have larger stomachs, kidneys, livers, and appendixes but smaller lungs.

6. Women have more emotional swings because of menstruation, pregnancy, lactation, and menopause.

7. Women generally have larger active thyroid glands than men, which makes them more resistant to colds and more prone to goiter problems. It gives women smoother skin and relatively hairless bodies. The thyroid gland produces a layer of subcutaneous fat, which contributes to important elements in personal beauty. A larger thyroid also makes women more emotionally responsive, causing them to laugh and cry more easily than men.

8. Women have blood with more water and fewer (20 percent fewer) red blood cells. Consequently, they often tire more easily and are more prone to faint.

9. Women's hearts generally beat more rapidly (80 beats per minute for women; 72 beats per minute for men), and women have lower blood pressure before menopause.

10. Woman can generally tolerate or are more comfortable in higher temperatures than men.

11. On the average, men possess 50 percent more brute strength than women (40 percent of a man's weight is muscle, contrasted with 23 percent of a woman's weight).[50]

Can these differences impact the marital relationship? Certainly they can.

Dr. Joyce Brothers pointed out:

> Are men and women really so different? They are. They really are. I spent months talking to biologists, neurologists, geneticists, research psychiatrists, and psychologists. . . . What I discovered was that men are even more different from women than I had known. Their bodies are different and their minds are different. Men are

different from the very composition of their blood to the way their brains develop, which means that they think and experience life differently from women. . . . Women are left-hemisphere [brain] oriented, more verbally adroit. The left hemisphere develops earlier, which gives them an edge in reading and writing. . . . Men use the right hemisphere more efficiently than women do. The converse is not true, however. Women do not use the left brain more efficiently than men. The male and female brains are by no means set up as mirror images of each other. What it adds up to is that we are blessed with two different ways of thinking and learning. The male brain is specialized. Men use the right hemisphere when dealing with spatial problems and the left for verbal problems. . . . The female brain is not specialized. Right and left hemisphere work together on a problem. This is possible because in the female brain, left-hemisphere abilities are duplicated to some extent in the right hemisphere and right-hemisphere abilities in the left. . . . The ability to zero in on a problem with both hemispheres makes women much more perceptive about people. [This is sometimes called intuition.] They are better at sensing the difference between what people say and what they mean and at picking up the nuances that reveal another person's true feelings.[51]

Aside from these neurological differences, there are also some chemical differences that impact the different ways men and women behave. Most often men ascribe their behavior to testosterone levels. One theory postulates that testosterone is released throughout the embryo to make females into males (all embryos are female, unless there is a release of testosterone for those who have inherited the 'Y' [male] chromosome), and the fetus begins to develop masculinization. This hormonal bath of testosterone actually changes the brain and alters its structure; the color of the brain changes. Moreover,

The corpus callosum, which is the rope of nerve fibers that connects the two hemispheres, is made less efficient. This limits the number of electrical transmissions that can flow from one side of the brain to the other, which will have lifelong implications. Later, a man will have to think longer about what he believes— especially about something with an emotional component. He may never fully comprehend it. A woman, on the other hand, will typically be able to access her prior experience from both hemispheres and discern almost instantly how she feels about it.[52]

So, women, this may be the explanation you have been looking for. Most of us men are just brain damaged—that's our problem! Aside from that, we're fine. Testosterone, by the way, doesn't just affect the way we think. Our tendency to take risks, to be assertive and aggressive, to compete, to fight, to argue, to be rough, to be tough, to brag, to enjoy watching cars crash, and to have an insatiable desire to light things on fire stems from the hormone testosterone.

Testosterone is not the only chemical that makes men different. Serotonin also contributes. Serotonin is a neurotransmitter that carries information from one nerve cell to another. This chemical soothes emotions and helps us control impulsive behavior. In studies, monkeys with low levels of serotonin made dangerous leaps from branch to branch. Rats with lower levels of serotonin were aggressive and often violent. Perhaps you have already guessed where I am going with this, but, generally speaking, women have higher levels of serotonin than men.[53]

Another interesting aspect when comparing the male and female mind is that men seem to have the ability to compartmentalize their thoughts. Put another way, imagine that the male mind is made up of hundreds of compartments where a man can store his experiences and memories. Therefore, during the course of the day, a male can get upset because he received a traffic ticket on his way to work and put that in compartment one; become frustrated because his computer was attacked by a virus and put that in compartment two; engage in a yelling match with his boss and put that in compartment three; and so it continues throughout the day. In fact, the rest of the day could be horrendous, and the typical American male will continue to file everything away into little compartments. On the drive home from work, he may get a flat tire, only to find out that the spare is also flat. When he finally makes it home, with black rubber marks all over his clothes and face, he may trip over all of the toys in the yard on his way to the front door, get mad, scream at the kids, and kick the dog. He may then go into his room to take a shower, only to discover that his wife has been doing laundry all day, so there's no hot water. What makes men incredibly talented is that, despite a horrific day, by 9:00 p.m. they can still be ready for prime-time romance. For men, intimacy can be a source of therapy.

Women are just the opposite. They could never get into a romantic mood after a disastrous day like the one described. A woman's mind is more like a gigantic ball of yarn where everything is connected. Often, for most women, what happened this morning is related to what will happen this evening. A woman can be mad at her husband for something he did during the Christmas celebration five years ago, and that alone can directly impact a romantic evening years later! In fact, forgetting a wife's birthday or a wedding anniversary can sometimes basically sentence a man to a life of cruel and unusual punishment. After all, what woman would want to be intimate with a guy who cannot even remember the day they were married?

Humor aside, for women, life is all connected. For men, few things are connected. Because of their brain structure, men and women process life's experiences differently. This is why it is so important that husbands and wives talk about what they think, how they feel about certain issues, and why they feel and think the way they do. Positive communication is the key to navigating these differences. Moreover, when you communicate about these issues, listening is more important than talking. Don't try to change the other person or solve problems—just listen. Listening is the key to understanding.

Another key point here is for husbands and wives to realize that these physical differences are real. Husbands, if you're driving down the highway and your wife insists on turning on the heat but you want the air conditioner on, understand that her need for heat is real. You can adjust by rolling the window down or by taking your sweater off. She wants the heat on because she is actually cold, not because she wants to start a fight with you.

At the same time, wives, understand that the reason your husband makes some of the decisions he does is because of the way his brain has been designed to work. He isn't trying to be unreasonable or uncaring. He is just doing the best with what he has been given. Our Heavenly Father made men and women different physically because of our divinely appointed roles and purposes.

Emotional Differences

Remember the movie *Sleepless in Seattle*? There is a great scene in which Sam (played by Tom Hanks); his sister, Suzy; and her husband, Greg, are at Sam's house discussing his love life. Sam tells Suzy and Greg that

his son, Jonah, called into a national radio talk show and told the host
that his dad needed a new wife. He explains that a woman named Annie
heard the broadcast and, consequently, wanted to meet Sam on top of the
Empire State Building on Valentine's Day. As Sam shared this experience,
Suzy said, "Oh, it's like the movie—*An Affair to Remember*." Suzy then
proceeds to describe the movie, and her emotions overtake her. She begins
sobbing as she relates the romantic plot. As she's weeping uncontrollably,
the men, Sam and Greg, look at each other in unbelief and shrug their
shoulders as they wonder what has come over Suzy. Jonah then asks Suzy,
"Are you all right?" She just continues to share the story and weep. After
Sam discounts the film as a "chick's movie," he and Greg decided to poke
fun at Suzy's emotions by discussing a real man's movie: *The Dirty Dozen*.
As they recount the movie's plot, they sarcastically begin to weep and wail.
That is what makes this scene a classic: two men crying over *The Dirty
Dozen*. Suzy picks up on the humor, and she, too, begins to laugh. Perhaps
she realizes that crying over a movie is certainly a "girl thing." Perhaps
some of you women who are reading this are crying right now; then again,
maybe your husbands are too.

This classic movie scene depicts a major difference between men and
women: most women have probably cried during a movie, while many
men probably haven't but perhaps wanted to! It's not that women are
just a bunch of crybabies; compared to men, women view and experience
the world differently—more emotionally. Perhaps you have many things
in common with your spouse. I assume many newlyweds can converse
with ease, have similar values and beliefs, enjoy the same music, and like
the same kinds of food. However, if you are like most newlyweds, you
are beginning to notice differences in personality, character, manners, and
habits that will come to the surface in one way or another. Once they have
been married for several years, many couples begin to wonder if they have
anything in common.

Let us consider some of the specific emotional differences between
men and women. Keep in mind that I am speaking in extremely general
terms to exaggerate the point. Typically, women are more inclined to be
personal than men. The female sex has a deeper interest in people and
feelings; hence, building relationships is one of their great needs and desires.
Women connect by talking. On the contrary, men tend to be preoccupied
with practicalities and facts. For instance, when a young child gets injured
and comes running to their mother, she will usually respond by taking

care of the child, doctoring the wound, and administering some tender loving care. However, when the same child with the same injury comes to their father, there is an insightful question that must be first asked: "Are you hurt?"—even though there is blood gushing from the child's leg. That inquiry is usually followed by, "How did this happen?" I don't understand why, but for some reason, most men like to know how the injury happened. Perhaps this is because we don't want the same thing to happen to us. After all, if there's a rusty nail, a sharp stick, or a booby trap in the neighborhood, we would like to be aware of it so we can adjust our travel plans. Men most often just want "nothing but the facts, ma'am." We are logical and reasonable. We try to keep our emotions under the surface.

When I was in the fourth grade, my dad received a transfer, and we were going to move from our home in San Antonio, Texas. We lived in one of those ideal neighborhoods back in the seventies, where every neighbor knew each other and often socialized together. I will never forget the day we left. Most of the women from the neighborhood were in our front yard, hugging each other, crying, and exchanging addresses. Meanwhile, the men were gathered around the moving van, examining the hydraulic lift on the back of the truck, wondering how much weight it could support.

Isn't that typical? Women are emotional "feelers." They connect deeply to each other and form emotional attachments. Men have emotions too, but we often hide them under the guise of discovering how a hydraulic lift works. If you don't believe me, go into a typical Relief Society room on any given Sunday. The women are often sharing, weeping, and consoling each other, talking about issues from childbirth to teenagers, from cough syrup to chemotherapy. Meanwhile, men are in their priesthood meeting often trying to figure out who's supposed to have the lesson that week. Once that's discovered, they will often spend more time spewing out facts and information rather than connecting with each other. This may be why many men in the Church do not know each other as well as we should— we typically do not connect or share personal information.

One family scholar has identified some of the key emotional differences between men and women:[54]

1. Women are emotional feelers; men are logical thinkers.

2. For women, language spoken is an expression of what she feels; for a man, language spoken is an expression of what he is thinking.

3. Language that is heard by a woman is an emotional experience; language that is heard by a man is simply receiving information.

4. Women tend to take everything personally; men tend to take things impersonally.

5. Women are interested in all of the nitty-gritty details; men are interested in the principles, the abstract, and the philosophy.

6. Women have a great need for security and roots; men can be nomadic.

7. Women tend to be guilt-prone; men tend to be resentful.

Some of the relationships men build with other men are based on competition (perhaps testosterone levels are to blame). For instance, if a group of men went bowling or golfing together, they would keep score to see who wins, and the loser would have to buy milkshakes for the winners. While eating afterward, men would brag about their best shots and harass those who had a bad day on the course. This is just a tradition. Women, on the other hand, would applaud each other's successes. Then they would go out to eat together and talk about something totally different, like church, family, friends, or perhaps a book they are reading.

There probably has never been a greater tennis rivalry as there was in the 1980s with Chris Evert and Martina Navratilova. Off the court, these women were good friends. After matches, they would often call or visit each other. The winner would always console the loser. Often, they would leave each other notes: "Sorry" or "You'll get me next time." Meanwhile, the two great male rivals at the time were Jimmy Connors and John McEnroe. There was no love lost between these two. They would stare each other down and try to intimidate each other before and after a match. There were no cards from Connors saying, "Don't worry, John; you'll beat the tar out of me next time."[55] Most men would rather beat someone in anything than give them a hug.

Emotionally, men and women are different creatures. Now that you're married, it's important to identify your emotional differences and discuss them with each other. You will need to learn to understand and accept these differences. Recognize that a company move, an illness, a misfortune, a financial difficulty, a misunderstanding at church, and myriad other things will affect you two differently. Women, learn to be patient with your husbands. Just because he isn't crying over an issue or expressing himself the same way you would doesn't necessarily mean he doesn't have strong feelings about the matter. Men, be patient and understanding with your wives. If she needs to cry, let her. Hold her and listen to her. That's what she needs.

Verbal Differences

In my counseling visits with couples, many women will often ask something like this: "What happened to the guy I married? During our engagement he was so thoughtful, courteous, and kind. Not only was he a good listener but a good communicator as well. Before we were married, we used to talk hours into the night. Now that we've been married for a few years, we never talk about anything, and when I try to, he usually responds with a grunt or mumble."

Most women don't understand that men do not need to talk as much as females do. According to some marriage and family experts, the average man speaks between 12,000 and 15,000 words per day. The average woman speaks about 25,000 words per day. Do you see the crash coming? By late afternoon, men have used up all of their words! Women, on the other hand still have 10,000 words that need to come in sometime after dinner! Men, you must learn to listen to your wife. After you have been married for a few years and her only conversations have been with a toddler and phone solicitor, you need to become a great listener.

A few years ago, I was doing some premarital counseling with a couple who had become engaged the week before. I asked the future husband, "So how did you ask her to marry you?" The man described his proposal in about five minutes. Later in the session, I asked the future bride the exact same question. You guessed it. It took thirty minutes to hear her version of the exact same story. Most women love conversation. They love to talk. They love to know about each other's lives. Men talk as a way to share information and usually not much more than that.

Women, when your husbands don't talk to you, it's not because they don't like you. More likely, it's just because they have slipped back into their natural mode of not talking as much. Sure, they could stretch themselves and talk late into the night when you were engaged. They had to. Whatever it would take, they were willing to do. You wouldn't have married them otherwise. And at that time, he was willing to do whatever he needed to do to win your heart over. If he needed to write poetry, he did; if he needed to communicate like Dr. Phil, he did; if he needed to buy you flowers and sing a serenade, he did. Most men have a conquest mentality. In the heat of the battle, men will do whatever it takes to win. However, once victory has been achieved, men tend to think of the next Mount Everest they need to climb. They have won your love and need to move to the next challenge. That is why many men seem to become disengaged several years after marriage.

Furthermore, men are not that good at "multitasking." After we win our wives over, we tend to focus on getting good grades and graduating so we can provide for our future families. After that, we may focus on conquering graduate school or becoming the top producer at our place of employment. Wives, you probably won't change that. It's in our DNA. However, you can help channel that energy in the right direction—and that is toward marriage and family life.

Most men will need reminders and encouragement to talk, and they need to be rewarded for doing it. Wives, let your husbands know how much you love it when they converse with you and share their feelings. On the other hand, husbands, recognize your wives' need to communicate, and give them time to share and open up. When your wife speaks to you, sit down and look directly into her eyes. When you come home each day, ask her how her day was and then really listen. It may take her a while to share her experiences. That's just fine. Listening to her will bring more satisfaction for both of you in your marriage.

The Way We View Time

Since you have probably been married at least a few months by now, you have more than likely had a dispute over time or tardiness. Often, women seem to run about five or ten minutes behind schedule—and I don't want to imply that men are never late, because we know they are. For years, Janie and I were frustrated with each other because I felt that we should be at church at least fifteen minutes before sacrament meeting began. Janie, on the other hand, believed that if we arrived before the opening hymn was announced, we were on time. When I was a bishop, I would often speak about punctuality and give talks on the importance of being on time. Once, right in the middle of my little speech, Janie and the girls came walking in. So much for that sermon! Most men come to realize that when a woman says they will be ready in five minutes, it may be more like twenty-five minutes.

Furthermore, research indicates that men and women view time itself differently. For men, time is linear. We view time as a straight line on a continuum. In a way, men view time as driving down a long highway, with mile markers, roadside stops, and occasional lookout points. In our minds, once we pass through an event, we are done with that chapter or page and check it off our list. Therefore, men can check off mission, school, marriage, birth of baby, first job, etc. To men, once we pass through an event or an experience, it is completed, and we are ready for the next one.

Women, on the other hand, tend to view time in cycles, rather than linearly. That is, time can be viewed as a spiral instead of a line. Some scholars contend that this tendency is directly connected to the female menstrual cycle. Therefore, women see time as a series of events that they go through again and again and again. For women, time is a repeated series of events. Therefore, what comes around may yet come around again and possibly again.

For example, several years ago our youngest child, Natalie, outgrew her baby crib. She was the last of eight children to sleep in that crib. At this point in our lives, we had several teenagers, and I was anxious for us to get out of the "baby stage" of life. We had to make a decision on what to do with our old, banged-up baby crib. Since I had a long commute from work each day, I often had much time to think. On my way home on a particular Monday evening, I was contemplating what to do with that crib. I decided we could have some fun getting rid of the crib and make a "ceremony" of the process for family home evening.

I thought of how fun it would be to take the crib into the backyard and let each kid take a whack at it with a sledgehammer or axe. We would smash the crib into splinters; then we would put all the wood scraps into a pile and light it on fire. I envisioned our family doing some kind of funny dance around the fire, with me leaping over the flames. For me, life was a journey, and time passed as a car travels down the highway. What I needed was a ceremonial bonfire to signify that our family was done with the baby phase of our lives. The bonfire would be a rite of passage into the next stage of adulthood. This ritual was certainly a rite of passage, or at least a great excuse for Brandon and me to play with fire for FHE.

When I told Janie about my incredible idea, she almost snapped. She couldn't believe what she was hearing. How could we burn the crib that all of our babies had slept in? To Janie, that crib was a time capsule of years of wonderful memories. It wasn't simply a piece of furniture—it was a symbol of motherhood and nurturing. Janie simply felt that I was a lunatic and wanted to have me committed. She thought my idea was the most ridiculous thing she had ever heard.

Besides, she explained, within the next several years, we would be grandparents. Where would our grandbaby sleep when our married children came to visit? Of course, for Janie the only appropriate place for any of her grandbabies to sleep would be in the very crib where her own children had slept. When Janie presented these ideas to me, I was flabbergasted. I was just starting to feel comfortable being a father. Just as I was figuring out what fathers do, Janie was announcing to me that I was going to be a grandfather, and I simply wasn't ready for that! How could I be a grandfather? Grandfathers are old men. My only visual of a grandfather was my own granddad, who had always looked like he was about eighty. Granddad walked around our house in a jumpsuit, used colorful language, told the same stories over and over again, and did the worst magic tricks ever. Grandfathers were not guys like me who jogged three miles a day, listened to contemporary radio stations, water-skied, and ate sushi. And they certainly were not guys who had children living in their homes. I just couldn't wrap my head around the idea that I would ever be a grandfather. That thought never even occurred to me until that day.

Perhaps you will discover experiences as a couple where you view time differently. Men and women certainly need to understand this concept. It will help resolve several issues in their relationship; it will also help them understand why they do certain things.

Approaches to Child Rearing

Men and women bring different traits and attributes into the ring of parenthood. For example, men tend to emphasize play, while women are more prone to caretaking. Men are often rough-and-tumble in their approach with their children, while women are generally more nurturing. Women tend to be more responsive to their children, while men tend to be firm. Women emphasize emotional security and nurturing in relationships, while men accentuate competition, risk-taking, and toughness. Working as a team, men and women make great parents when these roles are understood. There is no question that we need each other, particularly when it comes to raising children.

When our oldest daughter, Brittany, entered middle school, she qualified to be a member of the cross-country team. She was an excellent runner and won the city middle school championship. Then, as a freshman in high school, she made the varsity team. I enjoyed going to her meets and watching her compete. I took Brittany's cross-country career more seriously than Janie did. Every Friday night, I would encourage my daughter to carbo-load and then go to bed by 9:00 p.m. to be ready for her meets on Saturday mornings. Brittany had no interest in going to bed that early when she could hang out with her friends. She would occasionally remind me that I needed to chill out. However, I was grooming a future Olympian! At least, so I thought.

At each meet, I would strategically map the course and figure out where I could best cheer Brittany on. If I did it right, running at full speed, I could get myself to several places on the course before she finished the race. I would yell out crucial bits of advice, such as "run harder," or "compete." Rarely did I actually see her finish because I felt it was crucial that I yell encouragement to her that last quarter mile. On the other hand, Janie would cheer Brittany on from the starting line and then casually walk over to the finish line to wait to greet Brittany as she completed the race.

Once the race was over, I would come running up—draped in stopwatches, canteens, and maps—looking for Brittany and Janie. My first question was always, "What was your time?" Janie never knew. She was just there to give moral support and hugs. I don't think Janie even cared what Brittany's time was. She was just happy for her. I wanted to know if Brittany's time was faster or slower than the previous week. Of course, if her time was slower, I would introduce a regimen of running more miles during the week and a prescription cocktail of energy bars, vitamins, more pasta, and earlier bed times. Brittany finally had to explain to me that she really just enjoyed the camaraderie of the cross-country team and that she had no interest in becoming an Olympian or running in college. I backed off drastically at that point, when I realized that I was more worried about her athletic career than she was. This experience demonstrates my point: men tend to emphasize physical activity, competition, and risk-taking with their children, while women emphasize emotional security and relationships. Children will benefit when both of these approaches arc mingled together.

The Need to Be Needed or Cherished

Most women need to be cherished and to receive care and tenderness, understanding, respect, devotion, validation, reassurance, and a listening ear. Most men need to be needed, to receive trust, appreciation, admiration, approval, encouragement, and to be viewed as competent. If a man is not putting his wife first, treating her with kindness and respect, and simply adoring her, she will not feel cherished. Similarly, if a husband doesn't feel needed or appreciated or competent, he may feel worthless and may ultimately look elsewhere for fulfillment.

Right after Janie and I were engaged, we were driving home from Brigham Young University at the conclusion of the fall semester. We were heading toward our homes in the suburbs of Houston. At that time in my life, I was not mechanically gifted. I knew that running the air-conditioner was a drain on the engine and negatively impacted the gas mileage; therefore, I made my best educated "guess" and deducted that running the heater would cause the same problem. So as we drove home in a horrendous snowstorm, I elected to not run the heater in the car. I didn't understand that turning on the heater was basically a "freebie"—the heat simply comes from heat of the engine. Since I was short on funds, I thought I could save a few tanks of gas by not running the heater for the entire trip. Since we drove home in arctic conditions, the trip was quite miserable. During most of the journey, Janie protested, "I don't think running the heater has anything to do with your gas mileage." I assured her that it did and also explained that I *probably* knew much more about cars than she did.

Of course, as soon as we arrived at Janie's home, the first thing she asked her dad, after greeting everyone of course, was, "Dad, is it true that the heater is a drain on the mileage of the car?" Janie's dad laughed hysterically, looked at me, and winked. He figured, "Oh yeah, the old 'we can't turn on the heater so I guess we'll have to snuggle' routine!" I played along with the supposed joke but, of course, was humiliated that Janie had "called my hand," so to speak.

After we graduated from BYU, we bought a home in Mesa, Arizona, that needed some basic repairs. It seemed that everything I told Janie regarding fix-ups, she felt compelled to call home to Houston and check with her dad. It took a while for me to gain her confidence. The heater experience caused some collateral damage. Although my wife loved me, she thought I was clueless on repairs and mechanics, which I was. I couldn't help but feel inadequate and incompetent. It was embarrassing to have Janie call her dad to see how "off-course" I was. Over time I learned how to remodel our homes. Because Janie has believed in me, I have learned to believe in myself. So, thirty years later, we have now remodeled four homes, and Janie hasn't called Houston in quite some time. I am feeling more "needed" and "trusted" when it comes to home repairs.

Consider the following example from the lives of Spencer and Camilla Kimball. President Kimball came home for lunch, as was his custom, to eat and rest for a while. The phone rang, and on the other end was J. Reuben Clark Jr. He told Spencer to take a seat and then let Spencer know he had been called into the Quorum of the Twelve Apostles. Spencer was bewildered and numb. He could barely finish his phone conversation. He hung up the phone and began to weep uncontrollably. It was then that Camilla sat down on the floor next to Spencer, stroked his hair, and comforted him. He made it through the night, but only with the help of Camilla. He said, "My wife is my salvation. She comforted me and encouraged me and continued to say there was only one road to follow."[56] If it were not for the faith that Camilla Kimball had in her husband and her encouragement, he would have never been able to become the giant of a man he became.

Together in the Lord

Men and women were created differently by a loving Heavenly Father. The God-given differences between men and women should never drive them apart—those differences should bring them together. Men and women complement each other.[a] Specifically, we need each other's strengths for survival, for success, and for exaltation. The Lord made us different for specific reasons. Where one gender is weak, the other is strong. Together, we become a whole. Dr. James Dobson explained it this way:

> Consider again the basic tendencies of maleness and femaleness. Because it is the privilege and blessing of women to bear children, they are inclined toward predictability, stability, security, caution, and steadiness. Most of them value friendships and family above accomplishments or opportunities. That is why they often dislike change and resist moving from one city to another. The female temperament lends itself to nurturance, caring, sensitivity, tenderness, and compassion. Those are the precise characteristics needed by their children during the developmental years. Without the softness of femininity, the world would be a more cold, legalistic, and militaristic place.
>
> Men, on the other hand, have been designed for a different role. They value change, opportunity, risk, speculation, and adventure. They are designed to provide for their families physically and to protect them from harm and danger. . . . This is a divine assignment. Men are also ordained in scripture for leadership in their homes, to be expressed within the framework of servanthood.

---

a   Notice, I have spelled "complement" with an "e," not an "i." Men and women "complete" each other!

Men are often (but not always) less emotional in a crisis and more confident when challenged. A world without men would be more static and uninteresting. When my father died, Mom said with a tear in her eye, "He brought so much excitement into my life." That characteristic is often attractive to women.[57]

Perhaps this is why Paul wrote, "Neither is the man without the woman, neither the woman without the man, in the Lord" (1 Corinthians 11:11). President Kimball observed:

> Our Father made men and women dependent on each other for the full flowering of their potential. Because their natures are somewhat different, they can complement each other; because they are in many ways alike, they can understand each other. Let neither envy the other for their differences; let both discern what is superficial and what is beautifully basic in those differences, and act accordingly.[58]

Homework:
- Sit down together as a couple, and divide a sheet of paper into two columns. On one side of the page, brainstorm and write down your similarities. In the other column, write down some of your differences.
- Discuss as a couple how your differences can become assets in your marriage and especially to your future children.

Additional Readings:
- Jeffrey R. Holland & Patricia T. Holland, "Some Things We Have Learned Together," *Brigham Young University 1984–85 Speeches*, 15 January 1985.
- Brent A. Barlow, *Dealing with Differences in Marriage* (Salt Lake City, Utah: Deseret Book), 1993.
- John Gray, *Men Are from Mars, Women Are from Venus* (New York City, New York: Harper-Collins), 1992.

References
48 John Gray, *Men Are from Mars, Women Are from Venus* (New York: Harper Collins, 1992), 10.

49 President Gordon B. Hinckley, "Cornerstones of a Happy Home," (pamphlet, 1984), 5.

50 Brent A. Barlow, *Dealing with Differences in Marriage* (Deseret Book: Salt Lake City, 1993), 29.

51 Dr. Joyce Brothers, as cited in Brent A. Barlow, *Dealing with Differences in Marriage* (Deseret Book: Salt Lake City, 1993), 29–31.

52 James Dobson, *Bringing Up Boys* (Wheaton, Ill.: Tyndale House Publishers, 2001), 19–20.

53 Ibid, 25.

54 H. Norman Wright, *More Communication Keys for Your Marriage* (Regal Books, Ventura: California. 1983), 123.

55 James Dobson, *Bringing Up Boys* (Wheaton, Ill.: Tyndale House Publishers, 2001), 24.

56 E.L. Kimball & A.E. Kimball Jr., *Spencer W. Kimball* (Salt Lake City: Bookcraft, 1977), 191.

57 James Dobson, *Bringing Up Boys* (Wheaton, Ill.: Tyndale House Publishers, 2001), 27.

58 Spencer W. Kimball, *The Teachings of Spencer W. Kimball* (Salt Lake City: Bookcraft, 1982), 315.

CHAPTER 6
Managing Individual Differences in Marriage

"No man can be perfect without the woman, so no woman can be
perfect without a man. . . . I tell you the truth as it is in the bosom of
eternity. If he wishes to be saved, he cannot be saved without a woman
by his side."
-President Brigham Young[59]

IN THE PREVIOUS CHAPTER, I discussed what I would call "universal"
differences between men and women. I would like to be more specific in
this chapter. Some of the differences I discuss in this chapter will be absent
in your marriage; however, others will be present. Some of these issues will
be gender driven; however, other differences may occur because of your
unique personalities, world view, or perhaps the family you were raised in.

Take shopping, for instance. Most men I have met are not fond of
shopping. On the other hand, many women seem to enjoy it. For some
women, shopping should be an Olympic event. On the other hand, most
men would prefer to shop only on the Internet twice a year—Mother's
Day and Christmas. Some women view shopping as an all-day event; they
could be gone the entire day, never buy a thing, and call it a great success.
Meanwhile, most men view shopping like a deer hunt. They go to the first
store they see, set the object of purchase in their sites, throw their kill in
the basket, pay for it, tie it to the roof of the car, and haul it home.

Janie and I had to work through our "shopping" differences when we
were first married. Janie would drive all over town trying to find the best
bargains. Often, shopping for groceries would take most of our Saturday.
I, on the other hand, detest shopping and would like to make the event
as quick and painless as possible. Many times when we would shop
together, I would make life miserable for my wife, grunting, groaning, and
complaining every step of the way. We had to learn how to reconcile our
shopping differences. In our case, we learned that I was a better babysitter

than shopper. Janie learned to enjoy shopping on her own, and I enjoyed my time at home with our children.

Pack Rats

In most marriages, often one of the spouses is a pack rat, and the other seems to throw everything away. Perhaps it depends on whose stuff is weighing in the balance in order to make a determination as to who is the pack rat and who is not. Janie and I have had to work through this problem. Anything that I have not worn or used for a year, she throws in the trash or takes to Deseret Industries. Of course, Janie does most of this "spring cleaning" when I am out of town. For years, I kept my high school baseball cleats in our closet. I was most proud of those shoes because they still had dirt clods on the bottom from my last high school baseball game twenty years earlier. I went on a trip and haven't seen those shoes for a couple of years now.

After my grandfather died, he left me some of his wardrobe items, such as some old cardigan sweaters and a checkered blazer. I loved wearing these clothes because they reminded me of my grandfather, and I loved the "old school" look anyway. Janie, on the other hand, didn't see the sentimental value in the clothing. She thought I was just dressing up like a clown (with the checkered sports jacket) or Mr. Rogers (with the forty-year-old cardigans) for church each week. So, you guessed it—on one of my rare trips, Janie made a special delivery to Deseret Industries. In fact, she does such a masterful job at getting rid of my stuff that I usually don't notice my things are gone until a year or two after the fact.

I have observed this general rule in my marriage. Anything that Janie doesn't like of mine or that my family gives to me, she tosses in the garbage or hauls off to the dump. However, anything Janie's family gives us we must keep until the Millennium, whether it works or not. Years ago, Janie's family gave her a treadmill. Instead of using the treadmill to exercise, Janie would hang shirts on it when she ironed, and our children used it as a jungle gym. I would often suggest that we get rid of the treadmill, since it was in our bedroom and took up space we didn't have. Janie would have nothing to do with it. She told me that since her parents had given it to her, we had to keep it, no matter what!

Practical Solutions: Hanging on to things you will never use is not practical. Instead of doing what's best for the person who gave you the item, do what is best for your marriage. Have a general rule: if you haven't used something for the past year, get rid of it! This applies to both of you!

Energy Levels

Some spouses have more energy than others. In our marriage, I am definitely the hare. I tend to go about 100 miles per hour for most of the day, and then about 9:00 p.m., I start to crash quite quickly. By 9:30, I look like I've been ground into powder. Janie is the tortoise. She moves slow and steady most of the day but is able to last much longer.

Some are morning people, and some are evening people. I am a morning person. When I wake up in the morning, I'm ready for a new day. I will do some reading and then workout. When I arrive back at home, Janie and the kids are often still sleeping.

Janie prefers the evenings. When our children were younger, she learned to treasure the time between 8 p.m. and midnight because that was when she could get her best, most productive work done. Janie also takes a while to unwind before bed. Sometimes, she will lie in bed a good hour before she can fall asleep. Because of her late bedtime, she will sleep a little longer than I. With eight busy children, that means she usually sleeps until 6:45 a.m.

I try to be in bed about 10:00 p.m. each night, although that doesn't always happen. I have a favorite TV show I put on, but I rarely watch it. With my fan making some healthy white noise, I can be out cold in a matter of minutes. Sometimes, as I lie down in bed, Janie will want to discuss the day, talk about politics and religion, or solve the world's hunger problems. At that time of day, I am completely worthless. My mind is like Jell-O, and her words become hypnotic. Within three minutes, I'm out cold. On the other hand, I will try to have conversations with Janie at 6 a.m., but she's in a coma—which makes it difficult to converse.

Practical Solutions: You will probably marry someone who has a different energy level than you. Or they may be a morning person while you're a night owl. Don't try to change each other. Accept each other's individual differences in this area. Respect those differences, and learn to do things as a couple when you both have energy and strength. Find times to talk when you can both be tuned in. When you have children, one of you can drive carpools early in the morning, and the other can stay up late at night waiting for the children to arrive home.

Family-of-Origin Differences

Many of the differences you will deal with as a couple will be due to the fact that you were brought up in different families. This can become a huge source of contention if you're not careful. How you were raised is the foundation of many of your beliefs and opinions about marriage and family life. For example, when the late and renowned psychologist Carlfred Broderick was first married, he and his wife had to work through the protocol of how to handle sickness in the home. Most premarital couples do not discuss what happens when you get sick—it's usually not an issue. Like most of us, the Brodericks learned by trial and error.

In Carlfred's boyhood home, if you were sick, you became the "star of the show" and were given preferential treatment. Moreover, according to Carlfred, it was common knowledge in his family that fruit juice was the cure-all for everything. Everyone knew that the more serious the illness was, the more fruit juice would be required for healing. Thus, in Carlfred's home, the prizes went to those who were the sickliest. Fruit juice, television, a remote control, the fan, and Vicks VapoRub treatments could make a sick person feel like king for a day.

On the contrary, Carlfred's wife grew up in a more rural setting. In her family, if you were sick, you were sent to the back corner of the house so no one could hear you moaning and groaning. When you felt better, you could come out of the cave. Shortly after Carlfred's marriage, he became sick for the first time. In fact, he moved from his bed to the family room floor because his wife didn't seem to notice that he was sick. He began to moan and groan on the floor, but his wife didn't respond. She simply stepped over him while she vacuumed the room. After waiting to be served for some time, Carlfred finally asked his wife if they were out of juice. She responded by telling him that she thought they had some. Then finally, it clicked. She said, "Oh, you want me to get you some juice—is that it?" Eventually, she came back with a tiny, thimble-sized shot glass full of juice. He later learned that in his wife's house they rarely drank juice, and when they did so, it was in tiny glasses. In his family, juice glasses were the size of Big Gulps, and there was always someone standing near, ready to refill at request.[60]

Is there a problem with either of these techniques? Not necessarily. It is just a different way to solve the same problem. This is why couples need to talk and not be surprised when their partners do things that seem strange. Perhaps your spouse does something a certain way because that is the only way he or she ever saw it done.

One new husband married a young lady who came from a family of all girls. As she grew up, it wasn't unusual for all four girls to use the bathroom at the same time: two at the sinks, one on the toilet, and one in the shower. The morning bathroom scene was a flurry of activity, almost like a convenience store atmosphere—people coming and going all morning long. In fact, it wasn't unusual for the door to be left open while someone was using the toilet.

The husband, on the other hand, grew up in a very private family. Using the toilet was a personal and private experience. In his home, you would go into the bathroom with several magazines and newspapers, and the door was locked and dead-bolted. In his family, going to the bathroom was an experience that usually took some time. What do you suppose happened the first time this new, unassuming bride, walked into the bathroom while her husband was sitting on the toilet? It was the original "deer in the headlights look." I won't provide you with all of the detail. Suffice it to say that it never happened again.

Once again, there is no proper bathroom etiquette. There is no right way or wrong way. It is just a matter of previous experiences, background, and preferences. This is why couples need to talk. In this case, perhaps a wife could learn how to respect her husband's privacy. Also, a husband could explain that not wanting his wife in the bathroom while he is using the toilet does not mean that they cannot be close. He's just private in that area, and she will have to learn to respect that.

Since no two people are alike, disagreements can often result. For instance, a wife criticized her husband for the way he ate grapefruit—he peeled it like an orange. In her mind, only derelicts would eat grapefruit like that. She was worried that she would have to spend eternity next to a guy who ate grapefruit like oranges.[61] There are many small differences couples must contend with—how we eat corn, how we roll the toothpaste tube, how we feel about politics, and too many others to list.

Another significant difference that derives from family-of-origin practices is that of parenting issues. Some spouses have been raised in families where there was little discipline or where parents never raised their voices above a reverent whisper or where there was a healthy dose of affection. What if such a person marries someone who grew up in a family where there were strict rules, yelling, and little warmth? Most certainly, there will be parenting concerns that will need to be discussed and resolved. A healthy practice is for couples to try to take the *best things* from *both their families* and build on them. Aside from that, they should also incorporate ideas from other sources to bless their children. Even if you marry someone whose family does not belong to the Church, you can still learn things from them. No one has cornered the market on how to turn out successful kids.

Another common family-of-origin issue is traditions, such as birthdays and Christmas. Be prepared, because some newly married individuals believe that only *their* family knows the *true* way to celebrate Christmas. For example, some families allow a few Christmas presents to be opened on Christmas Eve. Other families may view Christmas Eve present-opening as criminal! There are other issues to work out, such as where to spend Christmas, whether to encourage a belief in Santa Claus, the emphasis on the holiday's true meaning, and so forth. In some families, Christmas decorations come out before Thanksgiving and stay up through New Year's Day. Other families are comfortable putting up decorations a few weeks before Christmas and taking them down the day after Christmas. Of course, there are also those who just leave their Christmas lights up year round and others who do not decorate at all.

Janie's family is very big on Christmas traditions. Every Christmas Eve is kicked off with a traditional scone dinner. After clean up, Janie's dad reads Luke 2, along with *The Night before Christmas*. Over the holiday period, Johnny Mathis Christmas music is constantly playing in the background. On Christmas morning, the children must line up in the order of age on the stairway to have their pictures taken. Only then can they come and see what Santa brought them. It is a rigid process and must be followed precisely. One deviation could cause serious trouble!

One Christmas, I was a little bored, so just for fun, I suggested, "What if we don't eat scones this year, and what if we don't listen to Johnny Mathis?" In fact, just for kicks, I suggested that we eat chili dogs and listen to Willie Nelson's Christmas album. I will not detail here how this story concluded, but we can say that I was summoned to a court martial on December 26 and asked to comply or be waterboarded.

Birthdays are another area where traditions need to be discussed. In Janie's house, there is no such thing as a birth*day*. For them, the true name of the celebration is birth*week*. In Janie's family, the birthday child ate all of their meals from a special plate. There was also a traditional spanking machine, dinner with parents, favorite breakfast, favorite cake, favorite snack, and practically a parade down Main Street. In my family, when it was your birthday, you had a cake and some presents, perhaps went to Chuck E. Cheese's, and received a coupon for a free round of

"Goofy-Golf" if you were good that year. The Ogletree birthday process was over in two hours.

Therefore, when we were first engaged and began to celebrate each other's birthdays, I had to be taught the "true" practice of birthday celebration. Some traditions are easier to convert to than others, especially when it's *your* birthday! The point is that this and other family-of-origin issues are areas that most couples don't think to talk over before they are married. Once married, couples need to discuss and work through these traditions.

Practical solutions: In all family-of-origin issues, couples must be careful not to defend their turf and feel like their family had the market on parenting, vacations, holidays, and Sunday dinners. What is best for your family now? That is the issue. Take the best from both of your families, tweak it, improve it, customize it, and make it your own tradition.

Community Differences

Some couples come from extremely different communities. I know of a couple—and I'm sure there are many like this—where he came from a tiny town in Idaho and she came from a huge metropolitan area in Texas. His idea of a good time was watching a video and playing some board games. The small area he grew up in was about sixty miles from civilization. On the other hand, her idea of a good time was going shopping at a huge mall and eating out at a nice restaurant.

When they were first married, this couple had many discussions about continued courtship after the wedding. It seemed that he was perfectly happy to stay home and watch videos, while she wanted to get out and do something. Many of their problems stemmed from the fact that they grew up in different communities and learned to enjoy different forms of entertainment. Furthermore, later in their marriage, he wanted to move out into the country and raise their children on some acreage, while she preferred raising their children in the suburbs. They compromised by purchasing a home on some acreage within the city limits. Expect differences in your marriage to arise because of *where* you were raised.

Practical Solutions: Learn as much as you can about your spouse's home turf. Come to know the things they love about their home community and roots. Learn to love that place. Ask your spouse questions, and learn details about some of their favorite community things. If both of you take this approach, you will always honor and respect the place where your spouse is from. Make sure your future children visit that community and learn to love it as you both do.

Religious Differences

Many couples reading this book may assume that religion won't be a problem in their marriage. After all, since you most likely married a Mormon in the temple, you won't have any religious issues, right? Wrong. Just because you are members of the same faith doesn't mean you won't have disagreements on how you live your religion. For instance, some individuals grow up in homes where television viewing is fine on the Sabbath, while others feel that television viewing on the Sabbath is one step closer to apostasy. Some are raised in families where drinking caffeinated drinks is acceptable, while some feel that those who drink caffeinated beverages are allies of the "anti-Christ." Some feel that when you go on vacation, you don't need to attend church; others feel that when you travel, you need to find the nearest chapel.

Shortly before we were married, Janie and I had a discussion about the Sabbath day. I had only been a member of the Church a year when I went on my mission, and shortly after I returned, I began dating Janie. My only experience of living the Sabbath came from what I learned as a missionary. Therefore, my view of the Sabbath was very regulated and structured. I envisioned that my future family would wake up at 6:00 a.m. and read the scriptures then write in our journals. After some breakfast, we would go on a walk, with monogrammed sweatsuits with the initials C.O.G. (Children of God), eating wheat bread and honey, while singing hymns. After church, we would write to the missionaries and our congressman. We would cap off the evening with some genealogy and a role play from the Book of Mormon.

As I explained this to Janie, she laughed hysterically. Then she said, "Do you want your children to hate you?" Of course, my answer was no. Janie then explained that she thought if our Sabbath was so regulated, our children would resent us instead of loving us and the Lord.

So I said, "Okay, smarty pants, how did your family live the Sabbath?"

Janie explained that they went to church; they had gospel discussions; they ate, laughed, played games, and watched movies together. Then came the clincher. She said, "Sometimes my dad would even watch football with my brothers."

It didn't take long. I said, "You know, I like your way. I can do that. I will make that sacrifice and go down with the ship."

Ways of Dealing with Disagreements

How you handle disagreements in marriage can sometimes cause further disagreements. Often when there is friction in a relationship, one spouse will prefer to retreat, where the other spouse will want to engage. If, in your marriage, one of you wants to talk immediately and one of you would rather process and think for a while before talking, give each other the needed space and respect.

In our marriage, Janie is the thinker and processer. She often will not say anything when there is a disagreement because she will think about it for a long time before she ever opens her mouth. I, on the other hand, like to resolve problems immediately. I assume we need to resolve the issue while it's "hot off the press." Otherwise it will fester. So I talk, and sometimes I actually learn how I feel by hearing myself discuss the issue.

The point here is that each couple needs to give their spouse the time they need to process the issue. If you are married to a spouse who needs more time, give that time to them. That way, you can both be cooled off and talk to each other more rationally. However, since some men and women like to postpone or avoid conflict, make sure you schedule a time when you can come back to the issue and discuss it. Then listen closely to what your spouse is saying.

Our Heavenly Father created us as unique individuals. Each of us has special gifts, talents, and abilities. Your goal is not to try to change your spouse so they become like you; your goal is to learn to appreciate and utilize your differences as strengths to build a strong marriage and family.

I have mentioned several of these kinds of situations in my own marriage. Allow me to share one more. Janie is very creative and has amazing vision. She has the ability to think outside the box. I can creatively think about some things, but not like Janie can. When it comes to fixing our homes, Janie can walk right in, look around, and say, "We can take that wall out, add a room here, and turn that space into a pantry." I will think, *Where and how did you come up with that?* However, in every case, she's right. Instead of arguing with my wife or being jealous that she has a gift I do not have, I have learned to encourage her to do her magic. In the last home we purchased, we walked in, and I said, "Okay, what do you see? What do you think we can do?" She began to come up with some plans while I went and got my sledgehammer. Together, we make a pretty good team. Learn to treasure the differences between you and your spouse, and use those differences as strengths.

Homework:
- List on a sheet of paper the differences in your families and how you were raised. Discuss how these differences can strengthen your marriage.
- Regarding your own personal differences, discuss how as a couple you could both benefit by your differences.
- What traditions would you like to incorporate into your new family, taking the best from both of your families?

Additional Readings:
- Dr. James Dobson, *Love for a Lifetime: Building a Marriage That Will Go the Distance* (Sisters, Oregon: Multnomah, 2003).
- The Mormon Channel, *Gospel Solutions for Families*, "Marriage Roles, Part 1," Episode 59; http://www.mormonchannel.org/gospel-solutions-for-families/marriage-roles-part-1.
- The Mormon Channel, *Gospel Solutions for Families*, "Marriage Roles, Part 2," Episode 60; http://www.mormonchannel.org/gospel-solutions-for-families/marriage-roles-part-2.

References

59 Spencer W. Kimball, *The Miracle of Forgiveness* (Salt Lake City: Bookcraft, 1969), 245.

60 Carlfred Broderick, *Couples* (New York: Simon and Schuster, 1979), 72–73.

61 Lola Walters, "The Grapefruit Syndrome," *Ensign*, April 1993, 13.

CHAPTER 7
Personality Issues in Marriage

"If any of us are imperfect, it is our duty to pray for the gift that will make us perfect."
-George Q. Cannon[62]

OUR CULTURE, SOCIETY, AND CHURCH are filled with many individuals with different personalities—and thank goodness for that. Personality is the spice of life; different personalities can bring excitement and strength to a marriage and family. In Church history, Joseph Smith was charismatic, quotable, and certainly a people person. His successor, Brigham Young, seemed to be more stern, practical, and an astute businessman. Both personalities were needed to establish the Church and spread the gospel message to the nations.

A significant piece of our LDS culture includes the different personalities that make up our wards and stakes. Several years ago, the movie, *Single's Ward*, became a favorite because it highlighted the different stereotyped personalities that can be found in many Latter-day Saint student wards. For example, there was the "overly zealous returned missionary—complete with white shirt and day planner," the "excited prospective missionary—who couldn't wait to serve in Boise, Idaho," the "obsessive girl chaser," the "stalwart, solid, and attractive woman," and my favorite, the "girl who was never going to marry that kind of guy."

I have often wondered how exciting it would be to create the movie *Residential Ward*. In my mind, that would be much more entertaining than *Single's Ward*. I have often asked my students at Brigham Young University if the wards and stakes that they grew up in had any stereotypical characters. My students have identified 1) "the Scouter," the man who has been the Scoutmaster in the ward for twenty-five years and wears his "knee-high" green shorts to ward activities; 2) "the food storage expert," who lives and breathes emergency preparation; 3) "the late family," who live right across the street from the church and still can't make it on time; 4) "the music man," who didn't make the cut when he tried out for the Tabernacle Choir but is determined to take mediocre talent found in the ward choir and have them perform in Carnegie Hall by the end of the summer; 5) and my favorite—"the testimony closer"—not to be confused with the monthly or regularly testimony bearer, this man or woman not only insists on taking time each month in testimony meeting, but they must be the last speaker. Of course, there are probably many more characters. Nevertheless, if someone could make a movie about this ward, I would be one of the first in line to watch it. Differing personalities certainly make life fun and exciting.

Bank on this: the person you are married to probably has a different personality than you. Moreover, as you and your spouse get older and mature in your marriage, you may find that your personalities diverge rather than converge. As you both learn to work with each other, you will compensate for the deficits in your personalities. For example, if one spouse tends to overreact, the other will perhaps become more laid back in order to balance out the marriage or the family. The more *he* overreacts, for example, the more laid back *she* will become. And of course, the more laid back *she* becomes, the more *he* feels he will need to overreact.

A few years ago, I counseled with a great couple in my practice. However, as they reached their early fifties, they were having a difficult time connecting. He was very social and wanted his wife to be involved with him in his hobbies and work and to cheer him on in his church basketball games. She, on the other hand, worked hard all day and wanted to retreat each evening by wrapping herself up in her favorite blanket, curling up in front of the fire, and reading a good book. She had no interest in attending his games, and he had no interest in staying home and reading books. This introvert and extrovert needed to compromise and work together and balance out their personalities.

If you think dealing with different personalities in marriage is interesting, wait until you have children. Some of your children will behave so differently from you and your spouse that you will often scratch your head and wonder where they came from. For example, I believe Janie and I are decent, hospitable, and mild-mannered people. We love our friends and neighbors and enjoy activities with our family where we can laugh and have a good time. However, a few of our children did not inherit the "happy-go-lucky" gene. We have a daughter who is one of the most aggressive people I have ever met. She played high school basketball, and although she was only five foot three, she was usually the most physical player on the floor. She wasn't afraid of anyone, and several times I saw her get in the face of another player on the opposing team and express her displeasure. She thrived on taking the winning shot—sometimes she made it, and sometimes she didn't. She was so competitive that sometimes she would cry when her team lost—even her senior year. That is how badly she wanted to win.

We also have a son who is the most competitive person I know. If he is playing a game—whether it is with a grandmother or young child— he would like to win 100-0. When he played basketball in high school, he didn't back down to anyone either, and he often wanted to take the winning shot. Sometimes I felt bad because he would take three or four shots in a game and miss each one. However, to his credit, he would keep shooting, and at the end of the game, he would have scored twenty-five points. I am just the opposite. If I took one shot and missed, I would never shoot for the rest of the game, and I certainly would never want to take the last shot.

I played baseball growing up, and I was often the lead-off batter. That was perfect for me because I never felt any pressure. However, sometimes late in games I would have to come up to the plate with two outs, a runner on base, and down one run. I would have preferred hiding in the dugout rather than have to bat with the game on the line. I never remember crying if we lost a game. I had so much fun, regardless of whether we won or lost. I even loved practice because I simply loved to play. Of course, I preferred to win, but a loss didn't affect me terribly. However, if my son lost a football game, our family would have to walk on eggshells over the weekend and pray for him to recover.

On the other hand, I have never wished that my children were like me because I realize that my own personality has flaws. In fact, I have learned more about life from my children who are most different from me. All of us will have different personalities to deal with in our marriages and family relationships, and that will make life exciting—and sometimes challenging.

The Origins of Personality

When it comes to personality development, many theories over the years have emerged. There are almost as many theories as personality types. For example, Sigmund Freud postulated that people are born psychologically unhealthy and are repaired by society. Freud's theory, in my opinion, doesn't hold much water, although I use many of his other concepts in my counseling practice.

A more humanistic theory would claim that individuals are born healthy and are ruined by society. Although this theory seems more applicable, it is also quite fatalistic. I could not get excited about a theory that suggests that when I am an infant, I'm on top of my game, and from that point on, my life will be in shambles.

Behaviorists suggest that people are born psychologically neutral and the interaction between nature and nurture will shape their personality and life experiences. I believe this theory explains a reasonable amount of human behavior, and there is much validity to what behaviorists teach.

However, behaviorism comes up short, especially with the philosophy that people are born neutral. Years ago an LDS psychologist from California began a comprehensive study of personality. Dr. Taylor Hartman proposed that personality is innate—that is, we come to this earth with our personalities. Yes, there are nature and nurture effects that mold and shape our personalities, but for the most part, we come to this earth with a personality already developed. Dr. Hartman further claimed that personality is developed based on a primary motive that cannot be learned or developed—we brought it with us from the womb.

Dr. Hartman's theory meshes well with Latter-day Saint theology. We understand that before we came to this earth, we lived in a premortal life. For instance, Abraham was shown many "intelligences" in the pre-earth life; among these were many who were noble and great (Abraham 3:22–25). Some were noble, and others weren't. That is because we had choice and agency in the premortal life, and because of that agency, some were able to progress more than others. Variables such as faithfulness and obedience would have shaped and molded an individual's character and personality.

It is not a stretch to imagine that our personalities began developing long before we came to this earth. For mothers who have borne more than one child, they recognize that even in the womb, children are all different. Our seventh child, Callie, created a completely different pregnancy experience for Janie when compared to our other children. This little girl was constantly kicking and flipping in the womb. She flipped positions so many times that the doctor had to turn her into the correct position more than once for delivery. When she was born, she screamed for about three hours straight. In fact, she screamed so much that after about an hour of trying everything we could do to settle her down, we asked the nurses if they would take her back to the nursery so we could catch our breath. Callie is now seventeen years old, but the personality she came to this earth hasn't changed that much. To put it mildly, she's a pistol.

As a father, I recognized the distinct differences in our children's personalities. Now that our children are older, and some are married and have children of their own, I thoroughly enjoy watching old family movies of our kids, mainly because none of their personalities have changed much over the years; in fact, their personalities from the moment they came to this earth are still intact. The way they act now is exactly how they acted as young children. I find this fascinating. Our children who were physically active as toddlers became great athletes and are physically active today; our children who liked to tease their siblings still do that as adults; our children who were easily moved to tears are still wiping their eyes.

Dr. Hartman was able to take substantial psychological concepts and simplify them so that even children could understand the principles of his model. Dr. Hartman proposed that there are four main personality types: reds, whose core motive is *power*; blues, whose core motive is *intimacy*; whites, whose core motive is *peace*; and yellows, whose core motive is *fun*. Since you are newly married, you are discovering the differences in personality between you and your spouse. Understanding the intricacies of your spouse's personality can be freeing and helpful. One of the greatest discoveries of my life was to learn that my wife wasn't trying to upset me on purpose—nor was I trying to upset her—but our personalities propelled us to act a certain way. I further learned that my children were not trying to make my life difficult; instead, their different personalities drove their behavior.

Reds: Power

Reds are the people who get things done. They are the movers and shakers of society. Reds are "our natural born leaders, the people who know how to get from point A to point B efficiently and typically with little fanfare. They are the power wielders."[63] Reds like to look good; they like to be right; they like to be respected; they hide their insecurities tightly; they like to please themselves; and they love challenging adventures. These individuals are active and productive, visionary, bold and fearless, determined, self-reliant, self-assured, and relentless. Unfortunately, reds can also be insensitive and selfish, demanding and critical, insecure, always right, competitive to a fault, manipulative, impatient, and poor listeners.

There are ten core strengths of the red personality. They are

1. Decisive	6. Leader
2. Assertive	7. Responsible
3. Action-oriented	8. Disciplined
4. Task-dominant	9. Confident
5. Determined	10. Proactive

Like every personality type in Dr. Hartman's personality profile, reds also have limitations. The core limitations of reds include

1. Selfish	6. Bossy
2. Insensitive	7. Aggressive
3. Arrogant	8. Argumentative
4. Always right	9. Demanding
5. Impatient	10. Obsessive

If you believe you're a red, do you have more of the strengths or the limitations? If you have more of the strengths, then you are a "healthy" red; however, if you have more of the limitations, then you are "sick" in your personality and need to make some changes.

The key with every personality type is to continue to progress and improve. It is not justifiable to say, "Well, I am just selfish, so what you see is what you get." No, none of us can say that. We need to identify the traits in our personality that aren't healthy and try to improve them. If I am a selfish person, then it is my responsibility to learn to be kind and considerate to others. The laboratory for such changes is in our homes, in our families, in our marriages.

Two of my children are reds. This has been an interesting journey for Janie and me because neither of us have many red traits. Our two reds always think they are right. Both of them could hit you in the head with a hammer and then convince you it was your fault you got hit. We have had to learn as parents to take the good with the bad. Both of these children are natural-born leaders: they accomplish many good things; they have goals and dreams and plans; and they are always heading out the door to climb a mountain, kill a wild animal, or drum up a cure for a disease. I admire both of them and have learned a great deal from them.

For example, my red son has tremendous business skills. From the time he was a teenager, he was well read and had incredible ideas for organizational success. As a teenager, he worked for some small businesses, and he would always come home and tell me why his manager was clueless or what he would do with the company if *he* was in charge. He is knowledgeable about things like marketing, debt-to-income ratios, and product lines.

Even though I am not a businessman, I have always had my own counseling practice. I learned to listen to my son's business frustrations and then apply his suggestions to my practice. Instead of arguing with him or fighting against him, I knew early on I could learn much from him if I would simply listen. That has blessed our relationship over the years.

My red daughter is always on the go. I'll come home from work, and she'll have lumber in the backyard to build something. Since she doesn't always know what she's doing, her twin sister and I end up being her assistants in these projects. However, thanks to her, our home has been blessed with some cool things. She is always ready to tackle a mountain or build an additional wing onto our home during a commercial break.

If you are married to a red, you will need to deal with facts and figures. Women, if you have a red husband and want to buy a certain home—don't try to convince him based on any emotion, such as, "I love this house; it's perfect for us!" Reds don't do emotion. Instead, you must use logic and facts. Tell them you want to purchase the home because the elementary school in the area is highly rated or the new-fangled air conditioning unit will save you a hundred dollars per month or the location will save you tons of money in gas as you commute to work and other activities. Reds fall for that stuff almost nine times out of ten.

What you shouldn't do if you are married to a red is embarrass them in front of others. Don't expect them to ask you for your opinion—they may be too busy or engrossed in a project to come up for air. Also, don't take their arguments or suggestions personally. When you are with a red, you have to talk to them directly—that's what they respect. I love discussions with my son because I don't have to tiptoe—I just tell him what I think. Often he disagrees, and we don't care. There's no emotion, no tears, and no apologies. And living in a home with nine women and a constant estrogen fog hanging over my head, it's nice and refreshing to just bat ideas around with my son and occasionally disagree with each other just for the heck of it.

Blues: Intimacy/Connection

Blues are good people—inherently good. Blues practically love everyone—well, almost everyone. Blues have a strong sense of right and wrong, and their moral compass is always pointing north. They are concerned about how you're doing, and they never forget a birthday. In fact, they never forget anything! They'll remind you in twenty years about a first glance in the greatest detail and be deeply hurt that you don't remember. "These sainted pit bulls are our blues, and they innately know that life is all about relationships."[64] A blue is the type of person that will help a stranded motorist, visit friends in the hospital, and feel guilty for forgetting to send someone a thank-you note. Blues have friends everywhere in the country, and they keep in contact with most of them!

Blues are committed, perfectionistic, admired, self-sacrificing and nurturing, self-disciplined and stable, and appropriate and sincere. However, blues can also be demanding, distrusting, complex, opinionated, emotional and moody, unforgiving and resentful, worried, driven by guilt, insecure, and self-righteous.

Furthermore, blues like to be valued and appreciated; they want to be understood and accepted. Blues typically reveal their insecurities and try to please others. They like to say that they don't care what others think, but the truth is—they care too much! Blues are sensitive people. When you cry, they cry too. They feel your pain, and they want to help. They are in tune to the needs of others. Blues are so sensitive that they can hardly watch the news—it's too disturbing.

There are ten core strengths of the blue personality. They are

1. Compassionate	6. Committed
2. Loyal	7. Dedicated
3. Sincere	8. Emotional
4. Thoughtful	9. Dependable
5. Analytical	10. Deliberate

The ten core limitations of the blue personality are

1. Worry-prone	6. Suspicious
2. Overly sensitive	7. Perfectionist
3. Self-righteous	8. Hard to Please
4. Unforgiving	9. Moody
5. Judgmental	10. Jealous

We have a blue family; I am primarily blue, Janie has some blue traits, and I have several blue children. Blues are wonderful because they think of others first, never forget holidays and traditions, and are anxious to help others. However, the negative side of the blue personality is where the trouble begins. As a blue, I am a worrier and can be hard to please. I also have a blue daughter who can cry at the drop of a hat and has a hard time forgiving others. At the same time, she loves everyone and spends her life helping those around her. She will do anything for anyone. She is the poster girl for blue.

If you are married to a blue, you will want to show them appreciation and help them feel secure. By praising a blue, you can be their friend for life. Blues are extremely loyal; you can strengthen your marriage by returning that loyalty. Don't make a blue feel guilty—blues feel guilty all the time anyway, so they don't need any more help with this one. Also, blues tend to hold grudges, so don't expect them to forgive quickly but try to help them to. I know sometimes my children have gotten upset with me when I have made jokes or referred to something they did years ago. Once, my son said, "Dad, let it go—that happened when I was nine." I knew he was right.[a]

Whites: Peace

I am married to a white. These are wonderful people. They are meek, they are humble, and they are the salt of the earth. Whites don't talk much, but when they do open their mouths, everyone should listen because it's going to be good. Whites like to listen and observe. While the reds and blues are fighting for the microphone, whites are content to work behind the stage, perhaps pulling the curtains or dimming the lights. Dr. Hartman further explained, "Whites resent being imposed upon and have absolutely no desire to impose their will on the rest of the universe. When life is hectic, just being in the same room with a person like this makes you feel calmer. Nothing seems to ruffle their feathers, and with their innate calm, they are often able to bring clarity to chaos."[65] Whites like to feel good inside. They like to be given space, they withhold their insecurities, and they like to be independent. Whites are content.

Whites crave peace; they are tolerant, kind, patient, gentle, even-tempered, and diplomatic. On the other hand, whites can be lazy,

---

a   Besides, he's a red, and reds are never wrong anyway.

unassertive, self-doubting, dependent, indecisive and impressionable, aimless, silently stubborn, unmotivated, and somewhat boring.

The ten core strengths of the white are

1. Kind	6. Good listener
2. Satisfied	7. Inventive
3. Even-tempered	8. Considerate
4. Agreeable	9. Diplomatic
5. Easygoing	10. Adaptable

The ten core limitations of the white personality include

1. Timid	6. Avoids conflict
2. Indecisive	7. Self-deprecating
3. Unmotivated	8. Indifferent
4. Silently stubborn	9. Ambivalent
5. Lazy	10. Uninvolved

Janie and one of our daughters have almost all of the strong traits of the white. They are kind, content, easygoing, go-with-the-flow, adaptable, and great listeners. In fact, I love whites because they know how to "chill out," something that is more difficult for me to do. Several years ago I was speaking at a conference out of town, so I called my family to check in with everyone. I asked my white daughter how things were going. She said, "Dad, with you not here, everything is great. Because Mom is so chill, all we do is watch movies, eat, and hang out." Of course, there's nothing better than being away from your family and finding out that they hope you don't come back anytime soon. What my daughter was really saying was, "Dad, without you here, we don't have to do our chores; we eat in the family room and go to bed any time we please." I realized from my phone call that I had some repenting to do. However, one of my red daughters made up for it by telling me that she loved it when I was home because she liked the rules and structure.

Whites are certainly low maintenance and like to fly under the radar. On the negative side, they have a hard time making decisions. When Janie and I go on dates, our conversation goes something like this:

Me: So where do you want to go eat tonight?

Her: I don't care—anywhere is great with me.

Me: Okay, great. Why don't we go to [really great Chinese restaurant]?

Her: No, why don't you suggest something else.

Me: Okay, how about we eat at [really, really awesome Mexican restaurant].

Her: No, I'm not in the mood for that.

Me: Janie, why don't you suggest something. I would like you to decide, for once. Just pick any place, and I am happy to go there.

Her: Well, I don't have any ideas. I don't know what I want.

Me: Okay, work with me now. How about [really great Chinese restaurant that I suggested in the first place].

Her: Okay, sounds good.

I will spare you the details of what happens when Janie gets a menu in her hands. Perhaps I could summarize the thirty-minute process by saying that I am ready to order after nineteen seconds, and then I wait for Janie to change her mind three times. Finally, she will ask the waiter for a recommendation. When the food comes, I completely enjoy my selection, and she explains to me that hers is terrible. Suffice it to say, whites have a hard time making decisions. They also don't like confrontation, so they tend to store up all of their frustrations inside, and then all at once, everything spews out like a volcano when they have reached their limit.

If you are married to a white, understand that they are extremely low maintenance—at least on the surface. However, if you are neglecting them, they will ultimately let you know it, and when that happens, it won't be pretty. Create an informal, relaxed atmosphere with your white partner—they sometimes have a difficult time with structure. Listen to whites, and react gently. Whites don't do well with confrontation. Don't force them to express their feelings quickly or immediately. Don't overwhelm them with too much at once—whites can get overwhelmed easily. I love my white wife because she balances out my blue overreactions and my zany yellow ideas. That is what I hope will happen for you.

Yellows: Fun

Remember when you were a teenager and there was always that one person you invited to everything you did? The only reason you invited them was because you knew if they came, everything would be fun. Yes, yellows make life fun for everyone. "Nobody *lives in the moment* quite like a yellow. They like people—all people—and people generally like them back. Luck is their middle name and magic is their game. Yellows are the frosting on life's cake."[66]

Yellows have the gift of not caring too much about anything unless it's fun and exciting. They could be failing three classes at school, lose their wallet, and discover that their checking account is overdrawn, but if you give them an ice cream cone, they will eat it while doing cartwheels and consider all to be right with the world. When a yellow walks into a room full of people, they simply assume that these individuals have come to watch them perform. Yellows like to look good socially, they like to be praised, they like to be noticed, and they love to always have fun, which is their core motive.

Yellows are fun-loving, happy, enthusiastic, carefree, charismatic and popular, optimistic, playful, and exciting. However, yellows can also be self-centered and uncommitted, irresponsible, chatterboxes, naïve and trusting, superficial, undisciplined, and disorganized.

The ten core strengths of the yellow personality are

1. Fun-loving	6. Trusting
2. Playful	7. Spontaneous
3. Carefree	8. Happy
4. Enthusiastic	9. Charismatic
5. Optimistic	10. Sociable

Here are the ten core limitations of the yellow:

1. Uncommitted	6. Vain
2. Self-centered	7. Afraid to face facts
3. Disorganized	8. Inconsistent
4. Impulsive	9. Unfocused
5. Undisciplined	10. Interrupter

I have a lot of yellow in my personality, and I like that because it has balanced me out, caused me not to take myself too seriously, and has given me the ability to make things fun at home. I am part blue and also part yellow. However, I have a daughter who is pure yellow, through and through. When she was a child growing up, we gave her the nickname "Funzie." This daughter was definitely the life of the party wherever she went, was always seeking out fun and adventure, and was the pied piper in our ward. By the time she was in high school, most of the Primary kids followed her around the church like lemmings.

Unfortunately, she also possessed many of the negative traits of the yellow. She was somewhat disorganized, undisciplined, and definitely afraid to face the facts. I will never forget the week before she left on her mission to Brazil. We kept urging her to pack her suitcases, organize her room, and get ready for her mission. However, she just never seemed to be able to pull any of that together. She was distracted easily and often procrastinated things that weren't fun and exciting. On days when she was thinking about packing, someone would stop by the house and invite her to do something more exciting, and she took the bait every time. Finally, on the day before she was to leave, she still hadn't packed anything. We asked her what she was going to do about that. She said, "I'm not sure, but I think I'm going skiing." So she left and skied for the day. Our oldest blue daughter couldn't take it anymore, so she and Janie completely packed my yellow daughter for her mission. Luckily, she learned many wonderful things on her mission that helped her overcome some of her negative yellow tendencies. At the same time, she harnessed her positive yellow traits and did much good. In fact, she organized a ward social in every area she served. Her capstone accomplishment—besides the people she taught and saw baptized—was organizing a rodeo in one stake. Yes, a legit rodeo! That's what yellows do. They organize rodeos!

If you marry a yellow, you will want to stay upbeat and positive with them. Coming down on them too hard will cause them to shut down emotionally and verbally. Encourage them in their positive yellow traits, and use those talents to bring to pass much good. For example, as a teenager, our yellow daughter choreographed the entire dance to *High School Musical*, and every youth in our ward participated. It was the big hit for the stake talent show. With yellows, you cannot be too serious in criticism. Don't try to control them, don't ignore them, and don't give them too much rope—they may hang themselves.

Beyond the Color Code
There is more to the Color Code than identifying your personality style. Each of us must seek to improve and become better. Being a healthy red or a healthy yellow is a great plan. However, what we really should strive for is to become more like the Savior. Joseph Smith taught, "If you wish to go where God is, you must be like God, or possess the principles which God possesses. For if we are not drawing toward God in principle, we are going from Him and drawing toward the devil."[67]

As we study more about our Savior, Jesus Christ, and about our Eternal Father, we learn that They are kind, gracious, merciful, slow to anger, patient, abundant in goodness, charitable, humble, and meek.[68] Our responsibility is to identify the weaknesses in our personalities and try to improve them. Since I am a blue, sometimes I worry. What is the opposite of worry? To me, it is being full of faith. To become more Christlike, as a blue, I need to learn to develop rock-solid faith. What if I am a red and understand that one of my weaknesses is selfishness? What is the opposite of selfishness? I believe it is charity. My responsibility would be to plead to the Lord for that most pertinent gift and seek to become like Christ. George Q. Cannon taught, "Every defect in the human character can be corrected through the exercise of faith and pleading with the Lord for the gifts that He has said He will give unto those who believe and obey His commandments."[69] President Cannon further taught,

> If any of us are imperfect, it is our duty to pray for the gift that will make us perfect. Have I imperfections? I am full of them. What is my duty? To pray to God to give me the gifts that will correct these imperfections. If I am an angry man, it is my duty to pray for charity, which suffereth long and is kind. Am I an envious man? It is my duty to seek for charity, which envieth not. So with all the gifts of the gospel. They are intended for this purpose. No man ought to say, "Oh, I cannot help this; it is my nature." He is not justified in it, for the reason that God has promised to give strength to correct these things, and to give gifts that will eradicate them.[70]

Our goal and mission should be to seek the traits we need to improve upon, plead for the Savior's help, and make changes. As we strive to become more like Christ, we can become healthier in our personalities. As a couple, I would recommend that you purchase Taylor Hartman's book, *The People Code*. You could also take the Color Code Test, which you can find online or in the book. Once you discover your primary and secondary colors, and the primary and secondary colors of your spouse, you should have a fun discussion. You should determine how you will help each other grow and develop into disciples of Jesus Christ. Identify your weaknesses and how your spouse can help you overcome some of them. Also, ascertain your strengths, and discuss how they can bless your marriage. Remember the words from Ecclesiastes, "Two are better than one . . . if they fall, one will lift up his fellow" (Ecclesiastes 4:9–10). In a marriage, we use our gifts, talents, and strengths to lift and build each other.

Homework:
- Discuss with your partner this question: How would you classify your parents—red, blue, white, or yellow? Why?
- Take the Color Code Test. You can find it online. Make sure it is Taylor Hartman's Color Code. What is your dominant color—red, blue, white, or yellow? Why?
- Read about Color Code interactions regarding marriage in Taylor Hartman's book, *The People Code*. Specifically, read how your primary color and your spouse's color interact.

Additional Readings:
- Dr. Taylor Hartman, *The People Code* (Scribner:New York, 2007).
- Hugh W. Pinnock, "Making a Marriage Work," *Tambuli,* February 1982, 13–16.
- President Spencer W. Kimball, "Marriage and Divorce," *BYU Speeches*, 7 September 1976.

References

62 George Q. Cannon, *Gospel Truth: Discourses and Writings of President George Q. Cannon*, ed. Jerreld L. Newquist, (Salt Lake City: Deseret Book, 1957), 155.

63 Dr. Taylor Hartman, *The People Code*, (New York, Scribner, 2007), 41.

64 Ibid, 61.

65 Ibid, 81.

66 Ibid, 100.

67 Joseph Smith, B.H. Roberts, *History of the Church of Jesus Christ of Latter-day Saints*, (Salt Lake City: Deseret Book, 1908), 588.

68 See Doctrine and Covenants 4, and Joseph Smith, *Lectures on Faith*, (Salt Lake City: Deseret Book, 1835), 3:19–20.

69 George Q. Cannon, *Gospel Truth: Discourses and Writings of President George Q. Cannon*, ed. Jerreld L. Newquist (Salt Lake City: Deseret Book, 1957), 155.

70 Ibid, 155.

CHAPTER 8
Resolving Conflict in Marriage

"I want to tell you that there are no marriages that can ever be happy
ones unless two people work at it."
-President Spencer W. Kimball[71]

THERE ARE CERTAINLY MANY SURPRISES in marriage. One such surprise
is learning to deal with conflict. Although you were probably initially
attracted to each other because of the many things you had in common
(i.e. could talk easily together, seemed to have similar values and beliefs,
shared similar opinions, liked the same music, enjoyed the same foods,
etc.), now that you have been married for a short period, differences in
personality, character, temperament, manners, and habits have all come
to the surface. The manner in which couples deal with differences and
conflict can make or break their relationship. Unfortunately, the number-
one predictor of divorce is the habitual avoidance of conflict.[72]

From a worldly perspective, when many couples have trouble in their
marriages, they simply walk away and try to find someone else who may
not argue with them as much. Unfortunately, it is too common in our
culture for people to give up instead of trying to fix their relationship.
Satan must love it when couples give up so easily.

As members of The Church of Jesus Christ of Latter-day Saints, our
plan is to be married for all eternity. So walking out when times are tough
or pulling the eject lever when we don't get our way are not viable options.
Unfortunately, even within the ranks of the Church, many couples end up
divorcing who really never need to. If there is friction in the relationship,
these individuals get nervous and wonder if their marriage has any chance
of survival.

President George Albert Smith once said, "You know, when I was
growing up I never saw a difference of opinion between my father and my

mother. I used to think it was a miracle, and after I had been married for twenty years, I knew it was a miracle."[73] Many individuals fall into the trap of believing that those who have happy marriages simply don't have any problems. *Every normal couple will have problems and disagreements to work through.* The way such conflicts are managed is the determining factor of whether or not the marriage will succeed. Please, don't let conflict ruin an otherwise good relationship.

A distant family member of mine divorced after six months of marriage. When asked why, she said, "We just fought and argued too much. I lived in a home where my parents never had a disagreement. I didn't think couples who loved each other would argue that much." Years later, this same woman, much wiser and mature, said, "I should have never divorced my first husband. I didn't realize until I was much older that, in fact, my parents did fight and argue; they just never did it in front of me. So I grew up thinking that if you had a good marriage, you would never contend with each other. I compared my first marriage with the fantasy of my parents' marriage, and I thought my marriage must be terrible."

What a tragedy. If only this woman could have realized that disagreements and occasional spats are normal parts of marriage. Perhaps it could be argued (no intended play on words) that her parents did her a disservice by hiding all their problems. Once again, every couple will have disagreements and differences. The issue is not "if" you will have disagreements any more than the issue is "if" you might get sick—everyone will. The issue will always be how you will handle it. The differences between successful and unsuccessful marriages is not whether or not there is conflict, but how those conflicts are worked through and resolved.

Researchers have determined that every married couple will have about ten unresolvable issues. If that couple divorces and each partner marries another person, guess what? They will also have about ten unresolvable issues with their new marriage partner—and ten old issues with their former spouse. None of us will marry a person where there simply are not any issues between us. That is impossible in a mortal world. Instead, we must learn how to resolve or at least tolerate the differences that are sure to come.

The Doctrine of Differences
One of the great myths in marriage is that disagreements, quarrels, and contention only occur in *bad* marriages. This simply is not true.

Disagreements, quarrels, and contention are present in *all* marriages. In fact, my professional experience has taught me that couples who divorce don't have any more problems than those who never divorce. Put another way, couples who stay married for their lifetimes have just as many problems as those who terminate their marriages. The main distinction between the two groups is that couples who stay married usually place a higher value on their commitment to each other and have learned to work through their problems.

Of course there will be differences to work through. We come from different backgrounds, and our different genders and personalities will cause misunderstandings. Potentially, there could be issues with money, in-laws, raising children, household management, sexual intimacy, communication quirks, meals, cars, yard work, and a host of other fun topics! However, being different doesn't imply that one person is right and the other is automatically wrong. If we want our marriages to work, we must be willing to compromise, to sacrifice, and to love unconditionally. Renowned Christian family scholar Dr. James Dobson has explained:

> Two people are not compatible simply because they love each other and both are professing Christians. Many young couples assume that the sunshine and flowers that characterized their courtship will continue for the rest of their lives. . . . It is naive to expect two unique and strong-willed individuals to mesh together like a couple of machines. Even gears have multiple cogs with rough edges to be honed before they will work in concert. . . . A good marriage is not one where perfection reigns: It is a relationship where a healthy perspective overlooks a multitude of unresolvables.[74]

Indeed, a healthy perspective will help you overcome many differences. Most couples have "cogs" they aren't even aware of. For example, Dr. Brent Barlow shared the following experience. After he and his wife had been married for just a few weeks, Brent's parents telephoned one Saturday morning to indicate that they were passing through town and would like to stop by and say hello. Brent began to "fluff" the place up, while his new bride, Susan, began to cook breakfast. Unknown to Brent at the time and to most of the male population in America, making the first meal for the in-laws is a stressful rite of passage for new brides. So when Susan dropped the first egg in the frying pan and the yolk broke, she instantly began to cry. Brent was insensitive to her tears and began to tell her to quit crying over broken eggs. This only made matters worse. He didn't understand that his new wife wanted the meal to be perfect. An argument ensued, and then the doorbell rang.

Brent and Susan went into the "Mormon Delay"[a] as they greeted their family and had a good visit. However, soon after their family departed, they were able to resume their argument practically right where they left off. As the day wore on, three weeks' worth of problems surfaced. By 11:00 p.m., Brent and Susan were discussing the finer points of their relationship, such as "Why did we get married in the first place?" and "How will our marriage survive?" Remember, all this over one stupid, lousy egg.

The next day Brent and Susan found themselves in fast and testimony meeting in their new ward. They were still feeling somewhat depressed from the night before and were wondering if their marriage had a chance. During the course of the meeting, an older gentleman bore his testimony. He let everyone in the congregation know that he and his wife had been married over fifty years and had *never* had an argument or expressed a cross word to each other. This only drove the Barlows into deeper despair. Here was a man publicly declaring that he and his wife hadn't had a disagreement in fifty years, and Brent and Susan couldn't even make it three weeks. They left church more depressed and dejected than when they arrived.

Later that afternoon, Brent phoned his sister who had been married several years. He asked her if she and her husband had ever been in an argument before. She let Brent know that of course they had arguments and disagreements—all normal couples do. Brent then related the story of the old man who hadn't argued with his wife in fifty years. His sister concluded that a) the old man was probably a liar or b) he was probably forgetful or c) if it really were true, what a dull and boring marriage.

With the encouragement of his sister, Brent and Susan were able to mend their differences. He apologized for not being as sensitive as he should have been, and she admitted that crying over broken eggs may have been somewhat dramatic. Thankfully, they were able to move forward and put their "egg issues" behind them.[75] However, there is a strong point to make here. Like many couples, the Barlows believed that those who have good marriages don't have problems or disagreements. Elder Joe J. Christensen, however, has wisely stated,

---

a   The ability Latter-day Saints have to rant and rave at their family and then answer the phone with a perfect and dignified, "Hello."

Occasionally we hear something like, "Why, we have been married for fifty years, and we have never had a difference of opinion." If that is literally the case, then one of the partners is overly dominated by the other or, as someone said, is a stranger to the truth. *Any intelligent couple will have differences of opinion.* Our challenge is to be sure that we know how to resolve them. That is part of the process of making a good marriage better.[76]

The doctrine of differences is clear. We learn from the Book of Mormon that there must be opposition (or an antagonist or resistance) in all things (see 2 Nephi 2:11). Just a thought, but why would marriage be excluded from "all things"? It's not. Opposition exists in the strongest marriages; in fact, opposition is what makes a marriage strong. *You cannot have a strong marriage without some form of resistance.* Strength comes from resistance, opposition, and pressure. Every time you tear a muscle down with resistance (e.g. lifting weights), the muscle rejuvenates itself, stronger than it was before. Marriage operates on the same principle. If it doesn't kill you, it will probably make you stronger. The very nature of bringing two people from different backgrounds and experiences together to live side by side for a lifetime will cause most normal people to "crack" every now and again.

One of the main objectives in coming to this earth is to experience problems and to learn how to resolve them. Otherwise, why come to earth at all? So here we are—a bunch of people with a bunch of problems. No one is excluded, not one person. Life was meant to be challenging and tough. There will be disappointments, failures, and sometimes despair. However, over time things seem to straighten out. As we learn to draw strength from the Lord and each other, our problems can be solved.

Even the people we most admire, including future prophets and apostles, must deal with problems in marriage. Do you remember what happened with Joseph Smith and Emma one morning while Joseph was translating the Book of Mormon? Evidently Emma had done something that offended Joseph. Soon after their disagreement, Joseph went upstairs to resume translating. However, he found that while still upset with his wife, he could not translate a single syllable. So what did Joseph do? He went out into the orchard and prayed for direction. An hour later, Joseph got up off his knees, went directly into his house and asked Emma to forgive him. Only then was he able to commence the translation of the Book of Mormon.[77]

Consider another example. Perhaps there hasn't been a more Christlike prophet than President Spencer W. Kimball. However, like Joseph and Emma, he and Camilla were not immune to disagreements. One summer Camilla wanted to save their extra cash for a new house. Spencer wanted to take the money and travel. They could not come to an agreement, so Camilla and the children stayed home while Spencer loaded up the car and went on a family vacation—by himself. Incidentally, it was reported that he had a great time.[78]

Truly, even the most admired couples have issues to deal with. Marriage is not easy for anyone, and adjustments will have to be made so the marriage can improve. After the glamour of the wedding and the drama of the honeymoon are over, you will have to settle into real life. President Kimball wisely counseled:

> Some think of happiness as a glamorous life of ease, luxury, and constant thrills; but true marriage is based on a happiness which is more than that, one that comes from giving, serving, sharing, sacrificing, and selflessness. Two people coming from different backgrounds soon learn after the ceremony is performed that stark reality must be faced. There is no longer a life of fantasy or make-believe; we must come out of the clouds and put our feet firmly on the earth. Responsibility must be assumed and new duties must be accepted. Some personal freedoms must be relinquished, and many adjustments, unselfish adjustments, must be made.
>
> One comes to realize very soon after the [wedding] that the spouse has weaknesses not previously revealed or discovered. The virtues which were constantly magnified during courtship now grow relatively smaller, and the weaknesses that seemed so small and insignificant during courtship now grow to sizable proportions. The hour has come for understanding hearts, for self-appraisal, and for good common sense, reasoning, and planning."[79]

Differences Can Destroy Relationships

Frankly, the ability to negotiate differences will determine whether your marriage will succeed or fail. Differences induce disagreements, disagreements engender conflicts, conflicts lead to anger, and anger destroys relationships. Diane Solle further explains:

What's sad is the reason couples avoid conflict is because they believe it (conflict) causes divorce. It's like the cartoon where the couple explains to the marriage counselor, "We never talk anymore. We figured out that's when we do all our fighting." In the beginning, we avoid conflict because we are in love and we believe that "staying in love" is about agreeing, about NOT fighting. We're afraid that if we disagree—or fight— we'll run our marriage off into the ditch. We believe that if we've found our soulmate, we'll agree about most things—and certainly about the important things. Later, we avoid conflict because when we finally do try to deal with our differences (talk about them) things get so out of hand and our fights so destructive and upsetting that we simply shut down.

After a few bad blow-ups, we become determined to avoid conflict at any cost. And, we start wondering if we married the wrong person. We think to ourselves: It shouldn't be this hard. Successful couples know how to contain their disagreements—how to keep their disagreements from spilling over and contaminating the rest of their relationship.

While it's true that we don't get married to handle conflict, if a couple doesn't know how—or learn how—to fight or manage their disagreements successfully, they won't be able to do all the other things they got married to do. Put another way, it's hard to take her out to the ball game if you're not speaking. Couples are often so determined to avoid disagreements that they shut down—quit talking, quit loving. Couples need to know what the research has found: that every happy, successful couple has approximately ten areas of "incompatibility" or disagreement that they will never resolve. Successful couples learn how to manage their areas of disagreement and live life "around" them—to love in spite of their differences and to develop understanding and empathy for their partner's positions. . . . Irreconcilable differences are part of every good marriage. Successful couples learn to dance in spite of their differences.[80]

Elder Robert E. Wells recommended several steps for couples to follow when addressing conflicts in their relationships:

1. Begin by sharing your gratitude for each other and reviewing blessings.

2. Discuss frustrations or problems. As you do so, keep in mind the words of Paul: "Let the husband render unto the wife due benevolence: and likewise also the wife unto the husband" (1 Corinthians 7:3). Be kind and considerate to each other.

3. One of you could begin by asking, "What can I do to be a better husband/wife?"

4. As you share areas where your partner needs to change or improve, be humble and nonthreatening. Don't assume that you are always right and your partner is always wrong. Remember it is not necessarily a matter of determining who is right and who is wrong, but of understanding each other. Understanding is the gateway to conflict resolution.

5. Do not bring a list of faults to such meetings. In fact, it may be good to limit your complaints to one or two.

6. If you are on the "hot-seat," don't be defensive. Continually ask within your heart, "Lord, is it I?"

7. When your spouse offers you a suggestion, you can respond by saying, "You're right. I need to do better in that area." Then write some things down on a sheet of paper and commit to your spouse some specific behaviors you will work on.

8. Once you have gone through these steps, let the other partner share their concerns, and follow these same guidelines.[81]

A Model for Help

There really is no secret or rocket science to resolving concerns. It's just like anything else you do in this life—it takes some effort, thinking, and inspiration. The key is being Christlike so you can have the assistance of the Holy Ghost. You must also become selfless—focusing more on your partner than on yourself.

I recommend that when resolving conflict in your relationship you should:

- Try *not* to engage in heavy discussions when you're tired, hungry, or not feeling well.
- Always allow your partner time to talk, and don't cut them off.
- Learn to become a good listener, and reflect your spouse's key points back to them so they know you are hearing them.

- Don't engage in heavy discussions when you are both mad. Take time to cool off, and strive to be rational and objective.
- Learn to seek, understand, and appreciate your partner's point of view.
- If you think you're right, you could be wrong.
- Don't **ever, ever** tell your spouse what they think or how they feel.
- You may want to write the issues down on paper so that you can stay focused on the core problem. Couples can get off on tangents very quickly in the heat of the moment.
- Never personally attack your spouse with name-calling, labeling, or mockery. Focus on behaviors and practices that need to change, not the integrity of your celestial partner.
- Learn the fine art of forgiveness.

I would like to share with you a model that will help you work through your differences. Try to remember that in your marriage, one of you is more logical and one is more emotional—usually. As couples try to negotiate through differences, most often the conversation will stay at an emotional level. If that is the case, then nothing will be accomplished. On the other hand, if the resolution process is too cerebral, then the resolution will lack heart and feeling. Often such resolutions do not last. This model will allow you to focus on both the emotional and logical components of the problem. The following is a simple three-step model I use in my counseling practice:

Steps: The Patient	Skills: The Doctor
1. Deal with Facts • State the problem • Don't attack the person	 • Focus on your partner, and don't be defensive • Ask "why" questions • Restate, or mirror
2. Deal with Feelings • Use "I" statements, and own the feelings • Let your partner know if they have stated your feelings correctly	 • Listen • Restate • Show empathy • Don't worry that you haven't shared your side of the story yet • Apologize

Steps: The Patient	Skills: The Doctor
3. Resolve the Concern • Brainstorm • Ask your partner what they think would resolve the issue • Commit to the solution	• Brainstorm • Ask your partner what they think would resolve the issue • Commit to the solution

This model will help you work through some of the differences you have; it is not much different than the way missionaries are trained to resolve concerns with investigators. Stephen R. Covey taught that parents should treat their children as if they were investigators.[82] Why not, then, treat your spouse, as if they were an investigator too? When was the last time you saw or heard of a missionary criticizing an investigator for not remembering an appointment or giving a nonmember the silent treatment for not living the law of tithing? One of the reasons the missionaries are so effective is because they are taught how to resolve people's concerns in Christlike ways.

You'll notice that the model is divided into two parts, a step side and a skill side. The person who has the problem should focus on the steps, and the person who is "in trouble" or in the "hot-seat," should focus on the skills. Moreover, the person with the grievance can be considered the "patient." The other spouse, the one that is being "vented" to, is the doctor. What does a good doctor do? A good doctor focuses and listens to their patient. A good doctor would not tell the patient what their problem is, nor would a good doctor interrupt a patient and say, "Oh yeah, well my arm hurts worse than your head." Nope, good doctors will forget about themselves and focus on the patient.

Here is a demonstration of how the model should work. Let's take Bethany and Will, for example. They have been married for three years. Bethany's entire family lives in Salt Lake City, while Will's lives in Washington State. Bethany's family is big, and they like to get together often. None of them has ever lived outside of Utah despite job offers to different places—they could never leave their family. Will's family is a little more transient. After they graduate from college, they are not afraid to take jobs all over the country. Will has siblings in Texas, California, Florida, Kansas, Utah, and Washington.

One of Will's concerns is that every single Sunday, they have to spend the entire afternoon over at Bethany's parents' house, eating, playing games, and discussing the BYU football team. Will feels that visiting is fine every now and then, but he is getting tired of this routine. He would like some time just to be with Bethany by himself. Even though Will noticed this pattern before marriage, he thought that once he and Bethany got established, the visits to her home would be less frequent. Instead, the visits have increased.

Will fears that he and Bethany will never have their own identity, be their own family, or have their own traditions. Not to mention that Will is considering a job offer that will involve a transfer to the East Coast. He wonders if Bethany will go with him or if she will want to stay in Utah with her family.

So let's see how this model works. Will and Bethany are driving from church to her parents' home for the traditional Sabbath activities. This is when Will decides to bring the issue up.

Step 1:

Will: Bethany, I don't want to make you mad, but there is something I want to talk you about. Do you mind if we pull the car over and talk for a minute?

Bethany: I don't mind. What are you thinking about?

(They pull the car over, and the conversation begins.)

Will: Bethany, I'm just not sure if I want to continue going over to your parents' house every Sunday.

Bethany: Why?

Will: Well, I just feel that there are certain things I would like to do on Sundays, and I don't think that spending all day at your parents' house is the best way to spend our time. I like going over there, just not every Sunday.

Bethany: What would you like to do?

Will: I would like to have some time to discuss our goals and progress as a couple. I would like time to study my scriptures, write in my journal, go for a walk, talk, read . . . you know, things like that.

Bethany: Okay, Will, so what you're saying is that you don't like spending all day Sunday at my parents' house because you would like to do some other things. Is that right?

Will: Bethany, that's pretty much it.

(Notice that they deal with the facts; Bethany doesn't let her agenda get in the way. She is not defensive, and she focuses on Will. If she turned the tables

and focused on herself, this conflict would not get resolved. Bethany is the doctor, and Will is the patient.)

Step 2:

Bethany: Will, how does it make you feel when I want to spend all that time at my parents' house?

Will: What do you mean?

Bethany: How do you feel? What are your feelings about me wanting to be at my parents' house all day on Sunday?

Will: Well, I guess it makes me feel like I don't want to be there.

Bethany: That's not a feeling word. How does it make you feel? You know, like happy, sad, ashamed, glad, rejected . . . What? Give me a feeling.

Will: I guess it makes me feel like you would rather be with your family than with me. So, in a way I do feel rejected, or that I come second in your life.

Bethany: Now we're getting somewhere. I can relate to what you are saying. I remember when I was on my mission, getting those doors slammed in my face. I felt rejection there, and I hated that feeling. I also remember being with a companion who was always being called on for her singing talents. She sang in wards, stakes, firesides, mission conferences. I always felt passed over or like some kind of second fiddle. Anyway, it's no fun being rejected or feeling like you're second place.

Will: I'm not sure if I feel second place, but I do feel that your family comes before me sometimes. Not all the time, but sometimes.

Bethany: Will, I am sorry if I have made you feel that way. I didn't mean to. In fact, I just assumed that you loved being with my family as much as I do. You seem to be right in the middle of those football discussions and playing computer games with my little brother.

Will: Yeah, I'm not saying I don't like that. It's just . . .

Bethany: Just not every Sunday.

Will: Right.

(Notice that Bethany helps Will identify his feelings because he isn't sure what they are. Once feelings are brought in, sometimes they serve as the solution. Also, notice how step two is the perfect time to apologize.)

Step 3:

Bethany: So what do you think we need to do here?

Will: I don't know. I don't want you to feel that you can't see your family anymore. I want you to be close to them. I don't want to get in the way of that.

Bethany: Well, I guess we could quit going over altogether or not go over on Sundays.

Will: Bethany, don't be drastic. For that matter, I guess I could quit whining and just suck it up.

Bethany: How about this. What if we only go over every other Sunday?

Will: Bethany, I told you I don't want to take you away from your family. They would hate me if they found out I was the reason you quit coming over. Besides, you would be the only member in your family from American Fork to Payson not there. That's not going to work.

Bethany: Well, what do you think would work?

Will: What if we keep going over, but instead of staying for six hours, we only stay for two?

Bethany: Okay, I can make that compromise. What are you willing to give up?

Will: If we stay just stay for a couple of hours, I promise I won't complain or gripe about going over there.

Bethany: Sounds great.

(Notice the compromise and commitments made.)

What might have happened if Bethany and Will didn't use this model to work through their problems? Consider the following dialogue:

Will: Bethany, I don't want to make you mad, but there is something I want to talk you about. Do you mind if we pull the car over and talk for a minute?

Bethany: I don't mind. What are you thinking about?

(They pull the car over, and the conversation begins.)

Will: Bethany, I'm just not sure if I want to continue going over to your parents' house every Sunday.

Bethany: Why?

Will: Well, I just feel that there are certain things I would like to do on Sundays, and spending all day at your parents' house isn't the best way to spend our time. I like going over there, just not every Sunday.

Bethany: Will, I can't think of a better way to spend the Sabbath than with my family. Sunday is a family day. If you really love me, then you will spend Sundays with my family.

Will: It's like you think your family is the "only true family" on the earth. We never do anything with my family.

Bethany: What do you want to do, hop in the car and drive to Seattle to visit them? It's not my fault they live fourteen hours away.

Will: Look, your family makes me nauseated, okay.

Bethany: Well, you're making me nauseated.

As you can see, this is going nowhere fast. When couples are focused on themselves, they will never be able to resolve their differences. Tiny molehills can become mountains when partners are selfish. Another tip is to speak softly. When voices are elevated, feelings get hurt, and problems are not resolved.

Now, what we haven't addressed is this question: "What if Bethany has an issue with this topic? When does she get to talk about it? She has been completely focused on Will, but at the same time, it seems that she was never allowed to share her own vantage point?" In step three, before solutions are made, it is the perfect time for Bethany to say, "Before we resolve this completely, can I share some of my own concerns?" This is where they go back to step one and switch roles. Now Will becomes the physician, and Bethany becomes the patient.

There will be occasions in your lives when this model will not work. If this doesn't work, then let your partner talk for five uninterrupted minutes, while you just listen. When they are finished, you get your turn. When things really get out of hand, write each other a letter. That's not a bad thing to do regularly anyway.

As you learn to put your spouse first and strip yourself of your own pride, you will succeed in your marriage. You will be able to successfully resolve the conflicts that enter into your relationship. Of course, you must be humble, unselfish, and willing to work at it. In every marriage, couples can negotiate their differences if they are willing to swallow their pride, accept responsibility for their contribution, and apologize quickly.

Homework:
- Discuss as a couple how you have resolved differences in the past with other people, such as mission companions or roommates.
- Use the model presented in this chapter to solve a conflict along the lines of finances, intimacy, or household duties.

Additional Readings:
- C. Ross Clement, "Breaking the Cycle: A Case Study of Conflict in Marriage," *Ensign*, September 1981.
- Richard Miller, "Repentance and Forgiveness in Marriage," *Ensign*, September 2011.

- "Lesson 4: Responding to Challenges in Marriage," *Marriage and Family Relations Instructor's Manual*, 18–22; https://www.lds.org/manual/marriage-and-family-relations-instructors-manual/part-a-strengthening-marriages/lesson-4-responding-to-challenges-in-marriage?lang=eng&query=Conflict+in+marriage.
- "Reconciliation and Forgiveness in Families, Part 1," Episode 47, The Mormon Channel, *Gospel Solutions for Families*, http://www.mormonchannel.org/gospel-solutions-for-families/47-reconciliation-and-forgiveness-in-families-part-1.
- "Reconciliation and Forgiveness in Families, Part 2," Episode 48, The Mormon Channel, *Gospel Solutions for Families*, http://www.mormonchannel.org/gospel-solutions-for-families/47-reconciliation-and-forgiveness-in-families-part-2.

References

71 Spencer W. Kimball, *Teachings of Spencer W. Kimball*, ed. E.L. Kimball (Salt Lake City: Bookcraft, 1982), 307.

72 See Diane Solle, www.smartmarriages.com/divorcepredictor.html.

73 George Albert Smith, as cited in William E. Hartman, "Marriage—The Great Mutual Improvement Association," *BYU Speeches of the Year*, 1961, 5.

74 James Dobson, *Love for a Lifetime* (Sisters, Oregon: Multnomah, 2003), 63, 69.

75 See Brent A. Barlow, *Just for Newlyweds* (Salt Lake City: Deseret Book, 1992), 36–39.

76 Joe J. Christensen, *Conference Report*, April 1995, 86; emphasis added.

77 B.H. Roberts, *A Comprehensive History of the Church* (Salt Lake City: Deseret Book, 1930), 1:131.

78 Edward L. Kimball & Andrew E. Kimball Jr., *Spencer W. Kimball* (Salt Lake City: Bookcraft, 1977), 115.

79 Spencer W. Kimball, *Marriage and Divorce* (Salt Lake City: Deseret Book, 1976), 12–13.

80 Diane Sollee, www.smartmarriages.com/divorcepredictor.html.

81 Adapted from Robert E. Wells, "Overcoming Those Differences of Opinion," *Ensign*, January 1987, 61–62.

82 Stephen R. Covey & Truman G. Madsen, *Marriage & Family: Gospel Insights* (Salt Lake City: Bookcraft, 1989), 150–151.

CHAPTER 9
Meekness in Marriage

"What of the meek? In a world too preoccupied with winning through intimidation and seeking to be number one, no large crowd of folk is standing in line to buy books that call for mere meekness. But the meek shall inherit the earth, a pretty impressive corporate takeover—and done without intimidation!"
-President Howard W. Hunter[83]

EVERY MARRIED COUPLE SHOULD BE committed to growth in their marriage. It is not enough to treasure the good days and ignore the bad ones. We must be striving for constant improvement. One way for couples to enhance their marriages is to incorporate Christlike virtues into their relationship, such as kindness, charity, humility, and forgiveness. One Christlike attribute that can make a significant difference toward joy and satisfaction in marriage is often overlooked—that of meekness.

From the Sermon on the Mount, Jesus taught, "Blessed are the meek: for they shall inherit the earth" (Matthew 5:5). According to the Greek translation found in footnote a, we learn that meekness implies gentleness, forgiveness, and benevolence. Put another way, the gentle, the kind, and the forgiving will one day inherit this earth when it becomes the celestial kingdom. The meek are those who are at peace; they seem to be able to endure harsh words, incivility, unfairness, and injustice.

Moreover, the meek do not seek to retaliate—they seek to understand and help others. Elder Bruce R. McConkie further explained, "The meek are the god fearing and the righteous. They are the ones who willingly conform to the gospel standards, thus submitting their wills to the will of the Lord. They are not the fearful, the spiritless, the timid. Rather, the most forceful, dynamic personality who ever lived—He who drove the money changers from the temple . . . said of Himself, 'I am meek and lowly in heart.'"[84] Thus, meekness is not weakness. Instead, meekness is strength, power, and self-control.

Consider the following example of meekness:

A Church leader once toured a facility that housed a huge hydraulic crushing machine that could reduce old cars into small cubes. For a demonstration, the guide asked the man to remove his watch. The operator then placed it in the machine and adjusted the controls, and the top blade came crashing down, stopping just a millimeter above the watch. Next the sides slammed together, but once again they stopped just shy of the crystal. Then the operator removed the watch and returned it unscratched. Much pleased with the demonstration, this good man turned to those with him and said, "We have just witnessed the greatest demonstration of meekness I have ever seen. *Meekness is great power under complete control.*"[85]

Meekness isn't being powerless, weak, or even wimpy. Instead, meekness implies self-control and self-discipline. The meek individual can control his tongue as well as his passions. For example, President Harold B. Lee explained that "a meek man is defined as one who is not easily provoked or irritated and forbearing under injury or annoyance. . . . *The meek man is the strong, the mighty, the man of complete self-mastery. He is the one who has the courage of his moral convictions, despite the pressure of the [group]. He is humble minded; he does not bluster. . . . He is the 'salt' of the earth and shall inherit it.*"[86] Elder Neal A. Maxwell added that meekness "involves shoulder-squaring self-discipline, and what follows is the special composure that meekness brings."[87] Therefore, to be meek is to be in control, competent, composed, and confident.

What would be the single attribute that would help us become more like our Savior, Jesus Christ? Kindness? Charity? Love? Faithfulness? Elder Alexander B. Morrison suggested another possibility. "I submit that perhaps the most Christlike of all attributes of character is that of meekness, or in other words, humble submissiveness."[88] Meekness is not simply a nice quality to have. To become meek is critical to our salvation and exaltation. In fact, Moroni taught, "None is acceptable before God, save the meek and lowly in heart" (Moroni 7:44). To develop this incredible quality will take some time and effort, but just think how our spouses and children would benefit by our own quest for meekness.

Meekness is the root of kind words and gentle actions. Those who preside and lead in meekness do as the Savior did—tending, protecting, and nurturing the flock (see Matthew 2:6, footnote *d*). The meek do not raise their voices; they do not lead by shouting or shoving. They lead by example, and they lead by love.

Of all the attributes that would bless a marriage, meekness may even outrank charity and kindness. A spouse who practices meekness will exercise kindness when provoked. Such a person is in control, both physically and emotionally, has a gentle spirit, and is patient and charitable—even when he or she doesn't feel like it! Imagine how these attributes would bless and strengthen a marriage.

Defensiveness

One major challenge to all marriages is defensiveness. According to marriage expert Dr. John Gottman, it is criticism that leads to defensiveness, and defensiveness leads to withdrawal. In fact, Dr. Gottman has identified criticism and defensiveness as two key components that predict separation and divorce. Defensiveness is an automatic, emotional reaction which is hard to resist engaging in. Being defensive is, well, a defense mechanism. Gottman argues that "defensiveness is fundamentally an attempt to protect yourself and ward off a perceived attack."[89]

Unfortunately, when marriage partners become defensive in marriage, they first become closed off to some of the suggestions their spouse is providing. When spouses are defensive, they obstruct the useful communication needed between husband and wives to resolve conflict. When we are defensive, we are not attempting to understand our partner; instead, we spend our time defending ourselves. Moreover, even if your partner is critical of you, sometimes those suggestions may be very helpful for your growth and improvement.

Second, defensiveness creates contention in all relationships. When defensiveness and contention are present, the conversation is usually over—at least the productive part. Defensiveness leaves marriage partners feeling unheard or misunderstood.

Third, defensiveness keeps individuals from accepting responsibility for their actions. If a spouse is defensive, he or she is justifying the behavior or blaming someone else for the problem.

Finally, defensiveness keeps husbands and wives from putting their spouses' needs and happiness above their own. In essence, the defensive partner is saying, "I don't care what you need in the marriage, this is what I need." Defensiveness is self-focused. True love is when we focus on a partner's needs before our own. President Gordon B. Hinckley advised couples, "If you will make your first concern the comfort, the well-being, and the happiness of your companion, sublimating any personal concern to that loftier goal, you will be happy, and your marriage will go on through eternity."[90]

Defensiveness in Marriage

A close friend, I will call him Rob, shared this experience:

> Several years ago, I noticed something in my own marriage that began to bother me. I wish I could blame this problem on my wife, but I knew I was the problem. I became aware that each time my wife would question a decision I had made or take another approach or angle to an idea I had or simply not show her enthusiasm for something I had accomplished, I began to be defensive. I would immediately counter back with, "Why don't you ever like my ideas?" or, "Do I get a say in this?" or, "How come you never like the way I do things?"
>
> The more I defended myself, the more angry and resentful I was becoming. Then, one day with sudden clarity, I realized I was not being meek. Instead, I was being proud, selfish, and defensive. After all, my wife's ideas were not a direct attack on me—she was simply trying to help me improve my business, our lawn, or the ward, where I was serving as bishop. And frankly, her ideas were very good. I recognized that if I had been meek and humble, I would have received her counsel and wisdom as revelation from heaven. Instead, I often fought against her suggestions because I often felt inadequate or incompetent. Consequently, my wife felt she could never offer any suggestions to improve our marriage or our family. Soon we quit talking about the things that mattered most.
>
> My wife later revealed to me that she wanted to keep our conversations "safe" so we only discussed superficial things, like who would pick up the kids from soccer practice or take the dog to the vet.

It is clear from this example how the lack of meekness can stifle or hinder a marriage. If Rob would have stripped himself of pride and become humble, his wife could have helped him in his calling, in his business, and in their marriage. But because of Rob's unwillingness to listen and his rejection of his wife's ideas, all other areas of his marriage suffered.

Another friend I will call Steve shared the following experience. Steve had made some improvements on his home while his wife, Sherrie, was away at girls camp. He was excited for Sherrie to return home, knowing he had done several things that would make her happy. Steve finished tiling a bathroom, built some additional shelves in the pantry, and painted a bedroom. When Sherrie came home, she did notice the tile, and the paint, and the shelves. She complimented Steve on how good things looked and was happy that he would make such an effort for her. However, as they walked through the garage, which was still quite a mess, Sherrie said to him, "I thought you were going to tackle the garage while I was gone."

Immediately, Steve became defensive. He sharply responded, "I was up every night until midnight painting and tiling. I didn't have time to clean the garage. What did you want me to do, stay up until three each morning working on this dumb house?"

Sherrie became silent, and Steve realized he had fired a bazooka when a sling shot would have done the trick. His response did not demonstrate meekness but rather pride and defensiveness.

People who complain need something—they need comfort. Sherrie wasn't attacking Steve; she simply had a need. Her need was for the garage to be cleaned so they could have some order in their home. Sherrie was simply expecting to come home and have a place to put all of the camping gear. Besides, cleaning the garage was the one thing she had asked Steve to do while she was gone. Perhaps she shouldn't have been so critical after all of the hard work Steve had done; however, none of us can control how our spouses will react. The only thing we can control is how we respond to those reactions. Understanding that people who complain need comfort, Steve could have said, "Don't worry, honey, I didn't have enough time to get to the garage because I was so busy with the other projects, but I'll get to it this weekend. It will all work out." It would have been that simple! They could have hugged in the middle of the garage and perhaps had a tender moment together. Instead, they didn't speak to each other until later the next day.

Lord, Is It I?

Perhaps the greatest way to combat defensiveness can be found in the New Testament. As Jesus was preparing for his final hours, he told his disciples that one of them would betray him. In Matthew 26:22, we read, "And they were exceeding sorrowful, and began every one of them to say unto him, Lord, is it I?" In essence, each of the Apostles thought, "I wonder if it's me? I wonder what I could have done." What a fascinating concept in marriage! If we spent more time asking, "What is *my* contribution to this mess?" instead of blaming our partner, relationships would be much stronger and more fulfilling for both spouses. The only effective way to improve any relationship is to improve yourself.

This notion of changing yourself first is not new. In fact, it has been around for quite some time. In the Gospel of Matthew, we read:

> And why beholdest thou the mote that is in thy brother's eye, but considereth not the beam that is in thine own eye?
>
> Or how wilt thou say to thy brother, Let me pull out the mote out of thine own eye; and, behold, a beam is in thine own eye?
>
> Thou hypocrite, first cast out the beam out of thine own eye; and then shalt thou see clearly to cast out the mote out of thy brother's eye. (7:3–5)

From the LDS edition of the Bible, looking at footnote 3*b*, we learn that a mote is a speck of wood or a chip or splinter. On the other hand, footnote 3*c* helps us understand that a beam refers to a large beam used in the construction of homes. Put another way, "Why worry about the splinter in my eye, when you have a gigantic fifteen-foot beam sticking out of your entire face?" The Joseph Smith Translation adds the following verses to this sermon:

> And Jesus said unto his disciples, Beholdest thou the scribes, and the Pharisees, and the priests, and the Levites? They teach in their synagogues, but do not observe the law, nor the commandments; and all have gone out of the way, and are under sin.
>
> Go thou and say unto them, Why teach ye men the law and the commandments, when ye yourselves are the children of corruption?
>
> Say unto them, Ye hypocrites, first cast out the beam out of thine own eye; and then shalt thou see clearly to cast out the mote out of thy brother's eye. (Joseph Smith Translation Matthew 7:6–8 [in the Bible appendix])

How can we correct our spouses and chastise them for small specs of dust in their eyes when we may have a two-by-four sticking out of our own? Moreover, with that large beam in our own eye, *we have prevented ourselves from seeing clearly what reality actually is.* Our view is distorted because of our own mistakes, sins, and shortcomings. Therefore, before we grab hold of the pulpit, set the microphone just right, and give our best sermon, we may want to examine our own lives, our own pride, and our own selfishness. More than likely, our own issues are contributing as much to the difficulties as those of our spouses. Remember the question asked by the disciples of Jesus at the Last Supper? "Lord, is it I?"

Many wives, for example, feel that if they could just get their husbands into some counseling, perhaps the therapist could talk some sense into their mate, and the couple's problems would be solved. Perhaps some husbands feel that if their wives could just get in and talk to the bishop, then the marriage could get back on the right track. Generations have taught us, however, that no matter how hard we try, we never will be able to change our spouse. All we can really do is change ourselves.

Meekness in Marriage

In Alma 7, we learn how to live a life of meekness. Alma taught his followers,

> And now I would that ye should be humble, and be submissive and gentle; easy to be entreated; full of patience and long-suffering; being temperate in all things; being diligent in keeping the commandment of God at all times; asking for whatsoever things ye stand in need, both spiritual and temporal; always returning thanks unto God for whatsoever things you do receive.
>
> And see that ye have faith, hope, and charity, and then ye will always abound in good works. (Alma 7:23–24)

Perhaps these verses in Alma teach us what true meekness implies. Think of how humility, submission, gentleness, compliance, patience, and diligence could strengthen any marriage. If couples could apply these attributes in their marriage, their relationships would thrive! Their power would come from the Holy Ghost, which would strengthen their connection and love for each other. When a couple has the Holy Ghost as their guide, they have the strength to be patient, forgiving, gentle, respectful, nurturing, and healing.

Putting the Savior at the center of the marriage ensures that each spouse will seek to be meek and lowly of heart. Stephen R. Covey spoke of meekness and becoming Christlike in marriage when he wrote,

> If the God/Christ-centered person is offended, he blesses in return. He returns kindness for unkindness, patience for impatience. If he is afflicted, he chooses a response which enables him to grow and learn from the affliction, to suffer with meaning and nobility, a response which will have a greater influence on others than perhaps any other value. . . . If the person is praised, he gives thanks. If he is blamed, he appraises the matter to see whether there may be some blameworthiness in him, and if there is, he plans self-improvement. But he does not overreact and either accuse or blame in return, or condemn himself. . . . [Instead] he seeks to identify with Christ. Christ is his model. For instance, he studies scriptural accounts of the Savior's earthly life, and as he does so he visualizes each of the situations recorded. He empathizes with the people involved, seems himself as part of the action, feels himself in the more positive, disciple-type roles. He creates in his mind his response to present-day situations based on living by the principles represented by the scriptural accounts. . . . Gradually, as he comes to see the Savior as the perfect model and mentor, he identifies with that mental image and vision. In this way he acquires "the mind of Christ" and thus gradually learns to respond to life situations as He would have responded.[91]

In short, to become meek is to think the way the Savior would think, to act as He would act, and to do the things Jesus Christ would do, especially in our marriage and family relationships! Perhaps one of the finest examples of meekness in marriage comes from a conversation between Lehi and Sariah in the Book of Mormon. The account in 1 Nephi 5 describes some problems that Sariah and Lehi were having. Up to this point, Sariah had been a good camper. However, her sons had traveled to Jerusalem and had not returned. Sariah finally reached her breaking point as she laid out four major complaints: 1) Lehi was a visionary man (if it weren't for his visions, they wouldn't be out in the wilderness in the first place); 2) the family estate was gone (they had literally left everything to escape Jewish persecution); 3) their boys were probably dead (they had been sent to get the brass plates); and 4) Lehi and Sariah were probably going to die next.

How Lehi handled these issues is a testament of his Christlike nature and demonstrates how meekness can strengthen our marriages. It also serves as a model of how we should handle our own disagreements.

Regarding Sariah's first concern of his being a visionary man, Lehi essentially said, "Dear, I know I am a visionary man. If it weren't for the vision I had, we wouldn't be out here. However, I am grateful for the vision because if God had not warned me, we would all be destroyed" (see 1 Nephi 5:4). Notice there was no attacking Sariah's family or any weaknesses she may have had in the past. Lehi doesn't even pull rank by saying, "Hey, who's the prophet here anyway?" There was no temper tantrum or threat to sleep outside the tent. In fact, there was no defensiveness whatsoever. Lehi graciously and humbly listened and showed empathy as he responded, "Sweetheart, you have a good point. I can see that you are concerned, and I don't blame you in the least. I can only tell you what I know and what I have experienced; and I know I am sure of my inspiration. In fact, I've never been more certain. The Lord has shown me what would have happened had we remained in the city, and it's not pretty. I would not have believed it myself if the Lord had not been kind enough to show it all to me in a vision." In short, Lehi demonstrated true meekness.

Sariah's second objection concerned the loss of their family estate, their comforts, resources, wealth, and possessions. Lehi responded to this concern with, "I know we have lost everything of a material nature, but we are gaining a land of promise, a land that has everything we could ever want. It will be a great blessing to our family if you can be patient until we get there. It may not be easy, that I admit. But we will become wealthy again—perhaps not as we were in Jerusalem, but we have an important mission to accomplish. We are on the Lord's errand, and He will compensate us well for the loss of our property and home." Once again, no defensiveness, no criticism, no withdrawal. Lehi deals with Sariah's concerns patiently and humbly. Remember, people who complain need comfort, and Lehi was comforting Sariah by sharing his witness and testifying of the truth to the things she was concerned about.

Her third objection was that their children would probably be killed if they were not already dead. Lehi responded with his testimony: "I know that the Lord will deliver my sons out of the hands of Laban, and bring them down again unto us in the wilderness" (1 Nephi 5:5). It is as if Lehi said, "Yes, dear, you're right. It is dangerous. I know that their return may not be easy and is fraught with danger. But remember, Nephi and Sam are pretty level-headed. The Lord will inspire them, and they will return unharmed."

Finally, Sariah feared that the rest of the family would be killed as well. Once again, Lehi reassured Sariah that all would be well. He didn't retort with "Why don't you ever listen to me? We've just been through this." Lehi was compassionate and in tune with his wife's needs. In Nephi's words, "And after this manner of language did my father, Lehi, comfort my mother, Sariah, concerning us" (1 Nephi 5:6). Lehi acknowledged Sariah's worries and fears, and then resolved them with his faith and testimony. He did not give her a lecture or talk down to her. Consequently, she did not attack Lehi again because she had been comforted, meaning the Spirit of the Lord had assured her that everything would be all right.

When their sons made it back to camp, Sariah "was exceedingly glad" (1 Nephi 5:1); in fact, Nephi later records that "their joy was full, and my mother was comforted" (5:7). Because Lehi practiced meekness, the Spirit was able to attend their conversation and attest to his words. Subsequently, Sariah received her own witness: "Now I know of a surety that the Lord hath commanded my husband to flee into the wilderness; yea, and I also know of a surety that the Lord hath protected my sons, and delivered them out of the hands of Laban, and given them power whereby they could accomplish the thing which the Lord hath commanded them" (1 Nephi 5:8).

It is a credit to Sariah that she never again wavered or questioned Lehi's revelations. From that point on, she was totally committed to the cause of Christ and to her husband. In fact, later the Lord spoke to Lehi and commanded him to have his sons go back to Jerusalem again, this time to find women to marry. A lesser woman than Sariah might have said, "Look, Lehi, once was enough. You were lucky the first time, but this time could be a disaster." No, there was none of that. There was never a word of complaint.

In the Doctrine and Covenants, we read, "No power or influence can or ought to be maintained by virtue of the priesthood, only by persuasion, by long-suffering, by gentleness and meekness, and by love unfeigned" (D&C 121:41). First, notice how gentleness and meekness are coupled together in this verse. Indeed, gentleness and meekness are twin virtues. These qualities also seem to describe the Savior as well as any other words in our Christian vocabulary.

Second, this passage reminds us of a truth that Lehi knew. His power and influence with Sariah could not come by harsh words, manipulation, or force. Instead, Lehi's power and strength was in the Holy Spirit, which attended him because he spoke with gentleness and meekness.

Perhaps the next time you and your spouse find yourself getting into a heated discussion, remember Lehi and the way he comforted his wife, inspired her, and strengthened her with his own faith. This is the Lord's way for handling disagreements. Lehi is meekness personified. If you need to repent and make some changes in your marriage, take heart—even the very best couples need work and improvement.

Practicing Meekness

At the beginning of this chapter, I mentioned my friend Rob and how his defensiveness hindered his marriage. A few weeks later, Rob related to me that his wife is not a complainer. In fact, he said that she is actually a positive person. Because I knew his wife, I agreed with his assessment. Furthermore, since Rob was a good friend, I asked him, "Why would you be so defensive when your wife makes suggestions that will improve your finances or your home or a child's life?" Rob related to me that because of his own lack of confidence in some areas of his life, he perceived some of his wife's suggestions as a direct attack on him as a person. Rob said, "I felt that I was inadequate as a husband if the fence wasn't fixed, or I determined that I was a poor father if there was trouble with one of my children. Now, I came up with those conclusions on my own. My wife never implied any of that."

Like all husbands, Rob wanted his wife to be impressed with him—not to think of him as an incompetent husband and father. I assured Rob that I believed his wife thought he was a very capable and impressive person. I reminded him that when it came to his wife and children, he should think the best of them. I reminded him of Elder Jeffrey R. Holland's words, cited previously in this book, that he should assume the good and doubt the bad. Rob promised me that he would try to work harder on being less defensive and more responsive to his wife's needs. He would look for the good in his wife and assume the best. About two months later, Rob shared the following experience:

> I secured a new job out of state, and we were heavily involved in trying to fix up our house and make the lawn look nice so we could put the home up for sale. Because of my present church

calling as a bishop and my heavy involvement in running my business, my wife became exasperated with my busy schedule. One day, in frustration, she said, "We're never going to get this house fixed up so we can sell it."

My normal response would have been to say something like, "Well, sorry that I had to be up at the church all night, and sorry I have to work every day." However, I knew I had been wrong with my past responses, and I was working on becoming meeker and less defensive.

I put my arm around my wife and said, "Don't worry, honey, we're going to get this house fixed up. It's going to happen." I knew that was only half of the battle. She needed more than comfort; she needed a solution. I then assured her that I would take a few days off work, and we would hire a man in the ward to help us fix a few things. Instead of an argument, a hug followed, and then we went to work on our house.

After Rob shared this experience with me, I was proud of the changes he was making. I reminded him that most often, when our spouses complain, they are not implying that their husbands or wives are incompetent—they simply need comfort, assurance, and resolution.

The Apostle Paul taught that those who enjoy the fruits of the Spirit will have "love, joy, peace, longsuffering, gentleness, goodness, faith, meekness, temperance" and will "not be desirous of vain glory, provoking one another, envying one another" (Galatians 5:22, 26; see also Ephesians 4:2). In the Book of Mormon, we learn that "because of meekness and lowliness of heart cometh the visitation of the Holy Ghost, which Comforter filleth with hope and perfect love" (Moroni 8:26). Indeed, meekness is a fruit of the Spirit. Meekness can unlock other strong virtues as well. For example, to be meek is to be humble, kind, gentle, accountable, and comforting. It is to do what the Savior would do. Meekness is becoming Christlike.

The following suggestions will help couples practice meekness in their marriage.

1. *Learn to honor and respect each other*. Most of us want our spouse to be just like us—to see the world the way we do, to act how we act, and to feel passionate about our passions. Chances are, however, that you are married to someone very different from you. Instead of spending your entire marriage trying to change your spouse or trying to get them

to agree with you, learn to go with the flow to some degree. Trust your spouse and their position, honor them for who they are, and respect those differences. More of your conflicts and disagreements will be resolved through honor and respect than by arguing. Loving your spouse more than you love yourself is the first step to meekness.

2. *Be willing to listen to your spouse without feeling the need to defend your position.* When most men and women are in a disagreement, very little listening takes place. Instead, one spouse is preparing their argument while the other is making theirs. To listen without interrupting is an indicator of meekness. In fact, the next time you and your spouse have a disagreement, decide simply to listen rather than talk. You will be amazed at the outcome. Years ago, former Brigham Young University professor Brent Barlow posed a question to a group of priesthood brethren: "How many of you would like to receive a revelation?" Every hand in the room went up. Brother Barlow then suggested that every man go home that afternoon and ask their wives how they could be better husbands. That would be their revelation! He added, "I followed my own advice and had a very informative discussion with [my wife] for more than an hour that afternoon."[92] Learning to listen and reflect the concerns of your spouse is to respond with meekness.

3. *Recognize your own weaknesses, and try to improve them.* After all, we are probably not as kind, loving, and Christlike as we think we are. There is always room to improve and become more like our Savior. Elder Neal A. Maxwell has stated, "The pressures of life in a family will mean that we shall be known as we are, that our frailties will be exposed and, hopefully, we shall then work on them. . . . It is an encounter with raw selfishness, with the need for civility and taking turns, of being hurt and yet forgiving, of being at the mercy of others' moods and yet understanding, in part, why we sometimes inflict pain on each other. . . . The home gives us a great chance to align our public and private behavior, to reduce the hypocrisy in our lives, to be more congruent with Christ."[93] Meekness is the recognition that without God, we are nothing and that we need His help if we are to become like Him. To be meek is to be humble and recognize that without our Heavenly Father, we are nothing.

4. *Strip yourself of selfishness.* Selfishness is perhaps the cause of most of our misery and heartache. We understand that selfishness is the root

cause for disagreement, contention, and divorce. When we are selfish, we lose the Holy Ghost. On the other hand, the meek individual will put others, especially their spouse, before their own wants and needs. When President and Sister Hinckley had their sixtieth wedding anniversary, they were interviewed by the *Church News*. Sister Hinckley told the reporter, "You cannot be selfish in marriage. You have to have as your first priority the happiness and comfort of your spouse. If you work on that, then you are happy too."[94] To be meek is to be selfless—putting your spouse's needs before your own.

5. *Strip yourself of pride.* Pride is a deadly disease; it is the detonator for every sin we can commit. The proud believe they are always right and their spouse is constantly wrong. The proud believe that problems are caused by everyone else. We know from the teachings of modern prophets that to combat pride we must learn to cultivate humility.

6. *Accept responsibility when you make mistakes or cause problems.* For too many, accepting responsibility is difficult to do. It is as if men and women cannot have the "stain" of sin or fault on their shoulders. We need to get over that notion quickly. We are mortal, and all of us make mistakes—daily. Remember the words of John in the New Testament, "If we say that we have no sin, we deceive ourselves, and the truth is not in us" (1 John 1:8). Likewise, the Apostle Paul taught, "For all have sinned, and come short of the glory of God" (Romans 3:23).

I am reminded of a newlywed couple who was having a disagreement. The husband asked the wife, "So are you going to apologize?"

His young bride responded, "No, I am never going to apologize to you because I am never wrong."

When I heard this, I thought that this couple would have much to learn in the years ahead! With meekness, we would be more concerned about our own problems and less focused on the imperfections of those around us. Spouses who possess the quality of meekness will take responsibility for their behavior and be quick to apologize for their mistakes.

7. *Only if you sacrifice for a cause will you love it.* One great indicator of meekness is our willingness to make sacrifices. When the Apostle Paul taught, "Husbands, love your wives, even as Christ also loved the Church, and gave himself for it" (Ephesians 5:25), he was teaching the

principle of sacrifice. It is good periodically to ask ourselves, "What have I sacrificed lately for my spouse's happiness?"

Howard W. Hunter is a wonderful example of sacrifice and meekness in marriage. Before his marriage, President Hunter was a promising musician; in fact, music had been one of his greatest joys in life. However, on 6 June 1931, four days before his marriage to Claire Jeffs, Howard said he "packed up his saxophones and clarinets and his music and put them away." He later said, "Since that night, I have never touched my musical instruments except on a few occasions. . . . Although this left a void of something I had enjoyed, the decision has never been regretted."[95] In order to create a happy marriage, both husband and wife should be making sacrifices for their marriage and the family. Indeed, our love grows in proportion to the service, kindness, and affection we demonstrate. The meek marriage partner will seek to understand and meet the needs of a spouse—often at the expense of their own needs.

8. *Ask, "Lord, is it I?"* Each spouse contributes something to the problems in their marriage. Since no one can control their spouse's behaviors, the best place to begin the change process is with us. Some experts call this the "I Change First" Rule. Even though both partners have made some mistakes, the other spouse's mistakes should not concern us. The best thing we can do to improve our marriage is to improve ourselves. Our own behavior is really the only thing we have control over anyway.

9. *Seek the Spirit.* If married partners would each seek to have the Lord's Spirit in their lives each day, they could overcome many of the common challenges that face couples. Kindness and charity fade when spiritual resources are ignored or forgotten. Once couples lose the Spirit, their relationship deteriorates. They may become sarcastic or angry or critical or defensive or uncaring. On the other hand, when the eternal perspective of marriage is clear and the Savior is a part of the relationship, it is much easier to be kind and considerate.

The nearer we are to God, the more likely we will be to have his attributes. As we come to know the Savior, we can obtain the mind of Christ. When we begin to think how He thinks, and behave how He behaves, it is amazing what we can accomplish and overcome in our marriage relationships. When we have Christlike character traits, the Holy Ghost will be with us to inspire us and teach us how to act and what to say. Meekness comes to those who seek the Spirit and pray for humility.

Homework:
- Each of you write down the things you do that contribute to problems in your marriage. Share the list with each other.
- Identify in your personal journal some of the personality traits and characteristics you have that cause trouble in relationships. Ask your spouse how you can improve in these areas.
- Ask your spouse if there is one thing you could work on this week that would help you be a better marriage partner.

Additional Readings:
- Elder Ulisses Soares, "Be Meek and Lowly of Heart," *Ensign*, November 2013.
- The Arbinger Institute, *Leadership and Self-Deception* (San Francisco: Berrett-Koehler Publishers, 2002).
- James L. Ferrell, *The Peacegiver* (Salt Lake City: Deseret Book, 2004).

References

83 Howard W. Hunter, *Teachings of Howard W. Hunter* (Salt Lake City: Deseret Book, 1997), 266.

84 Bruce R. McConkie, *Mormon Doctrine* (Salt Lake City: Deseret Book, 1966), 474.

85 S. Michael Wilcox, "The Beatitudes—Pathway to the Savior," *Ensign*, January 1991, 19–21; emphasis added.

86 Harold B. Lee, *Teachings of Presidents of the Church: Harold B. Lee* (2000), 203; emphasis added.

87 Neal A. Maxwell, *Meek and Lowly* (Salt Lake City: Deseret Book, 1987), 15.

88 Alexander B. Morrison, *Zion: A Light in Darkness* (Salt Lake City: Deseret Book, 1997), 65–66.

89 John Gottman, *Why Marriages Succeed or Fail* (Simon & Schuster: New York, 1994), 85.

90 Gordon B. Hinckley, *The Teachings of Gordon B. Hinckley* (Salt Lake City: Deseret Book, 1997), 328–329.

91 Stephen R. Covey, *The Divine Center* (Salt Lake City: Bookcraft, 1982), 148–149.

92 Brent A. Barlow, "To Build a Better Marriage," *Ensign*, September 1992, 7.

93 Neal A. Maxwell, "The Value of Home Life," *Ensign*, February, 1972, 7.

94 Dell Van Orden, "Hinckleys to note 60th Anniversary," *Church News*, 19 April 1997, 3.

95 Eleanor Knowles, *Howard W. Hunter* (Salt Lake City: Deseret Book, 1994), 81–82.

CHAPTER 10
Making Marital Adjustments

"If [young people] would resolve from the moment of their marriage,
that from that time forth they would resolve and do everything in their
power to please each other in things that are right, even to the sacrifice of
their own pleasures, their own appetites, their own desires, the problem
of adjustment in married life would take care of itself, and their home
would indeed be a happy home."
-Elder Harold B. Lee[96]

EVERY MARRIED COUPLE WILL NEED to make adjustments after the
honeymoon is over. During the dating and courtship phases, you learned
how similar you were; it is during the normal course of life together that
you become aware of your many differences. Let me assure you that
these differences should not lead to disaster, but they certainly need to be
addressed.

Years ago, journalist Judith Viorst humorously described marital
adjustments:

> Before my husband and I got married, we never had fights
> about anything. What was there, after all, to fight about? On
> every fundamental issue—war, peace, race relations, religion,
> education, the meaning of the universe—we were in total, sweet
> accord. Surely we had no reason to think that this mellow state of
> affairs would not continue for the next forty or fifty years.
>
> From the moment we were married, we have managed to
> have fights about almost everything. What isn't there, after all,
> to fight about? We're still in total accord on those fundamental
> issues—but so what? That still leaves clothes, cooking, driving,
> sex, money, in-laws, children, and who gets to read the newspaper
> first. And there isn't the slightest possibility that this embattled
> state of affairs will not continue.

I hadn't planned it this way. My marriage, as I too frequently informed people in my premarital innocence, was going to be a mature, intelligent relationship. If, perchance, some small disagreement happened to trouble the serenity of our days, it would be resolved promptly by rational discourse. This was a swell plan.

Unfortunately, it had nothing to do with reality. Reality, I found out in the course of our honeymoon, was my getting resentful about having to lend him my hairbrush and his getting huffy about the way I left the soap in the washbasin instead of the soap dish. Honestly, I didn't know until then that we even had positions on hairbrushes and soap dishes—but we do indeed. . . . We have, it turns out, passionately held positions on hundreds of subjects too lowly ever to have been thought of until we started living, day in and day out, with someone who failed to share our cherished views.

He thinks a comfortable house temperature is 68 degrees. I think a comfortable temperature is 84.

He thinks a safe speed on the New Jersey Turnpike is 90 miles an hour. I think a safe speed is 45.

He thinks it's unnecessary to enter checks in the checkbook. I think that not entering each check should be punishable by death in the electric chair. . . .

Any couple is capable of escalating dumb disagreements to ferocious fighting. In our household, escalation often happens when it's too early in the morning or too late at night. Take 7:15 a.m., when, according to my youthful dreams, my husband and I were going to awake smiling warmly at each other and then launch immediately into a vivacious discussion of [current events]. Instead, I grope my way out of bed feeling exceedingly crabby and put-upon, while he coldly informs me that there isn't a single pair of matching socks in his drawer. . . . Theoretically, it might . . . be possible to see his remark as something other than an attack. But 7:15 a.m. is not one of my finer moments—and it is definitely no time to talk about socks. So I point out to him that just because his parents catered to all his infantile needs doesn't mean that I have to perpetuate this kind of crippling emotional dependency. The morning deteriorates from there. . . .

On countless occasions, in the afterfight afterglow, we both have made the most beautiful resolutions. I won't complain anymore when he's not on time. He won't complain anymore if I use his razor. I won't tell him he just went through a stop sign. He won't tell me I just destroyed the fried eggs.[97]

I think we can glean much from Judith's insights. However, she seems to convey the idea that the best way to have a happy marriage is to quit paying attention! From a gospel perspective, making marital adjustments provides opportunities for you to learn from each other, compromise, sacrifice, and invite the Lord into your relationship. Then your desire to improve and become better for each other will be strengthened.

Remember, a muscle grows by resistance. The muscle is torn down, and then it grows back even stronger than it was before. Marriage works the same way. There is no growth in any relationship without opposition, and there will be opposition in every single thing you encounter in this life (2 Nephi 2:11), including your marriage. View adjustments in your marriage as a chance to grow and learn.

Of course, it is normal that when two lives are suddenly blended together, nothing will ever be the same again! It can't. It's impossible. Another person to care for means another schedule to manage, another personality to deal with, and another way to do things. Everyone who enters the marriage arena must be willing to make changes and adjustments. The single life you left behind is gone. From now on, everything you do must be coordinated with your spouse's interest in mind. Although what I just described could sound confining, it's actually not. In fact, loving someone else more than yourself can be one of the most fulfilling experiences in life.

Be patient with each other. Remember, being married will be an adjustment for both of you. For the first month of our marriage, Janie seemed to be quite emotional. I finally got the courage to ask her what the trouble was, and she said, "I just miss my family." I had to learn not to take that personally. I knew she was close to her family, and I never wanted to stand in the way of that. For me, I found life in a basement apartment somewhat confining. After about three weeks of marriage, I asked Janie one evening if she cared if I ventured out alone just to hit some golf balls. I just needed to do some "man" stuff, and she was good with that too. She didn't take it personally that I wanted to leave her alone one night just to stretch my wings a tad.

The Magnificent Seven

I would like to address seven common areas of adjustment that most young married couples will encounter during the first year of their marriage. As these areas are mentioned, consider how you might resolve some of these issues.

1. In-Laws/Parents

The in-law/parent relationship is so significant that I devote an entire chapter to it in this book. However, I would like to briefly mention several key points at this juncture. Some of you will not have to worry about your parents or in-laws meddling in your lives too much because you will most likely live far away from them. However, others will live in close proximity to parents or in-laws, and that *could* pose problems. Moreover, some of your parents will find ways to interfere with your life no matter where they live. I recommend you create some boundaries with your parents and in-laws.

As a couple, you will want to forge your independence as soon as possible. If you are dependent upon parents for income, cell phones, housing, or other major expenses, I would recommend that you try to cut the umbilical cord as soon as you can and establish your identity as a couple. The hallmark of maturity is independence.

I have seen bucket loads of unnecessary strain and tension caused between parents and their newly married children. I am aware of parents who demand their newly married children come to Sunday dinner each week; I have seen newly married couples mooch off their parents—using them for food and gas as often as possible. Sometimes well-intended parents can become nosy and want to know things that are simply none of their business. I was recently privy to an informal study done with newly married couples in Southern Utah. More than seventy percent of the women said their husbands' families were too involved in their lives.

Shortly after Janie and I were married, we had the opportunity to go home to the Houston area for the summer, live with her parents, and work a job that would make us enough money to pay for our school expenses the following year. As tempting as the offer was—especially the prospect of free rent and food—I didn't feel good about accepting the opportunity. I strongly believed Janie and I needed to create our own identity and become our own team. Therefore, we stayed in Provo and worked our meager jobs. We struggled financially and came up short when it came to paying our tuition in the fall. However, I would not trade what we learned that summer for anything. Together we became closer and learned to rely on the Lord for help and strength.

My career has kept us away from our families for the majority of our married lives. We love our families, but we found great value in being able to raise our children and manage our affairs without anyone looking over our shoulders—so to speak. We developed wonderful friendships with ward members and neighbors, and learned in very direct ways that our Heavenly Father is there for us. Since our families lived so far away, we also relished the opportunities we had to be with them several times a year.

Having said all of that, I have also seen wonderful relationships created between parents/in-laws and their young married children. It can be done, but expectations must be discussed, and there must be boundaries. The key to developing a strong relationship in this area is mutual respect. Both parties must invest in these relationships if they are to be successful. Moreover, well-meaning parents must back out of the details of their children's lives. Mothers and fathers, when you visit your married children, you are a guest in their home. Young married couples, you must also treat your parents with the same respect you want from them.

2. Finances

Since both of you most likely come from different financial backgrounds, money matters will need to be discussed—and discussed regularly. President Gordon B. Hinckley taught, "An extravagant husband or wife can jeopardize any marriage. I think it is a good principle that each have some freedom and independence with everyday, necessary expenditures, while at the same time always discussing and consulting and agreeing on large expenditures."[98]

Perhaps a husband will want to spend extravagantly, while a wife is much more frugal. Some spouses will want to live by a strict budget, while others will spend for days without balancing the checkbook. The weekly couple's meeting previously mentioned in this book is the perfect setting to discuss finances, bills, and purchases.

Also, having a budget to live by is practically a miraculous way to save money. Too many couples spend every dime they make each month, without saving anything. Then when emergencies occur—which they will—or gifts need to be purchased or you need to travel a long distance to visit parents over the holidays, there is no money to make such purchases, and you may use a credit card instead. Before you know it, you can owe a small fortune on that credit card.

Furthermore, I have seen many couples over the years who want to have all of the same furnishings as their parents. They finally save enough for a home and then feel they need to go into debt in order to furnish it. Couples would do well to delay purchases, save money, and take the setting up of the home at a slow pace. One of the best ways to build wealth is to save money and postpone expenses.

Once again, husband and wife communication is the key to overcoming this potential barrier. You need to learn how you each feel about finances and set goals that will point you in the right direction. Discuss finances freely, and work together to meet your financial goals.

3. Friends

I believe that once you are married, your friends are going to change. Although you may find this hard to believe, it is very difficult to maintain friendships with those who are single as a married person. You will begin to notice the disparity between your new married life and the lifestyle of your single friends. Moreover, you will want to spend most of your discretionary time with your spouse—or at least, that's what you should want to do!

I had a wonderful group of friends that I associated with through high school and then at Brigham Young University. We played intramural sports and enjoyed hanging out together with our girlfriends. I was the first one of our group to be married. After I was married, I still played on an intramural softball team with many of my single friends. After practically every game, my friends invited me to their single activities. I respectfully declined their offers and looked forward to getting back home with Janie as soon as I could. Seeing this dilemma, the upcoming semester, I made sure I was on a flag football team with the married guys in my ward. It just made more sense.

Believe it or not, one of the most common problems I see in my counseling practice is when a newly married husband or wife wants to maintain close relationships with single friends. In my opinion, single friends can sometimes serve as a wedge between a husband and wife. As a general rule of thumb, if you can't engage in friendships together as a couple, you probably shouldn't be involved in such relationships.

Years ago, I counseled a newly married woman. She asked me this question: "Will you settle a debate between my husband and me?" I told her I would try my best. She then explained that every Tuesday night, she and her single friends went dancing together. Her husband was not thrilled with this social activity. Initially, I visualized this girl dancing and grooving with her girlfriends. However, she confessed that she was actually dancing with other men. She justified her behavior by telling me, "It was just dancing—nothing more." She asked if I thought her dancing activity was wrong. I told her, with all of the self-control I could muster, that she probably shouldn't be *dating* other men while she was married. She said, "I am not dating other men—just dancing with them." I explained that if she was dancing with other men, she was on a date. I further stated that even if she didn't want to call it a date, she shouldn't be dancing with other men or be hanging out with her single girlfriends at a dance club while her husband was sitting alone at home. She thanked me for the advice and left with a new perspective.

Once you are married, it would be wise to develop friendships with other married friends. You will meet these people in your wards and stakes. I know for Janie and me, we made many lifelong friends in our BYU married student ward. Many of these couples we still keep in contact with today—almost thirty years later. Once again, you still love your single friends. You don't shun them. You talk to them, and they are still part of your lives, but socializing with them solely will be more difficult after you're married.

Because of the power and influence of social media, you will also need to establish boundaries as a couple when it comes to Facebook and other social networking activities. I have seen many married couples in my counseling practice get into trouble by corresponding with "old friends" of the opposite sex on social networks. I know I wouldn't be comfortable if my wife was talking to other men on Facebook, and I'm sure she wouldn't approve of me talking to women. Either you need to have a joint Facebook account or have each other's passwords. You need to be completely transparent with your spouse when it comes to relationships of the opposite sex. You should be fiercely loyal to your spouse, and that could be difficult if you are developing inappropriate relationships through social media. Never let anyone get between you and your spouse. This includes maintaining relationships with old boyfriends or girlfriends.

4. Intimacy

I will not comment too much about intimacy in this section because I devote an entire chapter to it later. However, like anything else in your marriage, intimacy will need to be talked about. Couples can get into trouble in this area because of ignorance and unmet expectations. Many husbands go into marriage believing they are going to have a sexual relationship with their wives daily. Often, wives have the expectation that every sexual encounter with their husband is going to be worthy of the front cover of a romance novel. The key to working through this area of your marriage is being able to talk about it and share your expectations. However, instead of being completely worried about your own sexual needs, find out how you can meet the needs of your spouse in this area. By focusing on the needs of your spouse, you will find that your own needs will usually be met.

If your sexual life as a couple is the foundation upon which your marriage rests, you are heading for disaster. However, if you can build your marriage on the base of love, charity, friendship, kindness, and courtesy, the sexual part of your life will follow naturally. Furthermore, your affection for each other will be natural and not forced or manufactured. When a married couple is madly in love, best friends, attracted to each other, and meeting each other's needs, then a healthy sexual relationship is the normal result.

Another area of adjustment more common to women is what I call "Red Light—Green Light." For the first twenty years of their lives, our wonderful women of the Church have been taught regarding sex—"NO, NO, and double NO." And then, after a brief ceremony, the exchange of a ring, and a kiss over the altar, it's now "YES, YES, and double YES." Many women in the Church have a difficult time making the transition from being a virgin to a sexually active woman—and it happens so quickly. Men need to be soft, tender, patient, kind, respectful, and understanding.

For some men and women, it is helpful to understand the Church's view of the sexual relationship. Many outsiders who do not understand our faith have expressed their views that Mormon couples only have a sexual relationship to bear children. Nothing could be further from the truth. President Spencer W. Kimball taught:

> The Bible celebrates sex and its proper use, presenting it as God-created, God-ordained, God-blessed. It makes plain that God himself implanted the physical magnetism between the sexes for two reasons: for the propagation of the human race, and for the expression of that kind of love between man and wife that makes for true oneness. His command to the first man and woman to be

"one flesh" was as important as his command to "be fruitful and multiply."[99]

A good friend of mine is a psychologist in Colorado. He shared the experience of a prospective wife who was terrified of having a sexual relationship with her future husband. The psychologist talked to the couple for a short time, and then the future husband said, "Don't you worry about a thing. We will take it at your pace." What a wonderful response. If men could be more sensitive to their wives' fears and worries in this area, more women would be able to trust their husbands completely.

5. Division of Labor

Another common area of adjustment will be in the area of household duties. Like some of the other areas, this area can largely be driven by upbringing. I have met husbands who have been surprised that their new brides couldn't make toast; I have also met wives who were flabbergasted because their new husbands never lifted a finger to help with anything in the home—including picking up their own dirty laundry off the floor.

Perhaps she was never required to do much in the home she was raised in. Maybe her mother cleaned the house, made all the meals, paid the bills, and mowed the lawn while the children sat in front of the television all day and the father was mysteriously never around. Perhaps a husband grew up in a home where the mother did all of the indoor work, while he worked with his dad and brothers outdoors—and outdoors only. Maybe some spouses came from homes where the division of labor was very traditional, while others have a more contemporary perspective on household work.

In my case, my father was a hard worker. In fact, I don't know too many people who work harder than he did. However, I never once saw him do a dish, change a diaper, vacuum a floor, make a meal, or fold the laundry. On the other hand, Janie's dad had an office in their home, and his job in real estate allowed him great flexibility. He was the parent who often made the children's lunches for school and occasionally prepared meals because he loved to cook.

Do you see the crash coming? Early in our marriage I was changing diapers, vacuuming floors, ironing shirts, and doing dishes. Compared to my own father, I thought I was quite amazing—in fact, off the charts when it came to helping around the house! I often wondered when my Father of the Year medal was coming in the mail.

However, Janie's dad did all of those things, plus he cooked and drove all the carpools! So while I was out waiting by the mailbox for my medal to arrive, Janie was waving me up to the kitchen, explaining there was more to do—and in some cases, much more to do. Suffice it to say, we had a few adjustments to make in this area.

Some family scholars have ranked disagreements over household duties as the number-one cause of contention in marriages. Today, with more and more women working in professional jobs and obtaining their educations, there is more of a need to divide the labor. Since this area of adjustment is so common, it would be wise before you get married to discuss who is going to do the laundry, iron the clothes, clean the bathroom, make the bed, wash the dishes, shop, and take care of the yard. Once again, having a weekly couple's meeting and frequently discussing the household chores is a safe direction to take. Make sure the division of labor is practical and well-balanced. Wives, don't you dare spend hours getting the children ready for bed or cooking meals while your husband plays on the computer. Husbands, if you feel you are working ninety hours a week while your wife is home playing on Facebook, then you better have a chit-chat.

6. Parenthood

One of the most looming questions for newly married couples is, "When should we begin our family?" This decision, contrary to what your in-laws and parents may think, is between you and the Lord. However, having stated that, make sure you do include the Lord in this decision—don't decide for yourselves or make the choice to counsel with the Lord eight years after you're married. At a recent general conference, Elder Neil L. Andersen reasserted the Church's position on bringing children into the world:

> The family is ordained of God. Families are central to our Heavenly Father's plan here on earth and through the eternities. After Adam and Eve were joined in marriage, the scripture reads, "And God blessed them, and God said unto them, Be fruitful, and multiply, and replenish the earth." In our day prophets and apostles have declared, "The first commandment that God gave to Adam and Eve pertained to their potential for parenthood as husband and wife. *We declare that God's commandment for His children to multiply and replenish the earth remains in force.*" This commandment has not been forgotten or set aside

in The Church of Jesus Christ of Latter-day Saints. We express deep gratitude for the enormous faith shown by husbands and wives (especially our wives) in their willingness to have children. When to have a child and how many children to have are private decisions to be made between a husband and wife and the Lord. These are sacred decisions—decisions that should be made with sincere prayer and acted on with great faith.[100]

Often, antsy parents, in-laws, and other relatives stick their noses in the middle of this decision between husbands and wives. You should not pay too much attention to their counsel. In our case, we were told by a well-intending family member that we should wait to have children for several years. However, after Janie and I were married almost a year, we began to be prayerful about the decision, and it was our strong feeling that we should begin our family immediately. By the time we had been married three years, we had two children. I will never regret that decision.

The next question you will have to answer once you decide to have a child is how to parent. Now, here is the first revelation—even if you think you do, you probably will not know much about parenting. Sometimes men believe they will be excellent parents because one time in the mission field, they held someone's baby for two minutes and made it smile. Women will often feel prepared because they used to babysit their siblings or helped boil water once at girls camp. Friends, here is your second revelation—you will never be prepared to be a parent. However, don't let that stop you. If all of us waited until we were prepared to have children, no one would have any.

Face it; there has never been a book or owner's manual that has been written about *your* unique child. That's why you will need the help of heaven to prepare for this awesome task. Unlike the decision to be a parent, how to raise your child will require you to gather all of the resources you possibly can. Interview your parents, talk to your in-laws, and ask the greatest family in the ward you grew up in how they did it. Begin to read books and devour information.

Men, if your wives have some experience in parenting, listen to them and learn from them. When Janie and I were married, I realized I really knew nothing about parenting, raising kids, or dealing with babies. However, Janie was the oldest of eight children, and being a parent came naturally for her. She seemed to have it in her DNA. So I learned that if I wanted to be a good parent, I needed to watch my wife and listen to her.

This didn't mean I couldn't have my own ideas and suggestions—because I did occasionally have a few.

Over the past many years in my counseling practice, I have met LDS men who knew very little about parenting, but they insisted that they take the lead in this area. Metaphorically, this can be like letting a three-year-old drive a bulldozer. Some of these men wrecked their families and damaged their relationships with each of their children because they would not humble themselves and listen to their wives. Women, this same principle applies to you. If you lack many of the required skills to be a parent, and your husband was raised in a wonderful home—learn from him. Open up your heart, and let him teach you.

Like some of the other expectations we have discussed, you will have huge expectations in this area, and if you're not careful, they could rock your world. For instance, if you're like I was and believe that having a child is going to be like a trip to Disneyland everyday—you will get knocked out of Cinderella's castle quickly. I assumed that with a baby, I would sit for hours in a recliner, rocking my baby while watching *SportsCenter*. I imagined that all our baby would do is eat and sleep; however, I had no idea our baby would eat all night and sleep all day. As our children became older, I thought our days would be spent throwing balls, riding bikes, and reading scripture stories together—I had no idea our kids would fight with each other, throw up at three a.m., and ask me to help with math problems that were, frankly, over my head.

Anticipate now that there will be many expectations to navigate *just* with your children.

Next, you will have to work through the expectations you will have with your spouse. How much will they help with the children? Will husbands read to them and tuck them in bed? Will wives play with them outdoors, read stories to them, and make them sleep in their own beds? How involved will your spouse be with your children? How will they discipline your children? How will you discipline them?

I believe parenting is the most wonderful adventure in life. I used to believe that a mission was the ultimate school, but after thirty years of parenting, I believe that raising a family is the ultimate school—and a mission is pre-school. The most wonderful experiences, the most spiritual experiences, and some of the most difficult experiences you will ever face will be with your children. As a father, I have never laughed harder and never cried more. Thankfully, many of those tears, however, have been tears of joy. There are not many things that can draw a husband and wife closer together than raising their children in harmony with each other and with the teachings of the gospel.

7. Time Together

One of the most challenging areas of your newly married life will be learning how to spend meaningful and quality time together. During your dating months and engagement, you had plenty of time to spend together—so it seemed. In fact, maybe it felt like you spent every waking hour together. However, after you are married, reality will set in. You will realize that going to bed before two a.m. is probably a good idea. Many couples will still be in school or working and have other responsibilities. Time together can be greatly reduced if couples are not careful.

Now that you're married, you must continue the courtship—you must continue to do the things that caused you to fall in love in the first place. The most significant mistake many couples make after marriage is that they quit dating each other. President Harold B. Lee taught,

> Continue your courtship after marriage. Those who allow the marriage ceremony to terminate the days of "courtship" are making a well-nigh fatal mistake. If the new bride were to discover that her husband was just an actor before their marriage and now his quest is ended, he stands revealed as a cheap counterfeit of his former self either in appearance or conduct, that would indeed be a shocking experience. Evidences and tokens of your love and a daily proof of your unselfishness toward her and your family will make love's flame burn more brightly with the years. Do you girls suppose that the same attention to personal details is less important after marriage? Surely the same qualities and traits in you that first attracted him are just as important in married life in keeping alive the flame of his affection and romantic desire.[101]

Remember, before you were married, you did fun activities together—you had your favorite place to eat, you had the most perfect place where you could go and talk, you had your favorite song, you even danced together. Believe it or not, many couples get married and quit doing those things that caused them to fall in love. If you want your love to continue to grow, you will need to turn off the television, shut down the computer, and do some fun things together. Flirt with each other, write each other love notes, go on weekly dates, and dance like there is no tomorrow.

In 1 Corinthians 7:3, Paul taught the Saints in Corinth: "Let the husband render unto the wife due benevolence: and likewise also the wife unto the husband." Benevolence essentially implies kindness, charity, or generosity. So, yes, husbands should be kind to their wives, and wives should be nice to their husbands. However, in the LDS version of the Bible, the footnote for the word "benevolence" suggests continued courtship in marriage. So you must fan the flame of love by continually courting each other.

Husbands should initiate dating in the marriage relationship. This isn't to say that wives cannot plan dates, but the husband is responsible to ensure that this part of the marriage remains strong and consistent. Remember, husbands and wives should hold a couple's meeting each week to coordinate schedules, talk about finances, solve problems, plan gospel training in the home, and discuss their weekly date. Furthermore, couples should also try to break out of the mold of going to dinner and a movie on each date.

It would be well for couples who are trying to renew their relationships to engage in some of the activities they once did when they were engaged. Go putt-putt golfing or bowling or riding go-carts. Perhaps there are cultural activities that both spouses enjoy, such as visiting an art museum or attending a concert. The point is that there are many activities couples can engage in besides dinner and a movie. Recent research documents that couples who engage in novel activities that are fun and exciting—from hiking to dancing to travel to concerts to skiing—enjoy higher levels of relationship quality.[102]

Several years ago, in speaking to Church educators, Elder Jeffrey R. Holland related how difficult and stressful life was for him and his wife, Patricia, while they were graduate students at Yale. At the time, Elder Holland was serving in the stake presidency, directing the institute program, attending school full time, was married, and had a couple of children. Meanwhile, Patricia was the Relief Society president, wife, and mother and watched other people's children to make ends meet. However, this powerful couple decided that no matter what, every Friday night would be their night together. Elder Holland reflected,

> But on that one night for a few hours we would be together. We would step off the merry-go-round. We would take a deep

breath or two and remind ourselves how much we loved each other, why we were doing all of this in the first place, and that surely there must be a light at the end of the tunnel somewhere.

I do not remember those dates ever amounting to much. I literally cannot remember ever going to dinner, but we must have. We certainly must have at least gotten a pizza occasionally. I just don't remember it. What I do remember is walking in the Yale–New Haven Arboretum, which was just across the street from our student housing. I remember long walks there holding hands and dreaming dreams of what life might be like when things were less demanding. Down at the end of the street was a Dairy Queen, where we would occasionally end up for a cone or, on really good nights, a root beer float.[103]

Elder Holland explained that both he and Patricia needed those nights just to give them a sense of sanity and purpose. It was a time to reconnect and celebrate what mattered most in their marriage. Those Friday night dates were something the Hollands both looked forward to, and the time they spent together was renewing and healing. Elder Holland concluded, "A drugstore psychologist once said that people need three things to be emotionally healthy: someone to love, significant things to do, and something pleasant to look forward to." He then challenged the men, "Brethren, make sure your wife has something pleasant, something genuinely fun, to look forward to regularly."[104]

Renowned marriage scholar John Gottman discovered that couples who devoted five extra hours a week to their marriage gleaned tremendous benefits—especially when compared to couples who did not spend extra time to strengthen their marriage. During these "Magic Five Hours," as Gottman labeled them, couples concentrated on five things: 1) before leaving for the day, learn one thing that will happen in your spouse's life that day, 2) engage in a stress-reducing conversation at the close of the day, 3) do something daily to communicate genuine affection and appreciation, 4) demonstrate physical affection during the day, and 5) have a weekly date. Although these activities require a minimum time investment, the dividends will make a significant difference in each spouse's life.[105]

Joy in the Journey
I recommend that you begin your life together at a slow pace. Do not feel you have to be the perfect couple overnight. It takes a while to learn about

each other and to discover what makes each other tick. Don't focus so much on the destination, but enjoy every step of the journey. You may not be absolutely sure where you're going, but at least you're going together. With the Lord on your side, you will not fail.

It's no secret that good and healthy marriages take work. Just because you were married in the temple, you are not guaranteed a life of bliss and marital joy. Don't let apathy set in. In order for your marriage to be a happy one, you will have to work at it constantly. The good news is that "marriage work" is actually fun.

I would recommend the following as a newlywed starter kit. You can build your marriage on the proper foundation if you incorporate these steps.

1. Take turns praying together morning and night. Make sure you pray for each other—especially if you have had a difficult time with each other. It is difficult to go to bed angry if you have prayed together.

2. Find a regular time to study the scriptures and the words of the living prophets together. Read the *Ensign*, and discuss the messages. Gain valuable spiritual insights from each other. As you develop a spiritual intimacy, you will become closer in all other areas of your life.

3. Attend the temple together as often as you can. Some couples will be able to attend weekly, others monthly, and some yearly. Great strength, happiness, and satisfaction will come to you, and your marriage will be greatly blessed as you attend the temple together. No couple has ever walked out of a temple holding hands and saying, "Well, that was a complete waste of time." Marriages are rejuvenated through temple worship.

4. Begin the tradition of holding family home evening together. It doesn't have to be long, but if you get into the habit now, it will bless you and your family for eternity. Take turns sharing gospel stories, scriptures, and messages, and bearing testimony to each other. By the time children bless your marriage, you will be wonderful teachers of the gospel.

5. Date each other regularly. Take turns planning the date, and surprise each other by doing things that are creative. Have the same kind of fun with each other that you had before you were married.

6. Have a weekly couple's meeting. Plan out the coming week, talk about finances, review the calendar, and remind yourselves of your

goals—especially as a couple. Learn how you can best meet your spouse's needs and speak their love language.

Years ago, a man named Bob attended a session at the Jordan River temple. The session began late because of the arrival of President Ezra Taft Benson and his wife, Flora. As Bob watched President Benson and his wife, he couldn't help but notice how gently and kindly the prophet treated his aging wife. Bob felt strongly as he witnessed the Bensons' care and concern for each other that their marriage was truly celestial, and it was the type of marriage he wanted someday.

As the session ended, Bob thought, "I wonder what their secret is?" As he entered the celestial room, he met President and Sister Benson.

President Benson asked me if I was getting married in the near future. I answered, "Yes, sir, tomorrow."

President Benson then told me: "Always treat your wife as if you were in the presence of the Lord. And remember if you ever feel like having an argument, stop and ask yourself if it is worth destroying your marriage over."[106]

There you have it from a prophet. Always treat your spouse as if you were in the Lord's presence. If you do so, peace and harmony and happiness will bless your marriage and your family.

Homework:
- Discuss with each other some of the areas of adjustment you have encountered in your marriage.
- What corrective measures could you take as a couple to help make your journey smoother?
- How can you strengthen your marriage right now?

Additional Readings:
- Elder Hugh W. Pinnock, "Ten Keys to Successful Dating and Marriage Relationships," *Brigham Young University Speeches 1981*, 3 May 1981.
- Brent A. Barlow, "The Highs and Lows of Marriage," *Ensign*, October 1983, 43–47.
- Jeffrey & Patricia Holland, "Some Things We Have Learned—Together," *Brigham Young University Speeches 1984–85*, 15 January 1985.
- Brent A. Barlow, *Just for Newlyweds*, (Salt Lake City: Deseret Book, 1992).

References

96 Harold B. Lee, *Conference Report*, April 1947, 49.

97 Copyright © 1970 by Judith Viorst. Originally appeared in *Redbook*; condensed by *Reader's Digest*; as cited in D.E. Brinley, *Toward a Celestial Marriage* (Salt Lake City: Bookcraft, 1986), 97–99.

98 Gordon B. Hinckley, *Teachings of Gordon B. Hinckley* (Salt Lake City: Deseret Book, 1997), 652–653.

99 Billy Graham, *Reader's Digest*, May 1970, 118; as cited by President Spencer W. Kimball, "Guidelines to Carry Forth the Work of God in Cleanliness," *Ensign*, May 1974, 7.

100 Neil L. Andersen, "Children," *Ensign*, November 2011, 28; emphasis added.

101 Harold B. Lee, *Teachings of Harold B. Lee*, ed. Clyde J. Williams, (Salt Lake City: Deseret Book, 1996), 242.

102 A. Aron et al., "Couples' Shared Participation in Novel and Arousing Activities and Experienced Relationship Quality," *Journal of Personality and Social Psychology* 78 (2000): 273–284.

103 Jeffrey R. Holland, "Our Consuming Mission," *An Evening with a General Authority*, 5 February 1999, 2–3.

104 Ibid.

105 J.M. Gottman, *The Seven Principles for Making Marriage Work* (New York: Three Rivers Press, 1999), 260–261.

106 Bob Steinike, "How to Smoothly Adjust to Marriage," *Church News*, Salt Lake City, Utah, Saturday, 11 February, 1995.

CHAPTER 11
Sexual Intimacy in Marriage

"Marriage can be more an exultant ecstasy than the human mind can conceive. This is within the reach of every couple, every person."
-President Spencer W. Kimball[107]

HEALTHY INTIMACY IS A SIGNIFICANT component of a happy and satisfying marriage. However, I believe that many individuals go into marriage with only one concept of intimacy on their minds—and that is sexual. Intimacy is *closeness* and *connection*. Besides sexual intimacy, there are many other fundamental aspects of intimacy in a marriage. First, there is social intimacy. Couples who are socially intimate enjoy spending time doing things together. Their companionship is strengthened through fun activities and friendships. Second, there is emotional intimacy. This type of intimacy is developed as couples learn how to share their feelings with each other. At this level, love, validation, praise, and appreciation are shared in a culture of trust and understanding. Third, there is spiritual intimacy. Couples who enjoy spiritual intimacy have made the Lord a significant part of their marriage. They pray together, worship together, study the gospel together, and share their spiritual feelings and impressions with each other. Fourth, there is intellectual intimacy. At this level, couples connect cerebrally as they stimulate each other with information, knowledge, thoughts, ideas, concepts, and opinions. Such couples enjoy deep conversations and inspire each other to continue to learn, grow, and improve. Finally, there is sexual intimacy. Couples who are sexually connected share physical and emotional affection. They have a strong sexual relationship and can talk freely about their sexual needs.

If couples want to have a healthy sexual relationship, their intimacy must be strong and solid in the other five areas. For example, if couples have a strong socially intimate life, they will also be bonded sexually. If a couple's emotional intimacy is healthy, especially for women, then their sexual life will be enhanced. And so forth.

Marriage is not just for sexual relations; however sex is a profound means of expressing mutual love and commitment. Sex is designed to be a physical, emotional, and spiritual union for couples. Our Heavenly Father established marriage, and particularly sexual relationships in marriage, so that couples who face everyday challenges with school, employment, children, finances, physical handicaps, and so on will have a way to reconnect and renew their relationship as often as they desire. Just as good marriage increases sexual interest, healthy sexual relations add binding strength to the marriage partners.

A positive sexual relationship can be one of the highest forms of marital therapy. *Thus, a good, healthy sexual relationship is a symptom of a good marriage, not the other way around.* Sex alone cannot be a foundation for a successful marriage; however, if the marriage is strong, then a healthy sexual relationship can be the natural outcome. A truly happy marriage is built on the base of friendship. Intimacy is what brings couples together, and sex is the result of an otherwise happy marriage.

The Love Bank

Each one of us has a metaphoric *love bank*. Every single person we have a relationship with has a symbolic love bank account. All of us are constantly making deposits or withdrawals with each person we have a relationship with. Pleasurable interactions create deposits. Deposits are positive in nature, complimentary, security-producing, happy, and healthy. Anything that gives your spouse energy, uplifts them, builds them, or charges them up is a deposit. Deposits include gentle touches, love notes, verbal expressions of love, and shared experiences together. Temperament, gender, birth order, mood, and the time of day could influence one's personal definition of a deposit. Going for long walks in the woods with a spouse may energize an introvert in the same way a houseful of holiday company (entertaining) energizes an extrovert.

A withdrawal is anything sad, negative, deflating, or agitating. If you do something that drains energy from your mate—or sucks the life out of them—then you can rest assured you have just made a withdrawal. Withdrawals are characterized by negativity, criticism, ignoring, controlling, or not spending time together. Like deposits, withdrawals differ from temperament to temperament; in fact, something perceived as a withdrawal for one person might be a deposit for another person. But too much control or being absent too much, physically or emotionally, are always major withdrawals.[108]

Obviously if you want your marriage to thrive, you will need to make more deposits than withdrawals. Unfortunately, there are too many couples who have a significantly depleted love account with each other. Too many couples are living on past deposits and haven't added to their marriage account recently. Perhaps they are too busy or too mad at each other or too disengaged or too distracted to make any new deposits. Perhaps they are too focused on serving in the Church or raising children. Maybe their work is too demanding. For whatever reason, it may have been a long time since they have made a worthwhile deposit. Consequently, their marriage has gone stale. Many contemporary couples live on marital credit— perhaps they haven't made a substantial deposit in years. Ultimately, such relationships reach the point of marital bankruptcy. The withdrawals have exceeded the balance. As a result, their overdrawn marriage becomes extremely volatile.

Here is the crucial principle of "love-banking": income must exceed outgo. You must deposit more in the bank than you withdraw every month. Marriage expert Dr. John Gottman recommends a 5:1 ratio of positive interactions to negative: that is, five deposits to every one withdrawal.[109]

I am not a financial wizard, but I am smart enough to know that every time I deposit five dollars into the bank and only withdraw one, eventually I am going to have a healthy balance. The same principle applies to marriage and every other relationship we have. Therefore, you and your significant other should take the time to discuss how to make a deposit in each other's accounts and what actions constitute a withdrawal. And, in case you're wondering when we are going to talk about sexual intimacy, we are discussing it right now. Sexual intimacy begins as you make deposits in each other's love bank during the day—it doesn't begin at ten thirty p.m. in your bedroom. Sexual intimacy begins as the sun comes up and we begin to fill our partner's love bank.

Just as a healthy garden needs sunlight, as well as water, fertilizer, and weeding, so will your marriage need careful attention. President Spencer W. Kimball taught, "Your love, like a flower must be nourished. . . . When marriage is based solely on [physical attraction], the parties soon tire of one another. . . . The love of which the Lord speaks is not only physical attraction, but spiritual attraction as well. It is faith and confidence in, and understanding of, one another. It is a total partnership. It is unselfishness toward and sacrifice for one another."[110]

Meeting Marital Needs

Most men and women have a difficult time understanding the needs of their spouse, let alone meeting those needs. A woman's marital needs are not similar to her husband's. A husband's needs in marriage are much different than his wife's. If each partner is trying to give what they think their spouse needs (something similar to what they need), they will fail miserably. If you want to have a happy marriage and a fulfilling sexual life together, then you will need to learn how to meet your spouse's needs. Otherwise, you will live in total frustration. Therefore, marital needs will need to be discussed and evaluated frequently.

The Top Needs of Men

According to Dr. Willard Harley, most men have five universal needs in marriage. I understand this is a stereotype and not all men will have these needs—but most will. I will make some short observations about each. These needs are placed in order of importance, according to Harley.

1. Sexual Fulfillment
    *   Many men speak a "physical touch" love language.
    *   Without sexual intimacy in marriage, men feel distant and unconnected to their wives.
    *   For men, the ultimate form of validation, love, and approval in marriage is when their wives have a healthy sexual relationship with them.
    *   Sexual expression in a marriage for a man is a significant form of approval from their wives.

2. Recreational Companionship
    *   Most married men need a wife who will join with them in their hobbies and interests.[a] The need to have a recreational companion is second only to sexual fulfillment. Men enjoy it when their wives engage in their recreation, whether it's racquetball or visiting museums or fixing an old computer.

---

a   Wives, remember how you did this before when your husband before your marriage? You were shooting guns, playing video games, and throwing footballs. It's time to get out your cleats again.

- Believe it or not, men love it when their wives help them build fences, paint rooms, or jump-start the car.
- Couples who play together stay together.

3. An Attractive Spouse
   - Most men are not looking to be married to a supermodel. They simply love it when their wives take time to take care of themselves, to keep in shape, and to dress up occasionally.
   - Some women let their appearance wane after they are married.
   - Some women may feel that because they have had several children, they are not attractive anymore. In actuality, any man that is worth his salt will feel that the mother of his children is more beautiful now than she was on her wedding day.
   - Wives, ask your husbands how important it is for you to look good.

4. Domestic Support
   - Most men like order in their lives. They enjoy a clean home, with structure and organization.
   - Men particularly enjoy when their children are well-behaved, the lawn is mowed, and the inside of their home looks neat and clean.
   - A man's home is his castle—a place where he can come home and escape from the chaos of the world and the rat race they call work. The home should be a refuge and retreat.

5. Admiration
   - Most men have a need to be appreciated and admired.
   - The person most men want to be admired by is their wife.
   - If a woman can give her husband praise and compliments and tell him often why he is a wonderful person, he will run through a brick wall for her!
   - Wives, do you wish to build up your husband? Do you want to strengthen his resolve to be a better spouse and father? Do you want to make him feel like you are glad you married him? Write him a note, and share with him the things you admire most about him—other than on his birthday or your anniversary. After he reads your personal message of love and appreciation, you'll notice that his feelings for you will increase.

The Top Needs of Women

As with men, Dr. Harley has identified the top five needs women have in marriage. Remember, these needs are stereotypical.

1. Affection/Cherished
   - Most women do not have the same needs that men do for frequent sex. However, there are women who need more sex than men.
   - What most women need above anything else is to be cherished, to feel that they are the most important person in their husbands' lives—that they come first.
   - Affection is one key way to show women they are cherished, valued, and loved.
   - When a husband shows affection to his wife, he is saying, "You matter to me," "I love you deeply," "I am concerned about you and your life," and "I will protect you."
   - Nonsexual touching is as important for women as sexual touching is for men.
   - Affection can be demonstrated by husbands in many ways, including cards, notes, flowers, dates, hugs, kisses, walks, hand-holding, and a host of many other things.

2. Conversation
   - Just as men need a recreational companion, so women need someone they can share their life with—someone they can talk to and converse with on deep levels and in a positive manner.
   - Women want to be validated and understood by their husbands. This occurs through verbal conversations.[b]
   - Women connect with others, including their spouses, by talking; men, on the other hand, connect by doing.
   - Men, set time aside each day to sit in front of your spouse—knee to knee—and talk with her. Remember, listening is the greatest communication skill there is.

3. Honesty and Openness
   - Women have a great need for safety, security, and trust in a marriage relationship.
   - In today's world of pornography, Facebook, and other temptations, women need to be able to trust their husbands completely.
   - A marriage cannot succeed without truthfulness, faithfulness, and trust.

---

b   Men, remember, before you were married, you talked with your future wife about everything under the sun for hours—sometimes past midnight! You can do this! It's still in you!

- Wives need their husbands to be open and honest with their feelings—especially their deepest feelings.
- Women experience true intimacy and fulfillment when they share their deepest feelings and expressions of love with their husbands.

4. Financial Security
   - Women do not need to be filthy rich, but they need the security of knowing there is money in the bank.
   - Women enjoy the security that comes from their husbands having a steady job and the ability to provide—in healthy ways—for their families.
   - Women also like to share in the financial responsibilities with their husbands—meaning they want to communicate over financial matters, prepare budgets together, pay bills together, and discuss future financial goals together.
   - The mismanagement of money negatively impacts marriages more than all other troubles combined, so make sure you communicate about your finances often.

5. Family Commitment
   - Wives need to know that their husbands love being married and that they want to have a family.
   - Women desire for their husbands to take the leadership role in the family. This especially includes spiritual leadership.
   - Women deeply desire that their husbands play a key role in teaching and training their children.[c]
   - A husband can ruin a marriage really fast by not showing love, affection, and appreciation to his wife. If he really wants to obliterate the marriage, he can be unfaithful to her, neglect his duties as a father, and rarely come home.
   - Husbands, do you want to strengthen and improve your marriage? Do you want to make your wife float on cloud nine? Then, without her knowing, plan a wonderful family day together—completely arranged by you. Pull the children out of school, go to a fun place, and enjoy your family! Your wife will feel cherished, and her love for you will deepen as she feels your commitment to the family.

---

c   Most women do not want a father and husband who watches family life from the sidelines; they want a "quarterback," who is involved in every play and has the ability to move the team downfield toward the end zone.

As you have read to this point in the chapter, you may be thinking, "This is all great and amusing, but I'm still wondering when am I going to read about sex?" So here is your revelation: WE JUST DID! In case you missed the point, perhaps you should read the previous section one more time. Almost everything you need to know about a healthy sexual relationship and happiness in marriage can be boiled down to meeting each other's needs. In fact, I will be bold enough to declare that the secret to a happy and successful marriage comes down to two things: 1) living the gospel of Jesus Christ and practicing Christlike attributes, and 2) understanding and fulfilling the needs of your spouse. The reasons couples divorce or live in sub-par, unfulfilling, unhappy marriages are 1) Christlike attributes are not being practiced; 2) commandments are not being kept; 3) a spouse doesn't know the needs of their spouse; or 4) a spouse doesn't fulfill the needs of their spouse. It's just that simple. If you want to be happily married, practice Christlike attributes, and meet the needs of your spouse.

Moreover, if these needs are being met, you drastically improve your desire and the desires of your spouse to be sexually intimate. Different levels of intimacy (i.e. social, intellectual, emotional, and spiritual) are fulfilled as you meet the needs of your spouse. The fulfillment of these needs places your marriage on a trajectory for a happy, fulfilling sexual relationship.

Remember, the five needs I listed are not a comprehensive list. Some individuals may need intellectual stimulation or emotional connection to be fulfilled. Others may need entirely different things to be happy. Nevertheless, as you come to understand the needs of your spouse and seek to fulfill those needs, you will be on your way to a happy, fulfilling sexual relationship. (This is barring that anything out of the ordinary has occurred in the past, such as physical problems than can hinder a healthy sex life; spiritual issues, such as guilt from previous sexual transgressions; or emotional issues, such as trauma from sexual abuse and other issues that would significantly impact sexual intimacy.)

Human Intimacy and the Gospel

I believe if more couples better understood the purpose and role of sexual intimacy in the gospel framework, there would be fewer problems—especially among the women of the Church—when it comes to sexual relations. The bottom line is that sexual relations are ordained of God, and couples should have a happy and fulfilling life sexually.

Former Brigham Young University professor Dr. Brent Barlow shared the following experience:

> Several years ago when I was a young missionary for the LDS Church, I received a new companion right from the mission home in Salt Lake City. A few days later we were tracting and met a Protestant minister who invited us in. After exchanging points of view on various topics, he asked us, "And what is the Mormon attitude towards sex?"
>
> I choked on my cup of hot chocolate, but my new companion seemed unmoved. "Well," said the minister after a few more sips of his tea, "could you please tell me the Mormon philosophy toward sexuality?" I was tongue-tied and believed my new companion knew next to nothing on the matter. There were a few more moments of silence, and finally my companion said, "Sir, we believe in it."
>
> It has been more than twenty years since that time, and I have been asked the same question by numerous students, friends, professional people, LDS members, and nonmembers. Still, I haven't yet been able to find a better answer than the one given by the missionary: "We believe in it."[111]

Indeed, we do believe in a healthy sexual relationship between husbands and wives. I was asked by a college student in one of my classes recently, "Is it okay to have sex when you are not trying to have a child?" My student was sincere and had obviously never been taught the role that a sexual relationship plays in marriage. Another student texted me and asked, *Since I'm getting married in a few weeks, do you think it would be a good idea to have my parents teach me about sex, since they never have?* These are not questions from middle school students—these are legitimate concerns from college students. Perhaps a significant reason why so many young married couples are sexually ignorant is because their parents have never taught them anything—and I mean anything.

Here are some key doctrines and principles regarding intimacy that we learn from presidents of the Church:

- President John Taylor: "Well, [Heavenly Father] has planted, in accordance with this, a natural desire in woman towards man, and in man towards woman, and a feeling of affection, regard, and sympathy exists between the sexes."[112]

- Joseph Fielding Smith: "The lawful association of the sexes is ordained of God, not only as the sole means of race perpetuation, but for the development of the higher faculties and nobler traits of human nature, which the love-inspired companionship of man and woman alone can insure."[113]
- President Spencer W. Kimball: "We know of no directive from the Lord that proper sexual experiences between husbands and wives need be limited totally to the procreation effort."[114]

Our prophets seem to be in complete harmony regarding the role that sex plays in the marriage relationship. Sex is not only the means for bringing children into the world, but a sexual relationship between husband and wife strengthens emotional and spiritual bonds and unifies a couple on many different levels—the least of which is physical. The sexual experience in marriage welds a couple together spiritually and emotionally.

Not only can sex solidify a marriage, but disagreements about sex—especially the frequency of it—can ruin a marriage. I have seen many couples in my practice over the years whose marriages were filled with sexual tension. In many cases, husbands felt frustrated and wives felt used because they could not agree on how often to have sex. Sometimes, wives have been the ones who felt the frustration of being married to a husband who frankly didn't want to have sex that often.

President Spencer W. Kimball taught, "If you study the divorces, as we have had to do in these past years, you will find there are one, two, three, four reasons. Generally sex is the first. They did not get along sexually. They may not say that in the court. They may not even tell their attorneys, but that is the reason."[115] Social science research confirms what he taught. In a study several years ago, 335 divorced men and women were surveyed. Forty percent of the women and fifty-six percent of the men said sexual problems led to their divorce. In fact, men ranked sexual problems as the number-one cause of their divorce or separation, while women ranked lack of communication and sexual problems as the two leading causes of their divorce.[116]

We come back to what I have previously mentioned in this chapter. If husbands and wives will practice Christlike virtues and seek to meet the needs of their spouses, they can attain happiness and fulfillment sexually. President Spencer W. Kimball taught:

Total unselfishness is sure to accomplish another factor in successful marriage. If one is forever seeking the interests, comforts, and happiness of the other, the love found in courtship and cemented in marriage will grow into mighty proportions. Many couples permit their marriages to become stale and their love to grow cold like old bread or worn-out jokes or cold gravy. Certainly the foods most vital for love are consideration, kindness, thoughtfulness, concern, expressions of affection, embraces of appreciation, admiration, pride, companionship, confidence, faith, partnership, equality, and interdependence. . . . While marriage is difficult, and discordant and frustrated marriages are common, yet real, lasting happiness is possible, and marriage can be, more an exultant ecstasy than the human mind can conceive. This is within the reach of every couple, every person.[117]

The sexual relationship in a marriage can "build" or "kill" the relationship. That is why it's crucial for couples to learn and seek to meet each other's needs. Ignorance in this area of your marriage will cause much unhappiness and frustration. This is why couples must also constantly talk and determine how to best help each other reach joy in this area.

Sexual Differences between Men and Women

Husbands and wives perceive the sexual relationship quite differently. Men and women will struggle to understand and respond to each other's needs and desires if they are not educated. What men and women expect from the sexual relationship in marriage often differs greatly. However, differences can be overcome if spouses are willing to talk, share, and resolve their problems. The sexual experience can be positive and fulfilling for both husbands and wives.

In general terms, men are often more driven to have sex than women are. On the other hand, women are more often fascinated with romance than men are. Men most often give love and commitment in order to get physical affection and sex. Conversely, women give physical affection and sex in order to get commitment and love. Moreover, men initially give and receive love to fulfill their physical needs, while women initially give and receive love to fulfill their emotional needs. "While these statements may sound like stereotypes, and of course not all relationships are so black and white, we have found that for most couples, there is at least some element of truth in these generalizations."[118]

Unfortunately, most newly married husbands do not understand that their wives need emotional intimacy before sexual intimacy. That is, women need to be cherished, adored, cared for, and communicated with—to feel emotionally connected with their husbands—before they can engage in a fulfilling sexual relationship. For example, a wife recently told me that her husband is a bishop and a busy businessman. Consequently, he is gone often, and she bears the brunt of the family duties. When he does have spare time, he wants to be intimate with his wife. Her response was, "I feel like I need to get to know him again before we can have a sexual relationship."

Contrary to women, men do not have to be emotionally engaged with their wives to be sexually intimate with them. Women need to feel loved before they can become sexually aroused; however, men need to feel sexually aroused before they can truly feel love—or even express deep love. Brigham Young University researchers Stahmann, Young, and Grover further explained:

> It's through sexual activity that men are emotionally and physically fulfilled. It's through a loving sexual relationship that their hearts are opened and they're able to express love to their wives. Sex allows men to become aware of their wives' need for love and emotional support. Unless partners understand this basic difference between men and women, it will be difficult for them to find a common ground so that the emotional and physical needs of both are fulfilled.[119]

The sexual needs men and women have are so different that unless they talk and discuss their needs and perspectives, their sexual relationship can become more of a burden than a blessing. If men believe their wives' sexual needs are similar to their own, they will fail miserably. Likewise, if women believe that their husbands' needs are comparable to theirs, they will be up a creek without a paddle. The only way to have a fulfilling sexual relationship is to talk about each other's needs and then strive to fulfill them.

Commonly Asked Questions among Newlyweds and Engaged Couples
During my time as a professor on the campus of Brigham Young University, I have often been asked appropriate and innocent questions from my students regarding sexual relationships. Some of these questions have come in the form of anonymous text messages or e-mails; others have been notes slipped under my office door. Lest you panic too much, all of

these questions have come in conjunction with an intimacy lesson that is part of the marriage curriculum for a class I teach. Usually, after the class, there are plenty of questions asked and perhaps many that are not.

I will attempt to address some of the more common questions I am often asked each semester. I need to make it clear that I am not posturing myself as an authority on this subject, and I certainly do not represent Brigham Young University or the Church as an authority on sexual matters. I will attempt to answer these questions by teaching principles rather than responding specifically to situations.

Question #1: I am about to get married. Should I ask my parents to give me the sex talk?

When I teach my students about sexual intimacy, I always ask how many of them have had a "sex talk" with their parents. What I have observed has been shocking. Less than half of my students each semester were talked to at some point by their parents about sex. Even fewer have had a sex talk shortly before their marriage. Parents—*this is not acceptable!* One way or another, our children are going to learn about sex. It will be much better for them to learn it from you than from their sexually inexperienced friends, movies, novels, or music. There is only one place where children can learn the sanctity and sacredness of a sexual relationship, and that is from kind, wise, and loving parents. Taught almost anywhere else, children could grow up with a skewed view of the sexual relationship. For example, movies will teach teenagers that you should have sex daily and that women are sexual objects—not daughters of God.

In the Book of Mormon, we learn that parents have a responsibility to teach their children to walk in the ways of truth and soberness (Mosiah 4:15). This would include teaching children about chastity, fidelity, and sexual relationships. My experience in conveying this message with my children has been positive—especially when they were older and could understand more. I have treasured our talks with our children on the night before they were to be married. In fact, those conversations were bonding experiences.

Therefore, if your parents haven't had the sex talk with you, *ask them for it*. In fact, demand it if you need to. That is your parents' sacred responsibility. Most parents will feel ashamed that they haven't talked to you sooner, and you will be providing them the chance to repent and change. My guess is that most parents wanted to have this talk but just didn't know how. Perhaps they were afraid or felt awkward. Your persuasiveness will give them the confidence to carry onward. If you don't have a trustworthy parent you can talk to, seek the counsel of a wise bishop or leader that you respect.

Question #2: How often should a married couple be intimate? What is too much or too little?

Supposedly, Abraham Lincoln was once asked, "Mr. Lincoln, how long do you think a man's legs should be?" Lincoln replied, "Long enough to reach the ground." How many times a week should couples engage in sex? That depends on the couple. They certainly should have a sexual relationship enough to be mutually satisfying. All of us are different and have diverse needs and desires. Hormones, fatigue, age, and a host of other variables impact the quality and quantity of the sexual relationship. Moreover, there are times when the husband is in the mood and the wife is not, and vice versa.

I believe a young, vibrant, healthy newlywed couple will have sex two to three times a week. Older couples can expect to have sex less, but they report in research studies that the quality of their sexual relationship is much higher. We do live in a day of sexual addictions. Anytime a person wants to have sex multiple times daily, each day, for weeks on end, then they could be addicted to sex.

Elder Richard G. Scott, speaking to the men of the Church regarding sexual intimacy, taught, "There are times, brethren, when you need to restrain those feelings. There are times when you need to allow their full expression. Let the Lord guide you in ways that will enrich your marriage."[120] Once you are married, sex is not a "free-for-all." Even in marriage—no, especially in marriage—self-control still needs to govern our behavior. Remember, Alma taught, "see that ye bridle all your passions, that ye may be filled with love" (Alma 38:12). Men and women should be sensitive to each other's needs and moods, and respond with kindness, patience, and understanding.

Another female student asked, "Do we have to have sex every day? What about the days you are exhausted, sick, pregnant, and those days when you are simply not in the mood?" Yes, wise and tender husbands will exercise self-control and will consider the needs of their spouse before their own. Husbands who demand sex when their wives are not feeling well epitomize selfishness. Remember, a key principle to a healthy sexual relationship is the care and concern of your spouse—you should worry about their needs more than your own. President Spencer W. Kimball gave this advice:

> Husband and wife . . . are authorized, in fact they are commanded, to have proper sex when they are properly married for time and eternity. That does not mean that we need to go to great extremes. That does not mean that a woman is the servant of her husband. It does not mean that any man has a right to demand sex anytime that he might want it. He should be reasonable and understanding, and it should be a general program between the two, so they understand and everybody is happy about it.[121]

President Howard W. Hunter added, "Tenderness and respect—never selfishness—must be the guiding principles in the intimate relationship between husband and wife. Each partner must be considerate and sensitive to the other's needs and desires. Any domineering, indecent, or uncontrolled behavior in the intimate relationship between husband and wife is condemned by the Lord."[122]

Question #3: Is it possible to know your sexual compatibility with your fiancé if you are keeping the law of chastity? If sexual contact is prohibited before marriage, how will you be good for each other?

Sexual compatibility before marriage is a myth. This concept is taught by the makers of Hollywood movies, romance novels, and magazines for women. In fact, I remember a high school coach telling a group of us on a bus that we needed to live with a girl before we married her so we could determine our *sexual compatibility*. Even though I wasn't a member of The Church of Jesus Christ of Latter-day Saints at the time, I instantly knew what my coach was teaching us was completely wrong.

Millions of couples in America live together before marriage, often without any intent of getting married, for the purpose of sexual compatibility. However, research confirms over and over again that married people report the highest levels of sexual satisfaction when compared to those who cohabitate.

You don't marry someone based on sexual compatibility any more than you would marry someone based on the kinds of pizza toppings they like. I guess you could do that, if you wanted to base the foundation of your marriage on sex. However, anyone who centers their marriage on sexual compatibility will eventually be significantly disappointed. Sex is a sandy foundation, and it cannot always deliver happiness and pleasure. If you choose to build your marriage on this false foundation, what will happen when a spouse is not in the mood for sex or doesn't look as physically attractive as you would like? Furthermore, what happens when a woman becomes pregnant and can't engage in sexual relations towards the end of her pregnancy or after the baby is born? The only true foundation to build a marriage on is foundation stones such as friendship, love, trust, and commitment.

After you are married and begin your sexual life together, you begin to learn many things about sex and about each other. As you communicate openly and seek to meet each other's needs, you will discover how to develop a mutually satisfying sexual relationship.

Question #4: What if you are fairly naïve and don't know what to do the first time you have sex?

First, I commend you for being naïve; that is quite difficult to do in today's world, where sex is openly talked about on high school campuses, in every commercial, and as the focal point of almost every television show that airs during prime time. Often, being naïve isn't a bad thing—especially when it comes to sex prior to marriage. I would worry more about the person who knows much too much about sex before marriage.

Second, I would recommend that you have a significant talk with a mother or father or bishop before you get married. They can educate you on the basics. Furthermore, there are books that can help you, but I will talk more about that later. We have to be careful with literature regarding sex.

Third, I would suggest that you take things slowly and naturally on your wedding night. Often, there is too much formality on the wedding night. Certain "clothes" are to be worn, and the event is practically staged and scripted. I would recommend that you let things just happen naturally. You will be married for a lifetime and have many years to practice and work together—especially learning together. The chances are, the person you marry will be quite naïve too—even if they think they are not. Learning together is one of the most intimate aspects of the sexual relationship.

Question #5: What are some good books and other resources that will prepare us for sex?

Although I am an advocate of reading and learning—especially about marital issues—I want to give a caution here about reading too much about sex before you get married. Talking about sex leads to sex. Let me repeat that. *Talking about sex leads to sex.* This principle is true for those who aren't married, as well as for those who are. Talking about sexual relationships gets the hormones going—especially for men. I have known many couples who have elected to read books together about sex and then ended up breaking the law of chastity shortly before their temple marriages.

Satan also knows that if he can get you talking and reading about sex, the easiest part of the battle has been won. Then he can practically push you right into the pit of anguish and despair with his pinky finger. I would recommend that the month before you marry, you could start to do some reading on your own. You really don't need to read books about sex together until your honeymoon. At that point, you should feel free to do all the reading you want to—although most people don't read too much on their honeymoons!

Douglas E. Brinley and Stephen E. Lamb wrote a bestselling book several years ago entitled *Between Husband and Wife.* This is a good book to read before marriage. I would also recommend *Becoming One,* by Stahmann, Young, and Grover. This book is also an excellent read, is not as lengthy as other books on the market, and was done in good taste. *After* you are married, I would recommend *And They Were Not Ashamed,* by Laura Brotherson.

Question #6: If you have been sexually active with someone else before you are married, should you reveal this to your future spouse?

Intimacy is based on a foundation of trust and friendship. So, yes, repentance is real—the Atonement wipes away those sins. Therefore, the person is no longer unclean. However, I believe it would be difficult to have an intimate relationship with someone if there are secrets. *Intimacy means full disclosure.* Therefore, if it were me, I would want my future spouse to know about my past. Otherwise, the relationship will lack the trust and transparency needed to thrive. Perhaps revealing the nitty-gritty details is not necessary. But it is important to know that there were problems in the past and that those problems have been taken care of.

Several years ago, one of my classes engaged in a stimulating discussion on this topic. A student quoted a religious instructor who taught that when you get married, the only thing you have the right to ask is, "Do you hold a current temple recommend?" I completely disagreed with that statement. After all, this isn't a casual date we are talking about—this is linking you for life and eternity to another person. You had better know all there is to know about that individual and perhaps a little more. Exaltation is at stake. To know who you are marrying for eternity and what their baggage is can impact your decision to marry them in the first place.

As we were discussing this principle in my class and the students were going back and forth, a girl in the back of the room raised her hand. She told us that several years earlier, her sister had married a returned missionary with a bright future. However, the man failed to reveal to his fiancée that he had struggled with a pornography addiction for most of his life—he simply left that little detail out. Several years after they were married, he was again fully engaged in his pornography addiction. Not long after that, he began having sexual relationships with other women. At that point, this man and his wife had several children. Ultimately, the wife divorced her sexually addicted husband, and their family was in shambles for the many years that followed. The wife told her sister, "If my ex-husband would have told me before we were married that he was a porn addict, I would have never married him and would have never had to put myself or my children through the hell that we have been through."

This story and many others like it are why I believe a full disclosure of past sexual transgressions is a must before making the marriage decision. Once again, the Atonement is real, and people can change—but that doesn't negate the fact that someone had a sexual relationship prior to their marriage. To be fair to their future spouse, they need to disclose that. Intimacy cannot develop without full trust and disclosure.

Question #7: Does the Church have any rules or guidelines pertaining to what goes on the bedroom?

I do not speak for the Church, but I would like to attempt to answer this question because so many of my students have asked it and others similar to it, such as "Is there anything husbands and wife cannot or should not do behind closed doors?" We belong to a church that teaches principles, and we as members must learn to govern ourselves. In so doing, we should seek the Spirit of the Lord in everything we do in order to make right choices

Doctrine and Covenants 58:26–27 teaches, "For behold, it is not meet that I should command in all things; for he that is compelled in all things, the same is a slothful and not a wise servant; wherefore he receiveth no reward. Verily I say, men should be anxious engaged in a good cause, and do many things of their own free will, and bring to pass much righteousness."

Our Church leaders have taught principles for us to follow but haven't commanded us in every little detail. We should hearken to the

Brethren, apply the principles they teach, and seek to "bring to pass much righteousness," especially in our marriage relationships. Some principles leaders have taught to govern intimate relationships between husbands and wives include the following:

- "Let us instruct young people who come to us, first, young men throughout the Church, to know that a woman should be queen of her own body. The marriage covenant does not give the man the right to enslave her, or to abuse her, or to use her merely for the gratification of his passion. Your marriage ceremony does not give you that right." —President David O. McKay[123]

- "If it is unnatural, you just don't do it. That is all, and all the family life should be kept clean and worthy and on a very high plane. There are some people who have said that behind the bedroom doors anything goes. That is not true and the Lord would not condone it." —President Spencer W. Kimball[124]

- "A husband should avoid any domineering or unworthy behavior in intimate relationships with his wife. Keep yourselves above any domineering or unworthy behavior in the tender, intimate relationship between husband and wife. . . . Each partner must be considerate and sensitive to the other's needs and desires. Any domineering, indecent, or uncontrolled behavior in the intimate relationship between husband and wife is condemned by the Lord." —President Howard W. Hunter[125]

In my counseling practice, I have visited with men and women who have violated these principles. In my opinion, they took a very selfish and carnal approach to sex, and that selfishness poured into other areas of their lives. Ultimately, their marriages became unstable, trust was lost, and grudges were held. Your responsibility as a couple is to discuss these principles taught by prophets and your own marital needs. If you can align your needs and the needs of your spouse with the statements of our prophets, you will have peace and happiness in your lives and in your intimate relationship. You will be fulfilled, and your love for each other will continue to grow.

Question #8: Is sex always painful for the girl, especially the first time and on the honeymoon?

This concept is often perpetuated by girls who aren't even married or have never had a sexual relationship. It could also derive from women who have had painful sexual experiences. When our oldest daughter was about to get married, Janie and I had a wonderful talk with her the night before her wedding. She confided in us that she was extremely anxious about her upcoming wedding night because of some horror stories she had been told. I asked my daughter who told her these terrible tales, and she mentioned the names of several girls I recognized as her friends. I said, "Wait a minute, Brittany, none of those girls are even married!" My daughter confirmed my suspicion, and we had a good laugh to lighten the moment.

All of our bodies have been created a little differently, and yes, there are some girls who have a difficult time and even a painful time when they begin to have a sexual relationship. However, most girls do not experience the horror and the pain my daughter was convinced of.

Before marriage, girls should have a visit with an OB/GYN. This specially trained doctor can fill you in on more details after a thorough examination. I would also recommend reading Brinley and Lamb's book, *Between Husband and Wife*, where they provide a thorough treatment of this topic.

Question #9: What if your wife believes that sex is evil and for worldly sinners?

Unfortunately, there are a fair number of mothers in the Church who have done a huge disservice to their daughters by teaching them that sex is evil and only those who are wicked engage in it. I am sure there have been youth leaders who have also taught that sex is a wicked and perverse practice. What we should have taught is that sex is good; in fact, it is one of the most wonderful experiences a married man and woman can share together. We should invite the youth to wait for sex because it is good—not to avoid it because it is bad. Sex, in and of itself, isn't a bad thing. What is bad is when individuals engage in sex without authority or permission. You can't have a sexual relationship before you are married because it isn't the right time and you are not authorized by God to do so. You must be married—preferably in the temple—before you engage in a sexual relationship. But sex is God-ordained and God-approved. Married couples are supposed to have a sexual relationship, and that should be a healthy part of their marriage.

To answer this question more specifically, I would recommend again the book *And They Were Not Ashamed* by Laura Brotherson. In her book, Laura explains the "Good Girl Syndrome" as follows:

Sex to Janet was dirty, immoral and wrong, something she'd been taught NOT to do. She wondered about the appropriateness of sexual relations even within marriage. Sex was okay if she and her husband were trying to have a baby, but any "extra-curricular" or "recreational" sex for pleasure felt dirty and unrighteous.[126]

The Good Girl Syndrome is a result of the negative conditioning that occurs from parents, church, and society as they teach—or fail to teach—the goodness of sexuality and its divine purposes. This conditioning leads to negative thoughts and feelings about sex and the body, resulting in an inhibited sexual response within marriage. *The Good Girl Syndrome* does affect men but is generally more prevalent and pronounced in women. *The Good Girl Syndrome* represents a distorted image of what a "good girl" really is or should be. The good girl should be applauded for her desire to do what is right, but the unintentional overemphasis on the negative consequences of immodesty and immorality and the negative images in society lead many to incorrectly internalize negative teachings regarding sexuality.[127]

Laura Brotherson then gives ten signs of The *Good Girl Syndrome*. They are

1. Underlying belief that sex is bad, wrong, dirty, or sinful

2. Inappropriate inhibitions, guilt, shame, or awkwardness associated with sexual relations within marriage

3. Discomfort, embarrassment, or inability to appropriately discuss sexual matters

4. Discomfort or distaste with sexual parts of the body and body functioning

5. Lack of understanding of the divine purposes of sex—such as that God intended sex for pleasure as well as for procreation

6. Sexual expressions of love are a low priority

7. Inability to relax and let go within the sexual experience

8. Lack of genuine enjoyment of sexual relations—participation out of duty

9. Lack of sexual understanding and "know-how"

10. An inhibited sexual response due to any of the above.[128]

In order to help someone overcome their misconceptions about sex, I recommend a thorough reading of the books I have mentioned. Sometimes, individuals need to see a counselor so they can unravel the years of distorted teaching and thinking, but it can be done.

Question #10: I find that when I want a sexual relationship with my wife, she doesn't, and when she does, I don't. How do we make our needs coincide?

This is a great question not only for newlyweds but even for couples who have been married for many years. First of all, if your sexual needs do not coincide, that simply means your relationship is perfectly normal. Most couples don't have needs that match up completely. If they did, they probably would never come out of the house.

Secondly, you will need to accept that this is how it will be—to a large extent. Since you are two different people of different genders, the hormones pulsating through your bodies are also very different. In fact, how you handle stress and fatigue are also quite dissimilar. Because of these reasons, and many others, you may not often be in the mood at the same time.

Third, what you need to try to do with your wife is set the mood and the tone, and don't wait until ten thirty at night to do so. Intimacy actually begins the first thing in the morning as you serve and help each other. It continues in the middle of the day as you call each other and talk, and flirt it up over the phone. Intimacy continues in the evening as you see each other after a long day, hold each other, and talk about important things. It will continue into the night as you touch each other and say nice things. Tell her what she means to you, and look at her directly as you do so.

Finally, this is something you should talk about with each other and try to resolve together. The problem is that men and women are simply wired differently. Most men would like to have more sex than they probably do, and women do not seem to need it as much. If a woman is viewing the sexual relationship through her own lens and not considering that her husband has a sex drive that causes him to want to be intimate with her quite often, then her husband will live in frustration—and sometimes desperation. If a man views the sexual relationship only through his perspective and doesn't consider his wife's need for affection and not necessarily sex—then she too will be frustrated. Couples need to talk, compromise, and try to meet each other's needs the best they can.

Along the same lines, a newly married young woman asked, "I want to be intimate much more often than my husband does. I know this doesn't mean he doesn't love me, but I feel bad sometimes because I thought it was supposed to be the other way around."

This question can be a little tricky because it breaks the stereotype that most adhere to that husbands are most often the sexual pursuer. In some marriages, the woman is the sexual initiator. Often, I have discovered that some women feel guilty about this, and some men feel uncomfortable with it too. Frankly, sometimes men could have a low testosterone level, or there could be other issues—sometimes as simple as fatigue or stress— that hinder them from wanting to have a frequent sexual relationship with their spouse.

If you are in a relationship like this, and it works, then don't feel bad—let things happen. Some husbands wouldn't mind having their wives initiate sex. It would not be a bad idea for your husband to have his testosterone level checked—which can be done with a simple blood test. You should also talk through the problem, discuss your needs, and see what you can do to be more sensitive to each other's desires.

Bonus Question: If your spouse or future spouse has been a victim of molestation, is there any sort of intimacy advice that you could give?
Unfortunately, there are those individuals who have been sexually abused as children or youth. This can often impede their sexual relationships as adults—which is completely understandable. This tragic circumstance brought on so much guilt, shame, and sickening feelings—why would they want to engage in an act that caused so much heartache and trauma in their early life?

I recommend you talk to a good counselor who can help with this problem. If your spouse—the victim—has never seen a therapist for their abuse, they probably should. Moreover, as a spouse, you should try to exercise patience, kindness, tenderness, and empathy. Getting upset or frustrated will only make the situation much worse. I know many individuals who have had such trauma in their lives and have been healed by the Atonement and had a happy and healthy sexual relationship.

Remember, the key to a happy marriage is meeting each other's needs and practicing Christlike attributes. These principles apply just as much in a sexual context as they do in every other aspect of marriage.

Homework:
- What are some things that constitute a deposit for your spouse? What is a withdrawal?

- Are you aware of your spouse's marital needs? Write on a sheet of paper each of your marital needs in order of importance. Then write down how that need could be fulfilled. In your couple's meeting, discuss what marital need you can work on this week.
- Are you aware of your spouse's sexual needs? Discuss this together.

Additional Readings:
- D. E. Brinley & S. E. Lamb, *Between Husband and Wife,*(American Fork, Utah: Covenant Communications, Inc., 2008).
- L.M. Brotherson, *And They Were Not Ashamed* (Boise, Idaho: Inspire Books, 2004).
- R. F. Stahmann, W. R. Young & J. G. Grover, *Becoming One: Intimacy in Marriage* (American Fork, Utah: Covenant Communications, Inc., 2004).

References

107 Spencer W. Kimball, *Teachings of Spencer W. Kimball* (Salt Lake City: Bookcraft, 1982), 305–306.

108 Gary Smalley, *Making Love Last Forever* (Dallas, Texas: Word Publishing, 1996), 253.

109 John Gottman, *Why Marriages Succeed or Fail* (New York: Simon & Schuster, 1994), 57.

110 Spencer W. Kimball, *Faith Precedes the Miracle* (Salt Lake City: Deseret Book, 1972), 130–31.

111 Brent Barlow, *Twelve Traps in Today's Marriage and How to Avoid Them* (Salt Lake City: Deseret Book, 1986), 152–153.

112 John Taylor, G. Homer Durham, *Gospel Kingdom: Selections from the Writings and Discourses of John Taylor* (Salt Lake City: Deseret Book, 1943), 61.

113 Joseph Fielding Smith, *Restoration of All Things* (Salt Lake City: Deseret Book, 1945), 261–262.

114 Spencer W. Kimball, *The Teachings of Spencer W. Kimball,* ed. Edward L. Kimball, (Salt Lake City: Bookcraft, 1982), 311.

115 Spencer W. Kimball, *The Teachings of Spencer W. Kimball,* ed. Edward L. Kimball, (Salt Lake City: Bookcraft, 1982), 312.

116 A. Burns, (1984), "Perceived causes of marriage breakdown and the conditions of life," *Journal of Marriage and the Family*, 46, 551–562.

117 Spencer W. Kimball, "Oneness in Marriage," *Ensign*, March 1977, 3–6.

118 R.F. Stahmann, W.R. Young, and J.G. Grover, *Becoming One: Intimacy in Marriage* (American Fork, Utah: Covenant Communications, 2004), 14.

119 R.F. Stahmann, W.R. Young, and J.G. Grover, *Becoming One: Intimacy in Marriage* (American Fork, Utah: Covenant Communications, 2004), 15; emphasis added.

120 Richard G. Scott, "The Sanctity of Womanhood," *Ensign*, May 2000, 37.

121 Spencer W. Kimball, *The Teachings of Spencer W. Kimball*, ed. Edward L. Kimball (Salt Lake City: Bookcraft, 1982), 312.

122 Howard W. Hunter, *Teachings of Howard W. Hunter* (Salt Lake City: Deseret Book, 1997), 134.

123 David O. McKay, *Gospel Ideals: Selections from the Discourses of David O. McKay* (Salt Lake City: Deseret Book, 1953), 471.

124 Spencer W. Kimball, *Teachings of Spencer W. Kimball*, ed. Edward L. Kimball (Salt Lake City: Bookcraft, 1982), 312.

125 Howard W. Hunter, *Teachings of Howard W. Hunter* (Salt Lake City: Deseret Book, 1997), 134.

126 Laura Brotherson, *And They Were Not Ashamed* (Boise, Idaho: Inspire Book, 2004), 1.

127 Ibid, 2.

128 Ibid, 4.

CHAPTER 12
The Transition to Parenthood

"I am deeply moved that God finds His ultimate purpose and meaning
in being a parent."
-Elder Jeffrey R. Holland[129]

BEING MARRIED *WITHOUT* CHILDREN IS a wonderful stage of life. As
newlyweds, you have the opportunity to get to know each other without
distractions, to enjoy each other's company, to have a great time together,
and to make memories. In fact, the life of newlyweds should be an extended
honeymoon—at least, to some degree. This time period should be full of
laughter, romance, expressions of love, and intimacy. Of course, it is also
a time of adjustment, challenge, and learning how to live with another
person. The first year of marriage is certainly not all fun and games, but
there are advantages to doing whatever you want, whenever you want.

However, not long after you make the transition from living single to
living with a spouse, another decision will need to be made—when do you
begin having children? For some couples, this decision has been on their
minds long before they were married. Others, perhaps, have not given
much thought as to when they will begin their family. Nevertheless, the
time will come when thoughtful consideration should be given to bearing
children and raising a family.

The Doctrines of Marriage and Family Life
Some of the deepest-held principles in the theology of The Church of Jesus
Christ of Latter-day Saints center on marriage and parenthood. We believe
strongly in the sanctity of marriage, and we are passionate that family
life is the core of human happiness. We teach that establishing a gospel-
centered home is one of the grandest aims in life. From "The Family: A
Proclamation to the World," the following doctrines are declared:

- "Marriage between a man and a woman is ordained of God and that the family is central to the Creator's plan for the eternal destiny of His children."

- "The first commandment that God gave to Adam and Eve pertained to their potential for parenthood as husband and wife. We declare that God's commandment for His children to multiply and replenish the earth remains in force."

- "We further declare that God has commanded that the sacred powers of procreation are to be employed only between man and woman, lawfully wedded as husband and wife."[130]

Long before this proclamation was publicly declared, latter-day prophets taught newly married men and women about their responsibilities in relation to parenthood. For example, President David O. McKay said,

> The Lord has told us that it is the duty of every husband and wife to obey the commandment given to Adam to multiply and replenish the earth, so that legions of choice spirits waiting for their tabernacles of flesh may come here and move forward under God's great design to become perfect souls. . . . Thus, every husband and wife should become a father and a mother in Israel to children born under the holy, eternal covenant.[131]

Joseph Fielding Smith stated that "the family is the most important organization in time or in eternity. Our purpose in life is to create for ourselves eternal family units. There is nothing that will ever come into your family life that is as important as the sealing blessings of the temple and then keeping the covenants made in connection with this order of celestial marriage."[132] Later, it was President Spencer W. Kimball who declared, "Supreme happiness in marriage is governed by a primary factor—that of the bearing and rearing of children."[133]

I want to attest to President Kimball's statement. The greatest joys of my life have been experienced in my family. I love being a husband, and I love being a dad. That doesn't mean I am perfect at either of those two roles. I have had my share of ups and downs just like anyone else. But there isn't anything much better in life than rocking babies to sleep, looking into their angelic faces, and wishing you knew what they must know. There isn't anything much better than teaching your baby girl how to walk by holding a Fudgsicle in front of her face; there isn't anything much better than giving your two-year-old son a horsey ride on your back across the living room; there isn't anything much better than playing hide-and-seek with your children in the backyard; there isn't anything much better than your four-year-old daughter with "bed hair" and a raspy voice coming in your bedroom at three a.m., wanting to snuggle with you because she had a bad dream; there isn't anything much better than placing your trampoline under your roof and jumping off the second story with your kids; there isn't anything much better than teaching your child to throw a ball, hit a pitch, or water ski and then watching them master those skills; there isn't anything much better than watching your children grow in the gospel and develop testimonies of their own; there isn't anything much better than going into your teenagers' rooms and finding them reading their scriptures; there isn't anything much better than being the biggest cheerleader at your daughter's cross-country meet or your son's football game or your other child's choir concert; there isn't anything much better than finding out from your wife that your burley, macho, beast of a son comes home from high school each day and asks, "When's Dad going to be home?"; there isn't anything much better than walking through your front door after a long day at work and having your children hug you and maul you and cheer that you're home; there isn't anything much better than realizing your children have your exact sense of humor, so you spend hours together just cracking each other up. And there is absolutely nothing better than doing all of these things with your best friend—your spouse—your partner for time and all eternity. This is a great plan our Heavenly Father created for us. People who purposely decide not to have children are really missing out on what life is all about!

Now this is not to say that everything in marriage and family life is wonderful and rosy—you already know it isn't. Of course, there are a variety of issues to deal with in the process of helping your children find happiness and success. For example, when babies are sick and cry through the night and you have to be at work early the next morning or your spouse has to function the next day on three hours of sleep, life isn't so fun. What about when one of your children decides that they want to quit school, and they are only in kindergarten? How about when your two-year-old crawls under your desk and unplugs your computer right in the middle of your master's thesis and you lose thirty pages of crucial work? How about when your three-year-old drives your car through the garage and does about $5,000 worth of damage? Not to mention fights with neighborhood children, poor report cards in middle school, pranks and dating in high school, your teenage daughter wrecking the brand new car you saved for years to purchase.ᵃ Yes, there are all kinds of issues parents can expect to have with children, but believe it or not, there's nothing more exciting than parenthood. It is the ultimate school. Even though life with children is sometimes difficult and there are challenges to face, most parents would never trade those experiences for the freedom they enjoyed before children. Our children are also our greatest joys, and developing intimate relationships with them is one of the grandest experiences life has to offer.

President Gordon B. Hinckley was fond of quoting Jenkins Lloyd Jones, who once wrote:

> Anyone who imagines that bliss is normal is going to waste a lot of time running around shouting that he has been robbed.
>
> [The fact is] most putts don't drop. Most beef is tough. Most children grow up to be just people. Most successful marriages require a high degree of mutual toleration. Most jobs are more often dull than otherwise. . . .
>
> Life is like an old-time rail journey—delays, sidetracks, smoke, dust, cinders and jolts, interspersed only occasionally by beautiful vistas and thrilling bursts of speed.
>
> The trick is to thank the Lord for letting you have the ride.¹³⁴

Certainly in parenting there are all kinds of delays, sidetracks, smoke, dust, cinders, and jolts. However, when those paydays come, and they do, the years of breathing in dust and cinders become completely worth it. Hopefully, parents are able to see the fruits of their labors as their children enter the mission field, marry in the temple, serve in the Church, and keep their covenants. Not all children will follow their parents' teaching; some will stray and even rebel. However, peace can come to all parents who have tried their best to teach their children the gospel of Jesus Christ.

Elder Bruce C. Hafen shared the following experience:

> When we observe the covenants we make at the altar of sacrifice, we discover hidden reservoirs of strength. I once said in exasperation to my wife, Marie, "The Lord placed Adam and Eve on the earth as full-grown people. Why couldn't he have done that with this boy of ours, the one with the freckles and the

---

a   Of course, these are all just hypotheticals. These things never have happened to me. (wink, wink)

unruly hair?" She replied, "The Lord gave us that child to make Christians out of us."

One night Marie exhausted herself for hours encouraging that child to finish a school assignment to build his own diorama of a Native American village on a cookie sheet. It was a test no hireling would have endured. At first he fought her efforts, but by bedtime, I saw him lay "his" diorama proudly on a counter. He started for his bed, then turned around, raced back across the room, and hugged his mother, grinning with his fourth-grade teeth. Later I asked Marie in complete awe, "How did you do it?" She said, "I just made up my mind that I couldn't leave him, no matter what." Then she added, *"I didn't know I had it in me."* She discovered deep, internal wellsprings of compassion because the bonds of her covenants gave her strength to lay down her life for her sheep, even an hour at a time."[135]

Hopefully our children *are* making Christians out of us. There is no better way to learn about the compassion of Christ than being a parent. There is no better way of understanding how our Heavenly Father must feel about us than by having children of our own. There is no better way to comprehend the plan of salvation and certainly no better way to appreciate the power of prayer. If you want to refine your nature and learn to become a Saint, have a few children, and you will be on your way!

Making the Decision to Have Children

As I mentioned before, I would advise you that you should not wait until you are *ready* to have children. If you waited until then, you would *never* have any! If you want to become a great parent, you will need to seek the Lord's help, as well as help from your parents and others who have survived parenthood. Discover as much knowledge as you can. And then go forward with faith. Like all the other challenging things you have done in your life, you will grow into the responsibility of parenthood. No one can ever be ready for parenthood—at least, not by themselves. My guess is that you'll be a much better parent than you give yourself credit for. After all, you've seen some pretty good parents in your lifetime. Emulate the traits of good parents you know, and bring your own knowledge and skills into the mix. I have a feeling you will surprise yourself!

President Spencer W. Kimball taught, "Too many young people set their minds, determining they will not marry or have children until they are more secure, until the military service period is over; until the college degree is secured; until the occupation is more well-defined; until debts are paid; or until it is more convenient. . . . But the excuses are many, mostly weak."[136]

Yes, many delay having children because of the inconvenience and the strain it may place on a marriage. However, selfishness must never be the cause of postponing our families. Great growth opportunities await. I have always believed it is best to begin having children early in your marriage. I would never tell you when to do that, but there is something to be said about having your children while you are young, energetic, and enthusiastic. That will pay you many dividends in the future. Janie and I were in our early twenties when we started our family. Therefore, we were in our midthirties when our children became teenagers. We enjoyed our children's music, parties at our home, their friends, and many fun family activities. I was particularly happy that I could engage in physical activities with my children, such as training with my daughter for her cross-country meets, playing basketball in the driveway with my children, and teaching them to water ski. I don't think I could have done those things in my fifties.

Moreover, Janie and I have learned that the older you become, the more time demands are placed upon your schedule—especially work and Church responsibilities. Enjoy those children while you are young! Your life will continue to become more demanding and complex, and tomorrow may never come.

Several years ago, I came across a piece on the Internet called, "11 Step Program for Those Thinking of Having Kids." Although it is somewhat exaggerated, I couldn't help but laugh since many of these scenarios had already happened in our family.

Lesson 1
1. Go to the grocery store.
2. Arrange to have your salary paid directly to their head office.
3. Go home.
4. Pick up the paper.
5. Read it for the last time.

Lesson 2
Before you finally go ahead and have children, find a couple who already are parents and berate them about their . . .
1. Methods of discipline.

2. Lack of patience.

3. Appallingly low tolerance levels.

4. Allowing their children to run wild.

5. Suggest ways in which they might improve their child's breastfeeding, sleep habits, toilet training, table manners, and overall behavior. Enjoy it because it will be the last time in your life you will have all the answers.

Lesson 3

A really good way to discover how the nights might feel . . .

1. Get home from work and immediately begin walking around the living room from five p.m. to ten p.m. carrying a wet bag weighing approximately 8 to 12 pounds, with a radio turned to static (or some other obnoxious sound) playing loudly. (Eat cold food with one hand for dinner.)

2. At ten p.m., put the bag gently down, set the alarm for midnight, and go to sleep.

3. Get up at midnight and walk around the living room again, with the bag, until one a.m.

4. Set the alarm for three a.m.

5. As you can't get back to sleep, get up at two a.m., make a drink, and watch an infomercial.

6. Go to bed at 2:45 a.m.

7. Get up at three a.m., when the alarm goes off.

8. Sing songs quietly in the dark until four a.m.

9. Get up. Make breakfast. Get ready for work and go to work (work hard and be productive).

Repeat steps 1–9 each night. Keep this up for 3 to 5 years. Look cheerful and together.

Lesson 4

Can you stand the mess children make? In order to find out . . .

1. Smear peanut butter onto the sofa and jam onto the curtains.

2. Hide a piece of raw chicken behind the television and leave it there all summer.

3. Stick your fingers in the flower bed.

4. Then rub them on the clean walls.

5. Take your favorite book, photo album, etc. Wreck it.

6. Spill milk on your new pillows. Cover the stains with crayons. How does that look?

Lesson 5

Dressing small children is not as easy as it seems.

1. Buy an octopus and a small bag made out of loose mesh.

2. Attempt to put the octopus into the bag so that none of the arms hang out.

Time allowed for this: all morning.

Lesson 6

Forget the BMW and buy a mini-van. And don't think that you can leave it out in the driveway spotless and shining. Family cars don't look like that.

1. Buy a chocolate ice cream cone and put it in the glove compartment. Leave it there.

2. Get a dime. Stick it in the CD player.

3. Take a family-size package of chocolate cookies. Mash them into the backseat. Sprinkle Cheerios all over the floor, then smash them.

4. Run a garden rake along both sides of the car. There, doesn't that look nice?

Lesson 7

Go to the local grocery store. Take with you the closest thing you can find to a preschool child. (A full-grown goat is an excellent choice.) If you intend to have more than one child, then definitely take more than one goat. Buy your week's groceries without letting the goats out of your sight. Pay for everything the goat eats or destroys. Until you can easily accomplish this, do not even contemplate having children.

Lesson 8

1. Hollow out a melon.

2. Make a small hole in the side.

3. Suspend it from the ceiling and swing it from side to side.

4. Now get a bowl of soggy Cheerios and attempt to spoon them into the swaying melon by pretending to be an airplane.

5. Continue until half the Cheerios are gone.

6. Tip half into your lap. The other half, just throw up in the air.

You are now ready to feed a nine-month-old baby.

Lesson 9

Learn the names of every character from *Sesame Street*, *Barney*, Disney, the *Teletubbies*, and *Pokemon*. Watch nothing else on TV but PBS, the Disney channel, or Noggin for at least five years.

Lesson 10

Make a recording of Fran Drescher saying "mommy" repeatedly. (Important: no more than a four-second delay between each 'mommy'; occasional crescendo to the level of a supersonic jet is required.) Play this CD in your car everywhere you go for the next four years. You are now ready to take a long trip with a toddler.

Lesson 11

Start talking to an adult of your choice. Have someone else continually tug on your skirt hem, shirt-sleeve, or elbow while playing the 'mommy' tape made from Lesson 10 above. You are now ready to have a conversation with an adult while there is a child in the room.[137]

This is certainly a humorous view of parenting. Hopefully, your experiences will be somewhat different. Nevertheless, there are many individuals who become anxious about being parents. They begin thinking about all of the things that could go wrong with the health of their future children or about whether they have what it takes to be parents. Some may feel that because their own parents were not great at raising children, maybe they will stink at it too. Some women may worry about their own health and perhaps ruining their well-shaped body that took years to develop. Instead of focusing on all the things that can go wrong, put your energy and trust in the Lord. Choose to believe how wonderful your life will be with children.

As you work with your spouse in deciding when to start your family, be sure to include the Lord in your decision. I see many couples today who have chosen to delay parenthood, yet *they haven't sought the Lord's will or guidance*. Because I know some of these couples well, we have talked about this subject at length. I have discovered that many young couples simply don't think to counsel with the Lord on such matters, or they postpone praying over the matter because they are afraid of what the answer may be. I have known some couples who go for several years without counseling with the Lord. I invite you to go to the Lord, receive an answer, and then move forward with faith. Remember, the Lord will never give you a commandment or directive you cannot keep. He will help you along the way!

The Lord will bless you and aid you when you decide to bring children into the world. To receive such an answer from the Lord demonstrates His trust in you. With the Lord's help, you will find that becoming a parent will be one of the most exciting times in your life!

The Transition to Parenthood for Men

The initial transition to parenthood is one of the most striking, marked, and drastic changes that most married couples will experience during their life span. Many psychological stress tests reveal that having a child is usually considered a top-ten stressor, and having a baby isn't the only challenge that can be occurring. Frequently, when men and women become first-time parents, there are many other life events taking place, such as college, new jobs, moves, graduate school, new homes or apartments, living far away from home, and a host of other variables.

Traditionally, men are not socialized into parenting roles like some women are. Little boys are not usually given strollers, dollies, and kitchen sets as gifts. Instead, they are provided with swords, balls, and video games. In fact, as boys become older, little thought is given toward their future roles as husbands and fathers. I believe many men never really think about their potential fatherhood role until their wives become pregnant.

Consequently, becoming a parent could overwhelm the stoutest of men. Perhaps some may reflect upon their own fathers and realize that they grew up short-changed, the realization that their dad was marginal at best. Perhaps others may worry they will never measure up and be the amazing father their dad was to them. Most men face the generalized fear that they will not have what it takes to be a parent.

I remember when we learned that Janie was pregnant with our first child. Of course, we were elated and anticipated a wonderful life together with our new child and the other children that would surely follow. However, for me, there were some major concerns to deal with. First of all, the basement apartment we lived in was a dive, and I couldn't imagine our new baby could survive in that musty old place without developing "chalk lung" or contracting some contagious disease. So I felt the pressure of upgrading our living quarters. I also knew that the old jalopy we drove around town was probably not fit for a baby, since we were constantly taking it to our mechanic for repairs. Then Janie hit me up with the idea that we would need a baby crib, a baby stroller, and a couple crates of baby wipes. The later we got into her pregnancy, the more expensive this venture became. I was financially overwhelmed and had no idea how we were going to purchase all of these things. As I have interviewed many new fathers, I have learned that their prime concern is how they are going to afford it.

There are also other adjustments men must take into consideration. Christian, a twenty-three-year-old returned missionary from Utah, told me that one of the modifications he had to make was adjusting to his wife's loss of interest in affection and intimacy during her pregnancy. He also explained that he had to adjust to his wife's lack of energy. Christian explained he would come home from work or school and discover that their home wasn't as clean as he had hoped it would be. At first, this bothered him, but when he learned that his wife was legitimately exhausted, he adjusted and began expecting less from her and pitched in more.

Men don't simply have to adjust to the child coming to their home, but they must also modify their expectations as their wife changes in emotion, health, energy, temperament, and appetite. One new father told me, "My wife would get emotional, and I had no idea what I did wrong. No matter what I did, I was wrong. But I knew I just needed to stick by her because she was having a difficult time."

Some men may feel that during this transition to parenthood everything around them is changing—and they're probably correct. Their wife is changing physically and emotionally; there is a baby growing in the womb; perhaps there is also a job change or home relocation. Maybe everything is changing for the new father—except for him. He may be the only constant in the family unit. This is why it is crucial for new fathers to be strong and stable. They need to be the rock for their wives to lean on, and they need to "ratchet it up" in terms of their output and performance in the home. Husbands, serve your wives, meet their needs, and nurture them. Men, you should be the greatest nurse and doctor in terms of your wife's care.

Advice to Men during the Delivery

Finally, the day of delivery arrives. Once again, no one can be ready for such an emotional and exciting day. Perhaps the new mother's water will break or she will begin having heavy contractions. That's when a man finally has an excuse to drive his wife to the hospital as fast as he possibly can. However, once you skid into the hospital parking lot, husbands have the responsibility and privilege to make their wives comfortable and confident.

Men, there are several things that you *should not do* during the labor and delivery process. If I were you, *I wouldn't* . . .

- Park two miles away from the hospital because you don't want to pay for parking. Making your wife walk that far while carrying her own luggage and being 9 ½ months pregnant is a crime you will pay for the rest of your life.

- Tell your wife what to do or counsel her on any matter, especially when it comes to delivering the baby because, frankly, you don't know anything about that.
- Read the baby monitor and tell your wife when her next contraction is about to come. Especially don't say, "And this one looks like a really big one."
- Leave the hospital for any reason whatsoever. For example, asking your wife, "Hey, do you care if I just go out and get a hamburger? Watching you in agony is making me hungry."
- Eat really tasty food in front of your wife.
- Tell your wife to smile for the camera while she is in the process of delivering.
- Tell her that you have chosen to name the baby, without her input or approval.
- Talk to the doctor about football while your wife is in heavy labor.
- Tell your wife that her pain can't be that bad.
- Tell your wife that you have an injury or a pain that is probably much worse than hers.
- Check your e-mail or play on your computer while your wife is in labor.
- Tell your wife to "push harder."
- Faint while your wife is in labor.
- Turn the sound up really loud on the TV in the delivery room because you cannot hear the program over your wife's moaning and groaning in agony—and frankly, she's just being really noisy.
- After the baby is born, tell your wife you're going to head home for a bit to sleep because you're really exhausted.

Men, there are many things you *can do* to make your wife comfortable during her delivery. If I were you, *I would* . . .

- Become as educated as you can on childbirth and show your wife how interested and excited you are about having a child.
- Be your wife's caretaker. Fight her battles for her. Be brave and go to the nurses' station to ask for more medication (not for you, for her!) or water or whatever your wife needs. When doctors and nurses may not be listening or are preoccupied, make sure they know how your wife is doing. Develop a dialogue with the doctors and nurses. Become friends with them so that they will share information freely. Don't be a pain, but the squeaky wheel gets the grease.

- Be there for your wife to nurture her, comfort her, and give her praise and encouragement. Ask her what she needs, and respond to what she may require.
- Help your wife stay calm and relaxed. Ask her how she would like you to do that. What you have in mind and what she is thinking may be completely different. Use appropriate humor, and show her that you are calm and relaxed.
- Be present. Many men sit with their wife in labor, but they are not in tune to the moment. Show your wife you're there for her. When she's not in severe pain, talk to her, watch a program together, or perhaps even play a game to get her mind off the labor temporarily. Take pictures of your wife and baby. That is your role!
- Be tough. Having a baby is a difficult and sometimes extremely painful and exhausting experience. If your wife is short with you, gets upset with you, or gives you a look that could kill, just roll with it and understand she is under major duress. Anything derogatory she says to you during the labor and delivery process must be erased from your memory!
- Step up to the plate, and get your wife a nice gift or write her a beautiful note or get her flowers. Make sure she knows how much you mean to her, how proud you are of her, and how excited you are to be a parent with her.

Having a baby can be one of the most wonderful experiences you will ever have. Men, don't worry that you may not feel any different on the day after your baby is born than you did on the day before they were born. The reason you may not feel any different is that you really haven't done anything yet! For the most part, your wife has done just about every single thing to bring your new son or daughter to the earth. You have been a cheerleader for the most part. However, now that your child is here, it's time for you to get off the bench and into the game!

The day after our oldest daughter was born, a woman in our ward came over to our house and said, "Well, Mark, how does it feel to be a dad?" Honestly, I wasn't feeling much more than exhaustion since Janie had been in labor all night and had the baby early in the morning. I didn't want to respond by saying, "I don't really feel anything," because that sounded harsh. So I exaggerated a bit when I responded, "It feels great." I felt guilty that I didn't feel this tremendous aura of fatherhood swirling about me.

However, instead of watching Janie have all the fun, I decided to start chipping in. I wanted to be an involved father. When our baby cried, I would take a turn rocking her and tring to comfort her. I also learned that I could change diapers and get up in the middle of the night to help with the feeding duties. After several weeks of these experiences, I realized I was forging a bond of love with my daughter that had become very strong. I was reminded that it is only when we sacrifice for causes that we will love them. The more I sacrificed for my little girl, the more love I had for her, and the better father I was becoming. The love for her and all my other children has come in the exact same way.

The Transition to Parenthood for Women

Women become mothers the moment they conceive. However, for the next nine months, the development of the baby is on autopilot for the most part. Women do need to eat right, get adequate rest, and exercise. Nevertheless, most women are relatively unaware that there is a baby inside them until a month or two into the pregnancy. However, the fact that they are nauseated, tired, and not feeling normal is ample evidence that something miraculous is occurring inside them. For women, within a short period of time, their pants don't fit like they used to, and their bodies start changing. From a physical standpoint, a woman's body will change more drastically in this short period of time than at any other time in their lives.

There are also emotional changes that occur due to hormones. Women may cry without reason, have weird dreams,[b] worry about their baby's health, or doubt their ability to be a great mother. Physically speaking, women must also deal with their growing bellies and possibly other weight gain as well. The most significant change for most women is the fatigue they experience during pregnancy. Getting up early, exercising, and then cleaning the house from top to bottom most likely isn't going to be a pregnant wife's routine. Furthermore, many women can experience other physical challenges, such as morning sickness, difficulty sleeping, heartburn, nosebleeds, varicose veins, stretch marks, leg cramps, back pain, pelvic pain, hip pain, Braxton Hick's contractions, difficulty breathing, and hemorrhoids—doesn't that sound fun!

Some women may have several of these symptoms, and many will have only a few of them. Husbands can learn to appreciate their spouses

---

b   These dreams usually have a theme of their husbands doing something really stupid.

even more when they see the sacrifices their wives are willing to make to bring a child into the world. A Tongan man named Kime told me that his wife began to feel less beautiful when her body began to change. However, he said to me, "When I saw my wife making these sacrifices, I began to love her more than I ever had. She became more attractive to me, not less."

Now That the Baby Is Home . . .

One of the most unnerving experiences for both of you is when you bring your baby home for the first time. There is no longer a round-the-clock staff of doctors and nurses to take care of your baby while you rest. If you have a mother who can come stay with you for a few days, consider that a great blessing. The first night you're home and trying to sleep, you may find yourself waking up and checking on the baby every thirty minutes to make sure they are breathing.[c]

Once you come home from the hospital, your marriage will never be the same again. You have now entered an entirely new world. Now the responsibility to raise a child rests solely on both of your shoulders. You are to feed, change, nurture, love, and protect your new baby. Men, you can't do that while you're glued to the television or a video game. Furthermore, your schedule changes from doing things you want to do when you want to do them, to being at the mercy of your baby's schedule. Mothers may find that they can only rest or get the house picked up when the baby is sleeping. Men may discover they have a really small window of time to be with their wives before the baby wakes up.

Women, you may still be tired and exhausted for some time. Besides that, you will probably also become sleep-deprived quickly. Often, new babies have their days and nights mixed up. They want to sleep all day and make funny faces at you all night. Your milk will come in, which can cause discomfort. You may have a demanding baby who will require more attention than you expected. Now, don't get too depressed. There are many people who are blessed to have low-maintenance babies. Pray for such a child, and if you get one, thank God each day! If your child requires more time and attention, find ways to enjoy the journey.

Men, this can be an emotional time for your wives. Some of them could become depressed after the baby is born. Others are simply overwhelmed. This is your chance to shine! Become an all-star here. Help feed your new

---

c Don't worry. By the time you have your last kid, your children have to come in and check on you to see if you are still breathing.

baby, and change diapers. Get the baby dressed and bathed; give your wife a break. A twenty-seven-year-old-mother, Erin, told me that after her baby was born, she just needed some "me time." That was her husband's opportunity to take the baby for an hour or two so she could catch her breath and get something done.

Young mothers I have interviewed have also told me how difficult it becomes to go out together. One new mother related to me that she and her husband thought it would be fun to go eat at a restaurant shortly after their baby was born. First, she said, it took about twenty minutes to get ready, as they gathered bottles, formula, extra diapers, and the baby's "blankey." Once they got to the restaurant, their beautiful little cherub began to scream and cry. Of course, there were some people in the restaurant who gave them the evil eye, so they had to ask for a to-go box and eat their dinner at home.

Usually, after a baby is born, couples have less time to spend in leisure activities together. With a new infant, couples can no longer go to a movie or out to dinner as easily. Some new parents may feel they are now anchored to their home by a ten-pound infant. For couples who do try to continue their life of fun and excitement, they may discover that a "night on the town" simply isn't worth it. If they leave their baby with a sitter, they may worry the entire evening if the baby or the sitter is all right. If the parents take the baby with them, their evening is often filled changing diapers, looking for the pacifier that rolled down the aisle at the theatre, or taking turns holding the infant while the other eats.

For example, another young mother told me that she and her husband decided to see a movie when their baby was a few weeks old. They convinced each other that since their baby always slept, they were sure she would sleep through the entire movie. Nope. The baby screamed the entire time, so the couple traded places, either holding the baby in the lobby or watching the movie alone. Great date!

Making the Transition Together

Marriage and family experts often discuss that during the transition to parenthood, not only does leisure time decline, but intimacy at every level is reduced, interaction is lessened, and overall marital satisfaction suffers. Even though these trends are common, your marriage does not have to follow this path of least resistance. These are things that are sure to happen if you follow the course of the natural man. You can fight against these trends, however, and your marriage can grow stronger. In order to pull this off, you will have to be mature and selfless. In short, you should try to become a saint, and now that you have a child, the Lord has given you the perfect opportunity to do so.

I recall that when Janie had our twins our marriage and family really changed. We went from having three children to having five in one day. With that delivery, we outgrew our house, our car, and my income. Initially, Janie was going to try to breastfeed the twins, but that task proved to be too overwhelming. Inevitably, one twin would be hungry, and the other wouldn't, or vice versa. Or as soon as one twin would eat and Janie thought she could get something done, the other twin became hungry. The most challenging part was when one was crying and the other wanted to eat. All of this was going on while our three older children—ages 5, 4, and 3—were shredding the house to bits. In order to bring order back into our lives, there was only one solution. We elected to bottle-feed the babies. That way, I could help at nights, and our other children could help with feedings during the day.

I well remember those two a.m. feedings with Janie and our twins. It was an incredible bonding time for us. We were up together, sacrificing together, and growing together. We had great conversations and became a strong team as a result. Not to mention that our children who helped feed the babies while I was at work also grew and matured quickly. It was a great experience to come home and see my five-year-old daughter and four-year-old son sitting on the couch feeding their infant siblings.

For those of you who are first-time parents, learn to work together. Men, feeding, clothing, and bathing the baby is just as much your responsibility as your wife's. There is no faster way to develop a strong love for your children than by doing things for them. The key to transitioning to parenthood successfully is talking, sharing responsibilities, and working together.

Men, your wife is not going to be able to devote as much time to you. She now has a baby to deal with. You can either pout about that or jump in and help so that you can enjoy your time together. Wives, yes, your husbands may resemble a lost puppy for a while. Try to remember that he still wants love and attention from you. See what you can do to make him feel like he is most important in your life, and be creative as you craft ways to spend more time together. For both of you, when your needs are not being met or you feel frustrated or disappointed in the way your spouse is behaving—talk about it. Discuss how you can remedy the situation. Commit to solutions. Instead of being a wedge between you, view the baby as a means of bringing you closer together.

My daughter Brittany recently told me that one of her favorite times of the day is when her husband, Tyler, comes home from medical school each day. Tyler will engage with his new baby daughter by talking to her and playing with her. Brittany related that she wasn't sure how great of a parent Tyler would be, so it became very satisfying to watch him grow as a father.

It takes mature adults to have a child. A husband cannot pout or feel cheated because he isn't getting the attention he needs from his wife. A wife cannot feel that by having a baby, her life has been ruined. It takes complete selflessness. Men and women must learn to sacrifice their own needs for the needs of their spouse and child. If couples are mature and can practice selflessness, then having a child is one of the most soul-satisfying experiences in life. You will love holding your baby and singing songs to him or her; you will love pushing your baby in a stroller as you walk down the street. For the first time in your marriage, you will really feel like a family, and great happiness will come from that.

Men, be prepared for the awe you will feel as your watch your wife grow into her role as a mother. Your wife will become more beautiful to you than she has ever been as she nurtures and cares for your child. Women, you can anticipate feelings of deep love and happiness as you watch your husbands rock your baby to sleep or talk to your child or bust through the door at the end of the day asking, "Where's my baby?" Having a new child can be one of the most positive experiences in a marriage. You have to make it that way.

Homework:
- Find a time to talk, and discuss what your life will be like with a baby. Express to each other what kind of parent you think your spouse will be.
- Write down some expectations you have for yourself and each other when it comes to parenting. What kind of parent do you hope to become? What about your spouse?
- Go online, or visit a book store or library, and get a book about the development of a baby from conception to delivery.

Additional Readings:
- Elder Neil L. Andersen, "Children," *Ensign*, November 2011.
- *A Parent's Guide*, http://www.lds.org/manual/a-parents-guide ?lang=eng.
- There are many great books for first-time parents.

References

129 Jeffrey R. Holland, "Because She Is a Mother," *Ensign*, May 1997, 36.

130 See "The Family: A Proclamation to the World."

131 David O. McKay, *Conference Report*, October 1942, 12.

132 Joseph Fielding Smith, "Counsel to the Saints and to the World," *Ensign*, July 1972, 27.

133 Spencer W. Kimball, *Teachings of Spencer W. Kimball* (Salt Lake City: Deseret Book, 1982), 328.

134 Jenkins Lloyd Jones, "Big Rock Candy Mountains," *Deseret News,* 12 June 1973, A4.

135 Bruce C. Hafen, "Covenant Marriage," *Ensign*, Nov 1996, 26; as cited in *Living a Covenant Marriage*, eds. Douglas E. Brinley & Daniel K Judd (Salt Lake City: Deseret Book, 2004), 4–5.

136 Spencer W. Kimball, *Teachings of Spencer W. Kimball* (Salt Lake City: Deseret Book, 1982), 328.

137 http://urbanmoms.ca/uncategorized/11_step_program_for_those_thinking_of_having_kids_or_for_anyone_who_has_had_kids_and_wants_to_laugh/.

CHAPTER 13
Dealing with Parents and In-Laws

"Therefore shall a man leave his father and his mother, and shall cleave
unto his wife: and they shall be one flesh."
-Genesis 2:24

IT IS A TRUISM THAT when you marry someone, you marry their entire
family. On your wedding day, you not only receive a new spouse but you
also acquire a new set of parents, siblings, grandparents, aunts, uncles,
cousins—you get the whole "kit and caboodle." In most cases, that will
be a wonderful opportunity for growth, happiness, and strength. Some of
you will live close to your parents and in-laws, while others will live far
away. However, no matter where you end up living, there could always be
potential issues to deal with in this simple yet complex family relationship.
Remember, when a husband and wife marry and leave the nest, it's not
only an adjustment period for them but for their parents as well. Perhaps
this is the first time parents will live far away from their married child
or come to realize that their daily interaction and influence with them is
over. I know for me personally, it has been a mixed set of emotions seeing
my children marry and move on. Of course, I was elated our children had
married wonderful spouses in the temple. At the same time, I also realized
my day-to-day interactions with them, and in some ways my influence,
would now be reduced. Leaving the nest is part of God's plan, and it has
been rewarding to watch my children mature in their marriages, accept
new responsibilities, and raise children of their own.

Parent and in-law relationships can be both a blessing and a challenge
for newlyweds—a blessing in that you have support and encouragement
to draw from. Not only is there much to learn from them, but hopefully
you will have many treasured experiences together—especially when they
become grandparents to your children.

However, parent and in-law relationships can also be challenging and somewhat fragile. In our LDS culture, we pride ourselves on having strong families, close-knit families who spend much time together. Sometimes it is difficult for parents to let their adult children go; other times, it is problematic for married children to leave their parents. *There is a constant struggle between a newly married couple forging their own identity and their parents who desperately still want to be a vital part of their lives.* Finding the correct balance is the key to healthy parent–married children relationships. In fact, Dr. Brent Barlow has written,

> One of the keys for stable relationships with parents and in-laws during the early years of marriage is to observe the simple principle of the Golden Mean: *Not too much and not too little.* For a couple after marriage trying to establish a proper relationship with parents, it means not too much and not too little involvement. . . . The key is to strike a balance in how much involvement to have.[138]

As a couple, you will need to discuss what that balance will be, and you will need to do what's best for both of you. You will need to strike the balance between independence and dependence; between forging your own identity and adopting practices and traditions from your own family; between seeing your parents/in-laws often and not seeing them as much as you used to.

Common Problems

It should be mentioned that every newly married couple *will not* necessarily have problems with parents and in-laws. Frankly, some parents and their adult children get along marvelously well. They simply have the right attitude, the right involvement, and the right boundaries,[a] and their relationship seems to flow nicely.

However, many couples have issues with their parents and in-laws. Often this is new territory for all parties involved. How involved should your parents/in-laws be in your new lives? How often should you reach out to them? When Janie and I were first married, not only did I inherit her parents and siblings, but I also got a new grandfather out of the deal—something I wasn't expecting. No, it wasn't Janie's parents who were calling us—it was her grandfather. And he would call us at six a.m. on a Saturday morning just

---

a   And perhaps the right distance!

to chit-chat. I always felt compelled to answer the phone because I assumed that if anyone was calling us that early, it must be an emergency. Nope, it was never anything serious! My wife's grandfather just enjoyed waking up at the crack of dawn and calling people on the telephone. So you never know what in-laws you will get to interact with!

As a marriage and family therapist, I have seen many young couples, and some older ones, struggle with parent/in-law relationships. Here are some examples of some common challenges:

- A young husband, who comes from a strong family background, believed that by enjoying time with his in-laws or doing fun things with them he was being disloyal to his parents. Therefore, he retreated from his in-laws and treated them poorly.

- A young wife allowed herself to be easily offended when her mother-in-law offered a suggestion or told her what to do. Consequently, their relationship deteriorated quickly. The young bride never wanted to be around her mother-in-law and avoided her at all costs.

- A young wife told her own mother every intimate detail about her marriage, but she would get mad at her husband when he would tell his parents anything—including superficial events— like where they ate on Friday night. The wife would say, "They don't need to know anything about that." Meanwhile, her mother knew everything about their sex life, arguments, and life plans.

- A husband never communicated with his parents or in-laws and kept them completely in the dark regarding everything going on in their lives. His parents and in-laws constantly wondered what they had done to offend the couple.

- A husband is more loyal to his parents than his wife. He has failed to defend his wife when she was accused, mocked, or challenged by his parents.

- Parents or in-laws are too intrusive and want to know everything about your life and get upset if you haven't called them in two days. Often these parents/in-laws want to know too much, and they always seem to have their nose in your business.

- Parents or in-laws take over your home or apartment when they come to visit. They tell you what needs to be cleaned, inform you that the trash needs to be taken out, and basically kick you out of your kitchen. Then they wonder why you never invite them over.

- Parents or in-laws expect you and your spouse to attend every family activity, family dinner, and holiday celebration in their home. If you don't, the guilt trip begins with a vengeance.

Several years ago, one of my students came to my office to talk about some concerns. He was dating a girl, and their relationship was becoming more serious. However, he was seeing some red flags when it came to her parents. He was torn because he was really in love with this girl, but her parents were making their relationship extremely difficult. With his permission, I share the following e-mail he sent me:

> I am currently dating a wonderful girl, and the topic of marriage has become a serious one for us. We have only been dating for five months, but thus far I have seen relatively few problems in our personal relationship. When problems do arise, it is usually because of her parents' involvement. I, of course, understand that loving and concerned parents want to be a part of the biggest decision their child is ever going to make.
>
> However, what I don't agree with are some of the views they hold. One viewpoint they have is the vital importance of extended family. They believe that living near extended family is vital to a child's upbringing—that every child ought to know his cousins, grandparents, aunts, uncles, etc., and to do this, one must live in close proximity to extended family. While I do agree that extended family is important, I also believe that building the kingdom of God takes a higher priority. My family lives away from the rest of our extended family because we have felt that that is where God wanted us. This, however, has not deterred us from having a wonderful relationship with our extended family through phone calls and lots of visits.
>
> Her parents seem think it is a major red flag that I am not wholly insistent on living near them but am rather open to living elsewhere. Of course extended family is important to me, but my future family (wife and kids) will come first, and I don't need to live near extended family to be close to grandparents, aunts, and other relatives.
>
> My second concern is that I don't even know if I would want to live near my girlfriend's family should we get married. From my stance and background, they are a little controlling. My girlfriend is an adult, but her parents still insist on selecting her

classes for her, and they try to choose her housing. Her dad comes to visit nearly every two weeks because his business allows him to. When he is in town, I simply don't see her because her dad fills the schedule to keep us apart. During Christmas my girlfriend would only be allowed twenty minutes of Skype time with me before her dad insisted we stop talking so they could have family time.

Perhaps in reading this, especially as a parent yourself, you may not think this sounds controlling, but I just get the impression they are just too obtrusive and insistent on getting their way. Thus, I worry that if we lived near her parents, we would never establish ourselves as a couple. My girlfriend's dad would find me a job near them. Her mother would become the leading lady of OUR life, telling us how to raise our kids or anything else that she feels to counsel us on.

And my girlfriend and I wouldn't be able to make life decisions without their approval or at least involvement in the decision process. What worries me the most is that my life would be spent living according to their wills and not according to God's.

Thank you for all of your help,

One Really Worried Dude

In my humble opinion, I believe that my student had much to worry about. From our conversations and this e-mail, it is clear to me that his girlfriend's parents are going to be a force to be reckoned with. I'm not sure if he ever did marry her, but if he did, I feel confident they have had some issues with her parents. Marriage is difficult enough as it is. Adding controlling and manipulative parents to the mix could make things very difficult to deal with.

Principles and Doctrines Regarding These Relationships

Principle #1: One of the Ten Commandments reads, "Honour thy father and thy mother" (Exodus 20:12). This is a critical doctrine that cannot be ignored. You should find ways to honor your parents and in-laws, even though you may sometimes disagree with them. To honor them is to show respect and admiration. Be part of their lives, and let them be part of yours. Remember that your parents and in-laws have had twenty or thirty more years of experience from the "School of Hard Knocks" than you have. Find ways to tap into their knowledge and expertise. Occasionally, make their day by asking them for advice or counsel. At this juncture of their lives, they may be feeling underused or undervalued. Perhaps the reason they pester you so much is because they desperately desire to be needed. When you encounter difficult challenges, draw on their strength and expertise. Several years ago, my sister-in-law encountered a severe challenge in her life. When the crisis hit, her first thought was, "I need to call my parents—I need their prayers." The prayers of her parents and other family members led to a positive outcome.

However, it should be stated that if parents or in-laws are abusive, manipulative, controlling, or critical, then they have lost their right and ability to be an influence in your life. To honor parents and in-laws doesn't mean you have to do whatever they ask, do everything their way, or fulfill every request they make. Your first loyalty is to your spouse and to your children. You also have the responsibility to protect your spouse and children from manipulative, controlling, or abusive parents. You don't have to visit them if you metaphorically get clubbed over the head each time you are in their presence. Honor is like respect—it must be earned.

Principle #2: In Genesis 2:24, we read, "Therefore shall a man leave his father and his mother, and shall cleave unto his wife: and they shall be one flesh." From modern revelation, we learn that "Thou shalt love thy wife with all thy heart, and shalt cleave unto her and none else" (D&C 42:22). Regarding this verse, President Spencer W. Kimball explained, "The words *none else* eliminate everyone and everything. The spouse then becomes pre-eminent in the life of the husband or wife and neither social life nor occupational life nor political life nor any other interest nor person nor thing shall ever take precedence over the companion spouse."[139] Nothing comes before our spouse—not even our own parents.

When President Boyd K. Packer would seal couples in the temple, he was prone to tell them:

> First of all, today, as you are sealed for time and for all eternity, you become a separate family on the records of the Church, and that is a separation in a very real sense. All of the ties that have bound you to your father and mother to this point we undo today. We untie them all. . . . Many of them we leave permanently untied. That is why your mothers will be crying today . . . because they know, in a very real sense, that they are losing and that they should lose you as you become a separate family on the records of the Church.[140]

After the marriage ceremony, the mission for a newly married couple is to create an identity—separate from their parents. You should create traditions and practices that will benefit your future children and draw them closer to the Lord. Learn to become a team. Discover your gifts, your talents, your skills, and your resources. You cannot do that if your parents are constantly bailing you out of every jam or interfering in your life. Together, with the Lord's help, you are to learn to solve your own problems. As newlyweds, you are to become more reliant on the Lord and less dependent upon your parents. Simply put, you are to become mature and independent. President Spencer W. Kimball further explained:

> Couples do well to immediately find their own home, separate and apart from that of the in-laws on either side. The home may be very modest and unpretentious, but still it is an independent domicile. Your married life should become independent of her folks and his folks. You love them more than ever; you cherish their counsel; you appreciate their association, but you live your own lives, being governed by your decisions, by your own prayerful considerations after you have received the counsel from those who should give it.[141]

Therefore, President Kimball would recommend that you don't start off your marriage living in your parents' basement, eating their food, driving their cars, and writing your research papers on their computer.

President Boyd K. Packer provided further counsel to newly married women when he stated:

> My young sister, you have had some very choice, intimate, cherished times with your mother, talking over things that are sacred and personal. Now all of these moments belong to your husband, and only rarely and on superficial things would you have to run back to mother—maybe for an occasional recipe or a remedy, but on all the sacred and deep important problems you belong to one another and you solve them between the two of you.[142]

It seems clear that our Church leaders are teaching us that it will be difficult to create a new marriage and family with your parents constantly looking over your shoulder. What I hear President Kimball and Packer saying is, "It's time to grow up." Once again, this does not suggest that you don't love your parents or that you don't enjoy your time with them. This doesn't even imply that you have quit visiting or calling them. What our leaders are emphasizing is that now the team consists of you and your spouse. Other members of the team will be added when you begin to have children. Your parents and in-laws are not necessarily on your team anymore—they have their own team to worry about. Like President Packer said, "You become a separate family on the records of the Church, and that is separation in a very real sense." Therefore, your in-laws/parents are not even your general managers or coaches. From now on, your parents/in-laws take upon themselves the role of cheerleaders! Their job is to cheer you on, encourage you, motivate you, and inspire you. They will be there whenever you need them, day or night, but marriage is a game you must play with them watching from the sidelines—they cannot come into the game and pinch hit whenever you feel tired, weak, or inadequate. Instead, the Lord will help you through all of this. He is always there. Rely on Him for help and strength.

Principle #3: The Apostle Paul taught, "When I was a child, I spake as a child, I understood as a child, I thought as a child: but when I became a man, I put away childish things" (1 Corinthians 13:11). Now that you're married, you are men and women, not boys or girls. You now must "man up" and take responsibility. It is not your parents' responsibility to pay for your housing, food, transportation, tuition, and baby formula. If you are man or woman enough to get married, then you get everything that comes with it, which includes the responsibility of providing for and taking care of each other.

Often, young married couples wish their parents would treat them more like adults. Likewise their parents wish they would act more like adults and be responsible. One seasoned mother made this observation regarding one of her newly married children:

> We would love to treat our married children like adults, but they send us very mixed messages. . . . Just a couple weeks ago, for example, one of our married children said that we needed to treat her and her husband more like adults. She accused us of still treating them like children. My husband and I agreed to treat them more like adults, but the next day they called up and said that they were out of gas and wanted to borrow $20 from us. A few days later they again told us to treat them like adults, but they called that very evening saying that they were hungry and wanted

to come over for dinner. We would love to treat our married children like adults, but they won't act like adults.[143]

Since many youth of this generation have grown up pampered, with little responsibility and work experience underneath their belts, they often feel entitled to have whatever their hardworking parents have. They forget that their parents have worked for decades to acquire some of the wealth and possessions they now enjoy.

If this means you need to take an extra job, work longer hours, or sell some of your belongings, then do it. Previous generations have been willing to do whatever has been required to make ends meet. Many have taken second jobs, worked as night security guards, cut coupons, thrown newspapers, eaten macaroni and cheese, and sold household items to pay their bills.

So be prepared to do whatever it takes, and the Lord will bless you! It may be years before you have a new car, a nice computer, a DVD player, an iPhone, a big-screen television, or a comfortable home. And that's all right. You will find out that one of the greatest times of your married life is the early years when you do not have many material possessions but you have each other—and you have the Lord—and that is all you need!

Managing Parents and In-Laws: Principles to Consider

1. *Discuss with your spouse the role you want your parents and in-laws to have in your marriage.*

   If your in-laws/parents live close by, you may decide you would like to see them every other week. Perhaps you will want them to come eat dinner with you occasionally, and you will most certainly want to eat with them. If your parents/in-laws live far away, you will need to decide how often you will call or Skype them. When you talk to them, will both of you be on the phone or just one? We have three married children. In one family, it is most often our daughter who talks to us. In another family, most often our daughter and her husband talk together. In our son's family, we talk to everyone—him, his wife, their children, and even their pet dog. So it just depends on what each party is comfortable with.

2. *Be guarded, yet deliberate, in what you communicate to your parents/ in-laws.*

   Remember, your parents and in-laws *only* know what you tell them. If you go to them every time you're angry and frustrated and having problems in your marriage, they will remember what you share with them. Furthermore, when you make up with your spouse or solve a problem with one of your children, your parents often don't know that, and they may continue to suppose there is trouble. There have been times when Janie and I have shared with our parents some concerns about our children. The good news is that in most cases, we were able to resolve the problem quite quickly. The bad news is that our parents didn't know that, and we didn't communicate that to them. So five or six months later, our parents were still asking us about problems with our children that no longer existed.

Furthermore, you don't want to portray your spouse or children in a way that would warp your parents' view. You always want your parents to think the best of your family. They will often see your spouse and your children through your eyes. Therefore, build your spouse and children up to your parents; give compliments and praise to your family members in front of your parents/in-laws.

3. *Do not revert into the role of a child when you are around your parents.*

Although this is natural for parents, it should be unnatural for you. You are an adult now, and you are entitled to your opinions, beliefs, and values. Sometimes these beliefs may be contrary to those of your parents/in-laws. For example, in seeing a grandchild act up, a father-in-law said to his son-in-law, "If he was my kid, I would whack his behind." The son-in-law had to speak up and say, "We're not going to spank our one-year-old son just because he's tired and needs a nap." That message surprised the father-in-law, but he got the message.

I have seen many newly married husbands and wives go back to age fourteen when they are with their parents. These newly married children ask questions that are so basic, it could cause parents to doubt the ability of their children. You want your parents and in-laws to see your growth, your maturity, your competence. Constantly reverting to a child when you are with them will cause them unnecessary worry, and they will interfere in your life much more than you will want them too. For some parents, seeing any weakness in their adult children will give them license to come into your life and take over.

So in order to demonstrate your maturity, "man up." Don't allow your parents to pay for everything when they are with you or to run your household while you sit on the couch and watch television. You need to demonstrate your strength and your independence.

4. *Don't blame your spouse for the things their parents do.*

After all, it's not your spouse's fault that his or her parents did something that was offensive or nutty. We will all naturally defend our families when someone attacks them, sometimes even if we know they are wrong. You can make it easier in your marriage by helping your spouse understand that you don't blame them for their parents' weaknesses or mistakes. Console your spouse when their parents do something that is wrong, and work together as a team in resolving the problem. Do not punish your spouse for their parents' transgressions!

5. *Be courteous, show gratitude, and give respect to your parents/in-laws.*

Try not to be critical of your parents/in-laws. Always give them the benefit of the doubt. Learn to focus on the good they do, and ignore the bad. Build a friendship with them. Take the initiative to invite them over for dinner or to call them or to send them a text message. Building a relationship must come from two directions—not just one. Keep in contact with them. In fact, I believe that contact with your parents and in-laws can prevent a multitude of sins.

Occasionally ask them for advice and counsel. After all, they're probably going to give it to you anyway. Ask them how they strengthened their marriage when they were your age or how they raised their children or how they enjoyed serving in the Church or how they remodeled their kitchen or about their view on finances. Call them sometimes just to chat; show genuine interest in their lives.

6. *Set proper boundaries in place.*

Remember, good fences make good neighbors. I have seen many LDS marriages struggle due to a lack of proper boundaries: grandparents harshly disciplining their grandchildren; mother-in-laws talking down to their daughter-in-laws; fathers treating their adult children like little children; mothers asking their newly married daughters to provide intimate details about the newlyweds' sexual life; mother-in-laws feeding the new baby candy when the daughter-in-law was a health-nut; newly married husbands going to their parents' garage, taking whatever he and his wife needed for a camping trip, and never returning any of the "borrowed" equipment; a newly married daughter borrowing money from her parents, promising to pay them back soon, but never doing so. The list goes on and on.

You must have healthy boundaries with your parents and in-laws. Your parents and in-laws cannot simply barge into your lives whenever they feel like it. You must discuss these boundaries and come to some kind of agreement. Likewise, you must also respect your parents'/in-laws' lives as well. They, too, have a life, responsibilities, and needs. The respect between families must flow in both directions. For example, a particular young married woman enjoyed going over to her in-laws' home to relax, watch movies on their big-screen TV, eat their food, and basically make herself at home. Her in-laws were happy because they wanted her to feel at home when she came to visit. However, this young woman had a difficult time returning the favor. Whenever her in-laws came to visit, she could hardly stand it. This young woman didn't want them messing up her apartment; she didn't like it when they ate her food, and she made it clear that she didn't want them sleeping over.[b] Her verbal and nonverbal messages made it clear that their relationship would be a one-way-street. Nevertheless, the parents took the high road and waited patiently for their daughter-in-law to grow up.

Boundaries are only as good as the weakest link on the chain. Therefore, husbands and wives must discuss boundaries and agree to carry them out—together. For example, when one couple had been married just a few months, the wife's mother would often call and ask specific questions about the newlyweds' finances. The inquisitive mother-in-law wanted to know their checkbook balance and how and why they had made certain purchases. Since the wife had grown up with her mother and was used to her intrusiveness, she gave little thought to the prying. However, when the husband found out, he felt extremely uncomfortable and invaded. He sat down with his new wife and explained that he didn't feel it was appropriate for his mother-in-law to know so many intimate details. As a couple, they decided to establish a boundary of what they would share with their parents and what they would keep to themselves. This proved to be useful—especially when this couple's children became teenagers and the overly ambitious mother-in-law still wanted to know more than she needed to.

It is imperative that couples establish these boundaries early on. It is easy to loosen up tight boundaries but almost impossible to tighten up loose boundaries. Consider another experience. Each time a wife's parents came to visit, her mother would take over the kitchen, and her father simply wanted to do repairs on her home. Meanwhile, these grandparents had little to do with their grandchildren. Eventually, after several years of frustration

---

b   She was the antithesis of Goldilocks!

each time the wife's parents would visit, it became time for an intervention. The young couple sat down with her parents and explained that they would really enjoy it if the grandparents spent time with the grandchildren when they visited. This would give the parents a break and allow the grandparents to develop relationships with their grandchildren. The parents retorted that they just wanted to "help their daughter." Their daughter then explained, "Mom and Dad, this is the very best way you could help me." *This points to a common problem: most parents want to help their married children, but they want to help in their own way—on their own terms—taking no thought of what their children may really need.* Since these particular parents were task oriented, they wanted to help by doing things for their married daughter. However, taking over the kitchen and replacing light bulbs is not what their daughter needed—she needed her children to have a relationship with their grandparents! When this couple communicated their need to their parents, their lives became more fulfilling and less complicated.

Years ago, President Hugh B. Brown wrote, "As each new marriage craft sets sail, there should be a warning call, which is familiar to all ocean travelers, 'All ashore that's going ashore,' whereupon all in-laws should get off the matrimonial boat and return only at infrequent intervals and then only as invited guests for brief visits."[144] As couples begin to sail across the Sea of Life—complete with wind, waves, and storms as well as beautiful views and amazing experiences—they will learn to rely on each other and solve problems together. They will learn to rely upon each other's gifts, talents, and strengths—something they couldn't do if they were sailing on their parents' boat or even being towed behind them. They will also learn to rely on the Lord as they turn to Him in good weather as well as the bad. Sailing across the Sea of Life, they will have plenty of opportunities to develop faith in the Lord and in each other. Although some of the winds and waves they encounter will be difficult, these experiences will help them forge their character and establish their identity as a couple.

Homework:
- As a couple, write down some of the strengths of both of your parents. Share your list with each other.
- Next, write down some of the weaknesses or challenges you have with your parents/in-laws. How could you resolve some of these challenges? What would be some healthy boundaries to establish between you and your parents/in-laws?

Additional Readings:

- President Spencer W. Kimball, "Marriage and Divorce," *BYU Speeches*, 7 September 1976.
- Richard B. Miller, "For Newlyweds and Their Parents," *Ensign*, Jan 2006, 27–31.
- Patricia Russell, "Building Good In-Law Relationships," *Ensign*, March 2000.

References

138 Brent A. Barlow, *Just for Newlyweds* (Salt Lake City: Deseret Book, 1992), 87.

139 Spencer W. Kimball, *The Miracle of Forgiveness* (Salt Lake City: Deseret Book, 1969), 250.

140 Boyd K. Packer, *That All May Be Edified*,(Salt Lake City: Bookcraft, 1982), 227.

141 Spencer W. Kimball, *Marriage and Divorce: An Address* (Salt Lake City: Deseret Book, 1976), 25.

142 Boyd K. Packer, "Family Togetherness—The Core of the Church," *BYU Education Week Devotional Address*, 13 June 1963, 3; as cited in Gerald N. Lund, *Selected Writings of Gerald N. Lund: Gospel Scholar Series* (Salt Lake City: Deseret Book, 1999), 108.

143 Richard B. Miller, "For Newlyweds and Their Parents," *Ensign*, Jan 2006, 27–31.

144 Hugh B. Brown, *You and Your Marriage* (Salt Lake City: Bookcraft, 1960), 138.

CHAPTER 14
Applying Christlike Virtues in Marriage

"To follow Christ is to become more like Him. It is to learn from His character. As spirit children of our Heavenly Father, we do have the potential to incorporate Christlike attributes into our life and character."
-President Dieter F. Uchtdorf[145]

WHEN I WAS A BOY, my dad took my brother and me fishing to the Gulf of Mexico. Our boat had a small cabin that could sleep several of us comfortably. The first night of our fishing excursion, my dad dropped the small anchor to keep the boat from drifting aimlessly in the ocean as we slept. However, during the course of the night, a large freighter ship drove past our relatively small boat. The wake of the ship moved our boat a significant distance from our comfortable spot. When we awoke in the morning, our boat was a long way from where we originally dropped the anchor. As it turned out, our tiny anchor was no match for the huge waves the ship created. That morning, my dad learned that if you want to keep your boat steady, you need to have a much larger anchor or at least be anchored to something more solid than a sandy ocean bottom.

Today we live in turbulent times, and unless we anchor ourselves to something fixed and solid, our marriages may not survive the cross currents, riptides, and waves that life is sure to bring. In a Christ-centered marriage, we anchor ourselves to the Savior by our faith, our covenants, and our obedience to gospel principles. That doesn't mean everything will work out perfectly or that we'll never have difficulties. In every marriage, there will be trials and challenges. However, with the help of Christ, we can overcome every test that comes our way. When we are anchored to the Savior, we can exercise faith, hope, and charity—and those attributes will strengthen every disciple of Jesus Christ. President Howard W. Hunter declared, "I am aware that life presents many challenges, but with the help of the Lord, we need not fear. If our lives . . . are centered upon Jesus

Christ . . . nothing can ever go permanently wrong. On the other hand, if our lives are not centered on the Savior and his teachings, no other success can be permanently right."[146]

Relationships Built on a Sure Foundation

From "The Family: A Proclamation to the World" we learn that "Happiness in family life is most likely to be achieved when founded upon the teachings of the Lord Jesus Christ."[147] What does it mean to have a marriage built on the foundation of Christ? In such a marriage, both husbands and wives practice Christlike virtues. Couples who center their lives on Christ are slow to remember the transgressions of their spouse and are quick to forgive. Christlike men and women practice mercy and compassion. In a Christ-centered marriage, couples pray together regularly in order to call down the powers of heaven; they read consistently from good Church literature including the scriptures and Church magazines. They gain spiritual strength by attending the temple often. When President Thomas S. Monson and his wife, Frances, were sealed in the Salt Lake Temple years ago, Benjamin Bowring (great name for a temple sealer, derived from "bow" and "ring"), offered the following counsel:

> May I offer you newlyweds a formula which will ensure that any disagreement you may have will last no longer than one day? Every night kneel by the side of your bed. One night, Brother Monson, you offer the prayer, aloud, on bended knee. The next night, you, Sister Monson, offer the prayer, aloud, on bended knee. I can then assure you that any misunderstanding that develops during the day will vanish as you pray. You simply can't pray together and retain any but the best of feelings toward one another.[148]

A couple who has built their foundation on the Savior also serves in the Church and assists their fellow men. They have stripped themselves of pride and envy and seek to put each other's needs before their own. Such a couple can be found practicing selflessness and meekness. President Kimball described such a couple this way:

> When a husband and wife go together frequently to the holy temple, kneel in prayer together in their home with their family, go hand in hand to their religious meetings, keep their lives wholly chaste, mentally and physically . . . and both are working together

for the upbuilding of the kingdom of God, then happiness is at its pinnacle.[149]

As I have worked with many husbands and wives over the past twenty-five years in my counseling practice, I feel comfortable estimating that more than 90 percent of the couples I have counseled did *not* follow President Kimball's counsel. They were *not* attending the temple, they were *not* attending their religious meetings, they were *not* living wholly chaste lives, and they were *not* working together in building the kingdom as they served their families first and then the Church. Consequently, they were *not* happy. Yes, initially the Savior was a part of their marriage; as a newly married couple, they were following President Kimball's counsel and living the gospel. But for some reason that all changed. Perhaps they became lazy or selfish or sinful. For whatever reason, these men and women shut off the flow of the Spirit, and subsequently, the life-blood of their marriage was gone.

Such marriages need not be. The good news is that if your marriage is off track, you can change. You can put things back together. You can invite the Savior back into your lives and marriage by doing that which He commands us to do. He can heal you and your marriage, and He can bless you again as He did at the beginning of your relationship.

The True Center

If our lives are centered on the Church, we will fall short and be frustrated when things get in the way of our Church responsibilities. If we choose to center our lives on our family, we may neglect our spiritual responsibilities altogether. The life centered on God and Christ is the only *sure center* available to man. With this kind of focus, we will never make a wrong decision with our family or the Church. Furthermore, despite all the trials life throws at us, we know that our Heavenly Father and His Son, Jesus Christ, will always be there for us. They have always been there, and They always will be. No matter how sore the struggle or the challenge, the Savior will never desert us—He is the one constant in our lives.

Seeing the world through the Savior's eyes, walking where He would walk, saying what He would say, and touching the lives He would touch—that is what it means to live a Christlike life. Paul exhorted the Corinthian Saints to possess the "mind of Christ" (1 Corinthians 2:16). Elder Bruce R. McConkie explained that having the mind of Christ is "to believe what He believes, think what He thinks, say what He says, and do what He does. It is to be one with Him by the power of the Holy Ghost."[150] Our thoughts govern our behaviors; by changing our thoughts, we can have the power to change our behaviors. If our thoughts are centered on the Savior, we obtain the power to behave like the Savior. Think of how the world would be different if married couples possessed the mind of the Savior.

A few years ago after an Education Week presentation, Dr. Brent Barlow related that a young man and his wife approached him and asked to talk. The man was a member of the Church in his early thirties who was a successful executive. He often worked sixty to seventy hours per week. His job also required him to travel a great deal during the week and on weekends. So besides not spending time with his family, he was missing church as well.

At first he tried to attend church at wards in the cities where he had to conduct business, but after a time he stopped making the effort. He became involved with a woman colleague at his office, spending a great deal of time with her. At first the relationship was supposedly businesslike and professional, but then they became emotionally attached to each other. A sexual encounter loomed as a likely possibility. Then, about the time he was promoted to the high-salaried position he was aspiring to, his wife filed for divorce.

The young executive said he made several attempts at reconciliation. He reluctantly agreed to see their bishop, who suggested that they needed professional counseling. That avenue was pursued but to no avail—the damage had apparently been done. They finally entered the waiting period before their divorce would be final.

The husband became a little tearful as he continued his story. He realized that he would lose his young wife by divorce and that subsequently his relationship with his little daughter would be limited. The divorce and final separation seemed inevitable.

So he made a decision. As a priesthood holder and returned missionary, he still wanted to retain his membership in the Church and reestablish his relationship with the Savior. In essence, he decided not so much to "come unto Christ" as to "return to Christ." During the few weeks before the finalization of the divorce, he began praying alone and fasting periodically. He stopped seeing and traveling with the woman at his office. He attended his priesthood and other church meetings regularly for the first time in several months. He started to study the gospel and get more involved in service. He examined his heart and tried to bring spirituality into his life.

He did all these things fully expecting that his wife and child would soon leave him. But unknown to him, his wife was observing him. (As he was telling me about this episode in their lives, she was holding on to his arm, also in tears.)

The wife then continued the story. She said she noted some sincere and genuine changes in him as he tried drawing closer to the Lord. When the time came for her to sign the final divorce papers, she called her attorney and said that she was going to delay the action another thirty days.

The husband made major adjustments with his employment, even taking a cut in pay. He had realized the significance of the statement, "For what is a man profited, if he shall gain the whole world, and lose his own soul [and wife and daughter]? or what shall a man give in exchange for his soul?" (Matthew 16:26). By the time the thirty days was up, the wife had decided not to sign the divorce papers.

Although their marriage nearly ended in divorce, the couple experienced something more important than their troubles as they began to center their lives on the Savior, His teachings, and His Church.[151]

There is a tremendous power in the gospel of Jesus Christ. God can heal and strengthen *any* family relationship. Couples who rely on the Lord and make Him a part of their marriage have the added strength and power that come from the Atonement. Because of the Savior's love, mercy, and forgiveness demonstrated to these individuals, they will in turn treat their partner in a similar fashion.

Developing Christlike Character Traits

When couples fail to center their relationship on the teachings of the Master, they have no promise or guarantee that things will work out. In fact, they don't even have the resources to correct their course. Without the Lord's Spirit, the power to be kind and compassionate is almost impossible. In such marriages, the "natural man" ultimately takes over, and the relationship begins to deteriorate. Kindness, charity, meekness, and forgiveness are fruits of the Spirit. When couples engage in selfish and prideful activities, they lose the Spirit, and thus they lose the ability to treat each other as the Savior would. Individuals without the Spirit become sarcastic, angry, critical, defensive, and uncaring. On the other hand, when we understand the eternal purpose of marriage and that the Savior is central to the relationship, the Spirit of the Lord is present and so is the ability to acquire and practice His attributes. When we begin to think as He thinks and behave as He behaves, it is amazing what we can accomplish as a married couple. When we take time to develop Christlike character traits, the Holy Ghost will be with us to inspire us and teach us how to act and what to say. The Spirit will infuse us with power and strength, and with the Lord's help, our marriage can be happy, joyful, fulfilling, and healing.

In Doctrine and Covenants 4, we learn some of the Savior's attributes: faith, virtue, knowledge, temperance, patience, brotherly kindness, godliness, charity, humility, and diligence (D&C 4:6). These are also the traits of our Heavenly Father. We are His sons and daughters. Because of our covenant relationship with the Savior and our literal relationship with our Heavenly Father, we have those traits too. They are in us! We have inherited them. Now we must find ways to discover those gifts and use them. The Lord will help us if we ask Him.

Christ-Centered Attributes
Although there are many Christlike traits that could heal any marriage, I would like to focus on five. If these virtues are practiced, I believe almost any marriage can be strengthened, transformed, and healed. You will discover that as you apply these attributes into your life, you will change and become a more devoted disciple. The Savior's attributes deepen our conversion and help us to become more like Him.

1. Commitment: The life of our Savior, Jesus Christ, was evidence of His commitment to 1) His Father and 2) to us. When Christ appeared to the Nephites, we learn that He "suffered the will of the Father in all things" (3 Nephi 11:11). Put another way, Jesus was so wholly committed that He did every single thing asked of Him. His commitment was so strong that His Father's will became His will too. Jesus was so completely committed to us that He was willing to carry out His pre-earth pledge to be our Savior, even when He learned how painful and difficult it would be. Jesus also expects us to be committed. He said, "If any man will come after me, let him deny himself, and take up his cross daily, and follow me" (Luke 9:23; see also Matthew 19:21; Mark 1:18; John 14:15). Likewise, we need to become committed to our eternal companions.

Commitment is always the first foundation stone for a strong marriage. Commitment implies staying power, strength, and endurance. Couples who marry in the temple are committed for "the long haul." For those married in the temple, this permanent commitment is really a covenant. Not only do we pledge ourselves to each other for eternity, but we are also committed to our Father in Heaven.

Committed couples will enjoy the good times in marriage—when life seems to be going well, when there is plenty of money in the bank, when both spouses enjoy good health, when the children are pleasant to live with. However, the true test of commitment is when life goes sour—the health of a spouse is compromised, there is tremendous financial strain on the marriage, or the children are driving you bonkers. In a covenant marriage, couples work together and make God the center of their lives. When troubles come, they cling to each other and to their Heavenly Father. The thought of exiting the marriage when times get tough does not exist. In such a marriage, couples are bound to each other and to God. Couples who are committed will be faithful to each other, put each other first in their lives, work with each other, solve their problems together, help each other and build each other up, teach each other, learn from each other, and stand side by side—no matter what!

In order for a marriage to work, you cannot have one eye on the exit door. You cannot always be looking for an out. If you are committed to your spouse, you will not be looking for an excuse to pull the plug. You cannot throw the "D" word around like confetti, and you can't be halfway invested. No marriage will succeed with one foot in and one foot out. Commitment in marriage must be revisited. Renewing our commitment must take place over and over again. Couples must also be committed to improvement and growing their marriage. It is not enough to base your love on how you felt about each other two years ago. How do you feel about your marriage today?

Some of you may remember Christopher Reeve[a] and his experience of being thrown from a horse, landing on his head, and consequently being sentenced to a life as a quadriplegic. Five days after the accident, he was coherent enough to understand the extent of his injuries. The doctors explained that he would need to undergo a surgical procedure to reconnect his skull to the top of his spine. This procedure was extremely risky, and the medical team explained that there was a chance he wouldn't survive the surgery. Chris told the doctors that he felt he should go forward with the operation.

As Chris began to ponder the gravity of his situation and a future life in a wheelchair, his wife, Dana, came into his hospital room. In his words,

---

a   Those from my generation will remember Christopher Reeve in his role as Superman.

We made eye contact. I mouthed my first lucid words to her: "Maybe we should let me go."

She said, "I am only going to say this once: I will support whatever you want to do because this is your life and your decision. But I want you to know that I'll be with you for the long haul, no matter what." Then she added the words that saved my life: "You're still you. And I love you."

If she had looked away or paused or hesitated even slightly, or if I had felt there was a sense of her being noble or fulfilling some obligation to me, I don't know if I could have pulled through. Because it had dawned on me that I had ruined my life and everybody else's. But what Dana said made living seem possible because I felt the depth of her love and commitment. I was even able to make a little joke. I mouthed, "This is way beyond the marriage vows—in sickness and in health." And she said, "I know." I knew then that she was going to be with me forever.[152]

2. Compassion: One of the Savior's most unmistakable traits was the compassion He demonstrated to others. In the scriptures, there is evidence that compassion means to "suffer with" or show empathy. Jesus was certainly empathetic as the illnesses and sore predicaments of many individuals touched His heart. Jesus was often "moved with compassion" (Matthew 9:36) before He healed the sick or helped someone in despair. Jesus Christ was the Good Samaritan; His mission was to strengthen the weak, heal the sick, comfort those who lost loved ones, feed the hungry, find the lost, forgive the sinner, and lift the burdens of the overwhelmed.

If we want to follow the Savior's example, we must do likewise in our marriages. We should try to lift the burdens of our spouses as well as heal, strengthen, and provide comfort and rest. We should be more concerned about our spouse than we are ourselves; we empathize with and try to understand what our loved one is going through. We should try to connect with our spouse's feelings of fatigue, frustration, and sometimes even failure. The truly empathetic spouse can feel a partner's pain and distress and will do anything possible to help relieve those burdens.

President Gordon B. Hinckley expanded this idea when he taught, "I am satisfied that a happy marriage is not so much a matter of romance as it is an anxious concern for the comfort and well-being of one's companion."[153] In Matthew 7:12, we read: "Therefore all things whatsoever ye would that men should do to you, do ye even so to them: for this is the law and the prophets." We call this the golden rule. In the context of marriage and family relationships, we are to treat our spouse and children how we would like them to treat us. This is one of the most successful formulas for any relationship—it works especially well in marriage.

Even so, there is a still a higher law, also found in the book of Matthew: "Inasmuch as ye have done it unto one of the least of these my brethren, ye have done it unto me" (25:40). I call this the Platinum Rule. It is not enough to treat others as we expect to be treated—the Golden Rule. The Platinum Rule expands that concept and teaches that we must treat others as if they were the Savior—and that includes the way we treat our spouse. Although this is a lofty ideal, it should be something you consider and put into practice. This is a celestial law; thus, all who live it will reap celestial rewards.

The Prophet Joseph Smith declared, "It is the duty of a husband to love, cherish, and nourish his wife, and cleave unto her and none else; he ought to honor her as himself, and he ought to regard her feelings with tenderness."[154] Joseph further taught the women of the Church, "When you go home, never give a cross or unkind word to your husbands, but let kindness, charity, and love crown your works henceforward."[155]

On one occasion, Joseph Smith had a conversation with Jesse Crosby regarding marriage. Joseph came to the Crosby home to return a sack of flour he had borrowed. Jesse was concerned that Joseph did too much "women's work" around the house. He had observed Joseph building kitchen fires, carrying out ashes, carrying in wood and water, caring for the children, and a host of other indoor activities. In Jesse's opinion, a man could lose his self-respect by doing such "menial chores," and the fact that Joseph was a prophet and leader of the Church just made matters worse. Therefore, Jesse confronted Joseph on these matters.

From Jesse's own account, he stated:

> The Prophet listened quietly to all I had to say, then made his answer in these words: "If there be humiliation in a man's house, who but the head of that house should or could bear that humiliation?"
>
> Sister Crosby was a very hardworking woman, taking much more responsibility in her home than most women take. Thinking to give the Prophet some light on home management, I said to him, "Brother Joseph, my wife does much more hard work than does your wife."

Brother Joseph replied by telling me that if a man cannot learn in this life to appreciate a wife and do his duty to her, in properly taking care of her, he need not expect to be given one in the hereafter.

His words shut my mouth as tight as a clam. I took them as terrible reproof. After that I tried to do better by the good wife I had and tried to lighten her labors.[156]

Jesse learned from Joseph what it means to be a compassionate marriage partner. Joseph further taught that husbands and wives "should be . . . companions, the nearest and dearest objects on earth in every sense of the word. He said men should beware how they treat their wives. . . . He also said many would awake on the morning of the resurrection sadly disappointed; for they, by transgression, would have neither wives nor children."[157]

When we have the Spirit in our lives, we can emulate the Savior and do what He would do. We can follow His loving and kind example and apply His compassionate teachings to our marriages. That is one way to bless and nurture a spouse.

3. Communication: Jesus was a positive, kind, and loving communicator; He spoke kind, healing, and edifying words to His disciples. In His communication, we know from the scriptures that He was loving (John 15:12), kind (Acts 10:38), slow to condemn (John 8:10–11), and non-judgmental (Matthew 7:1). Let's face it; Jesus wouldn't have been able to attract many followers if He was abrasive, rude, and flat-out mean to people.

When Jesus spoke, I imagine that love radiated from His words. I am sure He also communicated with meekness and humility. The Apostle Paul taught, "Let no corrupt communication proceed out of your mouth, but that which is good to the use of edifying, that it may minister grace unto the hearers" (Ephesians 4:29). I imagine Christ lived by that principle.

Most individuals understand the need for healthy communication in marriage. Communication is the means for building strong relationships. In fact, it has been identified as one of the most crucial skills for a happy and successful marriage.

For communication to be meaningful, couples must connect on an emotional level; hence, communication must be more than just sharing words and ideas. If couples want to move their marriages from the superficial to the deeper levels of communication, they must learn to converse the way Christ did. This is what it means to communicate with our spouse in Christlike ways. When talking to our spouse, we must learn that the way we speak and the words we say should be similar to what Christ would say if He were there.

4. Consideration: Jesus Christ was always aware of the needs and circumstance of the people who surrounded Him. Christ was sensitive to how others felt. For example, in 3 Nephi 17, Jesus had just taught the Nephites for a full day, and He was ready to return "unto the Father, and also to show myself unto the lost tribes of Israel" (17:4). What could be more important than to meet with Heavenly Father and the lost tribes of Israel? However, being sensitive to the needs of His followers, Jesus "cast his eyes round about again on the multitude, and beheld they were in tears, and did look steadfastly upon him as if they would ask him to tarry a little longer with them" (3 Nephi 17:5). Our Savior placed His own agenda to the side and met the needs of His disciples. He healed their sick, ministered to them, worshipped with them; angels came down from heaven. This proved to be one of the most significant spiritual experiences in the Book of Mormon, and it all happened because of our Savior's care and sensitivity.

In marriage, consideration is demonstrated when we think about the needs and feelings of our spouse before our own. The considerate marriage partner seeks to eliminate problems instead of causing them. Considerate partners are sensitive to their partners' needs and challenges, anticipating how to be helpful and remove burdens.

President Spencer W. Kimball taught that for a marriage to be successful there must be "continued courting and expressions of affection, kindness, and consideration to keep love alive and growing."[158] Brigham Young taught that we should treat our spouses the same way "an angel would treat them."[159] President David O. McKay taught, "Let us teach our young men to enter into matrimony with the idea that each will be just as courteous and considerate of a wife after the ceremony as during courtship. . . . Let them remember that gentleness and consideration after the ceremony is just as appropriate and necessary and beautiful as gentleness and consideration before the wedding."[160]

Consideration also includes continued dating and courtship, attempts to keep the marriage fun and exciting, and demonstrating how you cherish each other throughout your lives. Moreover, husbands and wives need to take care of each other, even when it is not convenient. One of the great love stories in The Church of Jesus Christ of Latter-day Saints was modeled by Howard and Claire Hunter. When the Hunters were in their seventies, Claire's health began to deteriorate. She developed a blood clot in her brain that led to several strokes and other medical problems. Despite his busy and demanding schedule as an Apostle, Howard would visit his wife in the hospital or at home several times daily. Ultimately, one of Claire's lungs collapsed, and the strokes rendered her unable to talk and walk. Nevertheless, Howard cared for Claire for ten years. All she could do was occasionally smile at him—that was their only mode of communication.

When Howard returned home from the Church Office Building or a trip, he would enter their home, find Claire, and would stand her up out of her wheelchair, hold her tightly, and spin her around to dance with her as they had done so many years before. He also took her regularly to her favorite hair dresser, and even though she could not communicate, he would talk to her and tell her about his day and share news with her about family and friends.[161]

At Claire's funeral, Elder James E. Faust, speaking about Howard and Claire, said, "The tenderness which was evident in their communication was heart rending and touching. I have never seen such an example of devotion of a husband to his wife. It has been a many-splendored love affair."[162]

Each us of can find joy in placing our spouse's needs before our own and ministering to them the same way that Christ would. Being considerate helps us overcome our own selfishness and pride, and draws us closer to the Savior.

5. Character: You may be baffled that I mention character as a Christlike attribute. However, never have my mind and heart been more influenced by a talk than the one Elder David A. Bednar gave entitled "The Character of Christ." In that message, Elder Bednar cited example after example from the scriptures of the Savior constantly turning outward when most of us would turn inward. Or, in other words, when most of us encounter a crisis, our immediate reaction is to circle the wagons and take care of ourselves. However, that is not what the Savior did. Consider one example:

In Matthew 4:1–11, Jesus experiences the three great temptations. We know from verses 1–2 that Christ has been fasting for forty days, and then Satan came to Him 1) with the temptation to turn stones to bread—thus enticing Jesus to satisfy his hunger, 2) with the temptation to leap off the pinnacle of the temple and land in the courtyard below—therefore inviting Jesus to gain a host of followers by dazzling them with a miracle or two, and 3) with the temptation to have all of the kingdoms of the world—thus enticing Jesus with the riches of this earth. Of course, Christ was able to resist each temptation by quoting a scripture to Satan.

Finally, in verse 11, we learn Satan left and angels came and ministered to Christ. Having angels appear to Jesus to strengthen Him sounds wonderful. After all, Christ was probably weak and exhausted after forty days of fasting and then dealing with Satan in such a direct way. However, that is *not* what happened. A careful look at the Joseph Smith Translation for verse 11 indicates that Christ "knew that John [the Baptist] was cast into prison, and he sent angels, and, behold, they came and ministered unto him (John)" (Joseph Smith Translation, Matthew 4:11 [in Matthew 4:11, footnote *a*]). In one of His direst hours, instead of being worried about Himself, Jesus was thinking of someone else. In this case, His mind and heart were directed to His cousin John, who had been imprisoned. Examples such as this can be found through all of the scriptures.

Elder Bednar continued to expand on Christ's character when he taught,

> One of the greatest indicators of righteous character is the capacity to recognize and appropriately respond to other people who are experiencing the very challenge or adversity that is most immediately and forcefully pressing upon us. Character is revealed, for example, in the power to discern the suffering of other people when we ourselves are suffering; in the ability to detect the hunger of others when we are hungry; and in the power to reach out and extend compassion for the spiritual agony of others when we are in the midst of our own spiritual distress. Therefore, character is demonstrated by looking, turning, and reaching outward when the instinctive response of the "natural man" (Mosiah 3:19) in each of us is to turn inward and to be selfish and self-absorbed. And the Savior of the world is the source, the standard, and the ultimate criterion of moral character and the perfect example of charity and consistency.[163]

Other examples include Christ forgiving those who crucified Him while He hung on the cross; healing the ear of Malchus as He was being dragged away from the Garden of Gethsemane by Roman soldiers; and promising a Comforter who would deliver peace to His disciples, just before He was about to be tortured. No matter how much He suffered and no matter how unfair life was, the Savior always looked outward instead of inward.

As I have contemplated these accounts in the scriptures, I was reminded of my mission president—L. Dale Hanks. More than twenty years after his return home from being a mission president, President Hanks was diagnosed with an extremely aggressive form of stomach cancer. He was told he only had a month or two to live. How would you react to such a diagnosis? Would you cry? Would you become hysterical right in the doctor's office? Would you throw things across the room? My mission president calmly walked down the hallway of the hospital, stopping at rooms and asking sick patients if they would like a priesthood blessing. President Hanks was more focused on the needs and troubles of those around him than his own significant personal problem.

How do we demonstrate character in marriage? Perhaps we could be kind to our spouse when we are angry or don't feel well. Maybe we could be show happiness and optimism toward our spouse when we are tired or exhausted. We show character when we feel we have been dealt with unfairly by our spouse but we give kindness and respect in return. Perhaps we could exhibit Christlike character when we have pressing deadlines and needs but we put our spouse's needs ahead of our own.

As previously mentioned, Stephen R. Covey taught that if we have a Christ-centered marriage, then we follow Christ's example. "If the God/Christ-centered person is offended, he blesses in return. He returns kindness for unkindness, patience for impatience. . . . If the person is praised, he gives thanks. If he is blamed, he appraises the matter to see whether there may be some blameworthiness in him, and if there is, he plans self-improvement."[164]

On the evening of December 29, 1876, the Pacific Express—a two-engine, eleven-car train—was travelling through Ohio during a heavy winter snowstorm. Among other passengers on board was a man named Phillip Paul Bliss and his wife, Lucy. Phillip was a Christian songwriter, and he and Lucy had been married over seventeen years.

About seven thirty p.m., as the train crossed a trestle bridge over the Ashtabula River, the bridge gave way, and all eleven cars plummeted into the icy river below. As water pressed up from the broken ice, the wooden cars, heated by kerosene stoves, were engulfed in flames.[b]

According to an eyewitness when the train fell,

---

b   Incidentally, the train wrecked just one hundred yards from the railroad station.

Phillip Bliss freed himself and successfully crawled through a window. However, when he turned around to free his wife from the train, she was trapped in the ironwork of the seats. Rather than escape, Phillip devotedly stayed by Lucy's side in an attempt to free her before they were both engulfed and consumed in the flames. Ninety other people were killed or later died in the Ashtabula River railroad disaster, the worst such incident in American history to that point in time.[165]

Even though Phillip Paul Bliss was not a member of the Church, several of his hymns appear in our current hymnbook. One of those hymns you will easily recognize—"More Holiness Give Me." At the most stressful time of his entire life, Phillip Bliss demonstrated perfect integrity by living true to his message and his beliefs.[166]

Although this story is dramatic, it begs the question, "Would I be willing to do such a thing for my spouse?" You will if your life is marked by selflessness, kindness, and charity. Most of us will not have to give our lives in a train accident to prove our love to our spouse. However, each of us can demonstrate our love and keep the romantic flame alive in our marriages by doing selfless acts of service daily.

Homework:
- How will you begin to practice living a Christ-centered life?
- Of the five attributes mentioned, which one do you feel you need to work on right now? Where do you need the most improvement?
- Ask your spouse which trait they feel you should work on now.

Additional Readings:
- Merrill J. Bateman, "Living a Christ-Centered Life," *Ensign*, January 1999.
- David A. Bednar, "Developing Christlike Characteristics," *BYU Hawaii Devotional,* 30 January 2003.
- David A. Bednar, "The Character of Christ," Brigham Young University—Idaho Religion Symposium, 25 January 2003, 2; See also *Act in Doctrine* (Salt Lake City: Deseret Book, 2012).
- Richard G. Scott, "The Atonement Can Secure Your Peace and Happiness," *Ensign*, November 2006, 40–42.

References

145 Dieter F. Uchtdorf, *Conference Report*, October 2005, 107.

146 Howard W. Hunter, *Brigham Young University 1988–89 Devotional and Fireside Speeches* (Provo, Utah: University Publications, 1989), 112.

147 "The Family: A Proclamation to the World"; www.lds.org/topics/family-proclamation.

148 Thomas S. Monson, "Hallmarks of a Happy Home," *Ensign*, November 1988, 70.

149 Spencer W. Kimball, *Marriage and Divorce: An Address* (Salt Lake City: Deseret Book, 1976), 24.

150 Bruce R. McConkie, *A New Witness for the Articles of Faith,* (Salt Lake City: Deseret Book, 1985), 206.

151 Brent A. Barlow, *Dealing with Differences in Marriage* (Salt Lake City: Deseret Book, 1993), 121–123.

152 Jack Canfield, Mark Victor Hansen, Mark & Chrissy Donnelly, & Barbara De Angelis, *Chicken Soup for the Couple's Soul* (Deerfield Beach, Florida: Healthfield Communications, Inc., 1999), 104–105.

153 Gordon B. Hinckley, "What God Hath Joined Together," *Ensign*, May 1991, 73.

154 Joseph Smith, *Elders' Journal* 1:61–62; as cited in *Encyclopedia of Joseph Smith's Teachings*, eds. D.Q. Cannon & L.H. Dahl (Salt Lake City: Bookcraft, 1997), 410.

155 Ibid, 368.

156 Words of Jesse W. Crosby, as cited in *They Knew the Prophet*, eds. H.L. Andrus & H.M. Andrus (Salt Lake City: Deseret Book, 1974), 145.

157 Ibid, 140.

158 Spencer W. Kimball, *Marriage and Divorce: An Address* (Salt Lake City, Utah: Deseret Book, 1976), 17.

159 Brigham Young, *Discourses of Brigham Young*, ed. John A. Widtsoe (Salt Lake City: Deseret Book, 1954), 197–198.

160 David O. McKay, *Gospel Ideals* (Salt Lake City: Deseret Book, 1953), 471–72.

161 Eleanor Knowles, *Howard W. Hunter* (Salt Lake City: Deseret Book, 1994), 268.

162 Ibid, 271.

163 David A. Bednar, *Act in Doctrine* (Salt Lake City: Deseret Book, 2012), 8.

164 Stephen R. Covey, *The Divine Center* (Salt Lake City: Bookcraft, 1982), 145.

165 Brad Neiger, *Brigham Young University 2005–2006 Speeches*, (Provo, Utah: Intellectual Reserve, 2006), 460.

166 Ibid.

CHAPTER 15
Keeping Your Marriage Strong

"True love and happiness in courtship and marriage are based upon honesty, self-respect, sacrifice, consideration, courtesy, kindness, and placing 'we' ahead of 'me.'"
-Elder Marvin J. Ashton[167]

MARRIAGE IS MOST OFTEN VIEWED in the media, academia, and social circles from a deficit perspective. That is, we most often talk about what is wrong with marriage, rather than what is right about it. Husbands and wives are free to discuss why their marriage stinks, researchers and clinicians focus on marriage problems, and television rarely portrays marriage in a positive light. Our nation is losing faith in marriage—the bedrock of our society. When marriage erodes, family life and personal happiness will be greatly diminished. Without marriage, individuals and families are is filled with heartache, suffering, distress, poverty, poor health, stress, and uncertainty.

As members of The Church of Jesus Christ of Latter-day Saints, we believe that "marriage is ordained of God and that the family is central to the Creator's plan for the eternal destiny of His children."[168] We also believe that "Marriage between a man and a woman is essential to His eternal plan."[169] We must be defenders of the faith, which includes defending marriage and family life. Our first and greatest contribution to defending marriage is to be happily married! Latter-day Saints should be shining examples when it comes to marriage and family life. We have been given everything we need to be successful in marriage: the scriptures, the teachings of latter-day prophets, the temple, and the examples of those who have gone before us. If we use these resources, we should be able to navigate the matrimonial seas with success.

As I conclude this book, I would like to share twelve principles that will strengthen any marriage. These principles and concepts do not originate from me. Instead, they come from years of research that has been replicated over and over again. In short, what researchers have discovered is that the most successful couples in America have incorporated these principles into their marriages.

1. Be totally committed to your marriage and your marriage partner.

Commitment is the foundation where every other element of the marriage must rest. Without commitment, there is no marriage. In my private practice, I have seen couples whose marriages were in shambles. However, I have been able to tell such couples with confidence, "Your marriage is in very terrible shape right now. However, if there is one thing you have, it is commitment. Because you have commitment, your marriage is going to improve."

On the other hand, if there is no commitment, the marriage has no chance. I have also seen couples where either the husband or wife was not fully invested in saving the marriage. In every case, those marriages have ended in divorce. In a marriage, you must be committed to several things: 1) to God, 2) to each other, 3) to your families, and 4) to constantly growing and improving the marriage.

I met with a man several years ago. He was the cause of most of the problems in his marriage but was unwilling to admit that. He never wanted to change or improve. He simply wanted his wife to meet his demands, and that was it. Since he owned his own business, one day I asked him, "Do you try to improve your business each year?"

He said, "What do you mean?"

I pressed further, "Do you sit down at the end of the year, take an inventory of where your business needs to improve and change, and then put a plan in action to improve your business?"

He said, "Actually, I do that about every six months."

I said, "Great. Why don't you do that in your marriage every month?"

He said, "Because I think my wife should just accept me as I am, and if she cannot, then the heck with it."

Needless to say, that marriage didn't last. If we want our marriages to endure, we must set our priorities straight and put as much time and energy into our relationship as we do our other passions.

Here are some behaviors to practice to strengthen your commitment to the marriage:

- Never look at anyone of the opposite sex with lustful eyes, and never seek to have your needs met from another person outside of your marriage and family.

- Back your commitment up with actions, not words. If your wife is the most important thing in your life, then demonstrate that by placing her first on your priority list. If your husband is most important to you, then show that by the way you treat him.
- Spend time together, do fun things together, and constantly make time to heal and strengthen your marriage. You can't say that your marriage is the most important thing in your life and yet never do anything together and let everything else come first.

Commitment suggests staying power. When trouble arises in the marriage, leaving or bailing out is never in question. The late LDS psychologist Victor Cline wrote, "In many years of working with couples and families in conflict I have come to the conclusion that the single most important predictor of a couple's making their marriage last and avoiding the divorce court is commitment—not compatibility."[170] Couples who are committed put each other first, and they demonstrate that by their actions.

2. Practice honesty, trust, and fidelity in your marriage.

We live in a world where it is extremely easy not to trust a spouse. Sometimes both men and women travel often with their employment. Pornography has saturated the Internet. Women are involved in activities that more often pull them out of the home. As a marriage therapist, every affair I have dealt with has been based on lies and deceit. That is where the problem originated. The happiest marriages are built on a high degree of honesty and trust. Make it a practice to tell the truth; always let your spouse know where you are and what you are doing. Nothing will destroy a marriage quicker than lies, half-truths, and cover-ups. President David O. McKay said, "To be trusted is a greater compliment than to be loved."[171] A strong marriage must have transparency and honesty—no exceptions.

Here are some behaviors to practice honesty, trust, and fidelity in your marriage:

- Open up to each other, and learn to share your deep feelings about each other, about life, church, family, friends, and so on. Opening up and sharing your life in depth will cultivate a habit of trusting each other with your feelings. It will also help you detect when things are not right with your partner.
- Make a commitment to your spouse that you will always tell them the truth, the complete truth—even when it's not convenient and even when it's painful.

- Never look at someone of the opposite sex in a romantic, sexual, or flirtatious way. To love your spouse with all your heart means with all of your devotion, passion, and energy. The Lord said, "Thou shalt love thy wife with all thy heart, and shalt cleave unto her and none else" (D&C 42:22). None else includes other men, other women, hobbies, recreation, and anything else you could think of except for God.

3. Be a responsible marriage partner.

To be happily married requires maturity. A mature marriage partner takes full responsibility for his or her spouse and the couple's happiness. I recently met a young married man who had taken little responsibility in his new marriage. His father bought the engagement ring for the future bride; his father pays their rent; his father pays for their food; his father pays their tuition; his father pays for their cell phones; in fact, his father pays for everything. The wife does have a job. Since all of their bills are being paid, she feels she should begin saving for their first child or a down payment on their home. Meanwhile, the husband stays home, watches television, and plays video games most of the day. He tries to attend school but ends up dropping out in the middle of every semester because things are too tough. Because of his lack of responsibility toward his spouse or their future, his wife has little respect for him. This is not the way a marriage should begin.

On the other hand, I know many young couples who work two jobs so they can support each other. Their days consist of working hard at a job, going to school, coming home and doing homework until midnight, and repeating this grueling schedule daily. Many of these couples drive used cars and live in basement apartments. However, since they are mature and responsible, they are happy.

Responsibility implies that you will help take care of each other and that your marriage will come first. Because of that, you may have to give up some hobbies. Furthermore, you are accountable for your actions that negatively impact the marriage. Therefore, to be responsible is to admit when you are wrong and to confess when you have made a mistake. Remember, when Jesus told His Apostles they would betray him, almost in unison, His Apostles said, "Lord, is it I?" (Matthew 26:22).

Ways to demonstrate responsibility in your marriage would include

- Doing the best you can to provide for yourselves so you can meet your expenditures honorably.

- Always seeking to understand the needs of your partner, and seeking to meet those needs.
- Being quick to apologize and be accountable when your marriage is struggling. Acknowledge your contribution to the problem and seek to fix it.
- Being prepared to take care of your spouse in sickness and health.

"The Family: A Proclamation to the World" reminds us, "Husband and wife have a solemn responsibility to love and care for each other and for their children." As marriage partners, we must be responsible for the nurturing of our spouse, and we must strive to make their life better and happier.

4. Be willing to be flexible in your marriage.

Another sign of maturity is flexibility—the ability to go with the flow and accept the hand that life deals you. Being flexible means accepting that you're not always right and that there may be better ways of doing things than what you suggested. Flexibility means that sometimes you may not get your way or you may have to alter your plans, your ideals, and your schedule. In marriage, you must learn how to lower your expectations and train yourself to be more realistic. Being flexible is a wonderful trait to learn to cultivate in marriage; it will become more necessary when you have children.

Here are some practices that could help you with flexibility:

- Don't be afraid to admit that the family you came from wasn't perfect. Take the best things from your family of origin, and do the same thing with your spouse's family. Take the best from both families to improve your lives as a couple.
- Don't get stuck in your own rigid beliefs and traditions. Just because you believe something needs to be done a certain way doesn't make it the right thing to do.
- Be open-minded, and seek to learn from each other.
- Learn to listen for understanding, not for words.
- Change things up every now and then just for the fun of it.

Perhaps your way of doing something isn't necessarily the best way. Avoid being a control freak by insisting that your spouse do everything the way you believe it should be done. Highly successful husbands and wives learn to be flexible, adapt to new situations, and just enjoy the ride. When marriage partners are too rigid and believe things have to be done a certain way, the fun and joy of marriage begins to evaporate.

5. Strip selfishness from your life, and seek to fulfill the needs of the other first.

The strongest marriages are marriages in which couples are selfless. Selfishness can destroy a marriage faster than anything else. President Spencer W. Kimball taught, "[In marriage] there must be a great unselfishness, forgetting self and directing all of the family life and all pertaining thereunto to the good of the family, subjugating self. . . . Total unselfishness is sure to accomplish another factor in successful marriage. If one is forever seeking the interests, comforts, and happiness of the other, the love found in courtship and cemented in marriage will grow into mighty proportions."[172]

Selflessness implies that you are willing to let your partner have what they need, that you can forgo your own wants and desires, that often you will not get what you want, and that you will put your best efforts into making your partner happy. Selfless partners serve their spouses.

In order to demonstrate selflessness in marriage, here are some behaviors to consider:

- Do things for your spouse without them having to ask you or tell you (e.g. dishes, vacuuming, ironing, cleaning, putting gas in car, taking garbage out, making meals, etc.).
- Ask your spouse what they need from you or how you can help them each day, and then seek to meet their needs.
- If you are a husband with children, take your kids to the park or on outings to get them out of your wife's hair. Give her a breather.
- Wives, if your husbands are extremely busy, see what you can do to lighten their load.
- Surprise each other, date each other, and serve each other.

A spirit of selflessness, generosity, and service should be cultivated in every marriage. President Spencer W. Kimball taught, "Some think of happiness [in marriage] as a glamorous life of ease, luxury, and constant thrills; but true marriage is based on happiness which is more than that, one which comes from giving, serving, sharing, sacrificing, and selflessness."[173]

6. Communicate in positive ways that matter to your partner.

Strong marriages are made up of couples who communicate often and positively. Marriage partners can get into bad habits of rarely communicating, talking only superficially, or being critical and negative with each other. In strong and healthy marriages, couples freely compliment and nurture each other.

Establish rituals in your marriage where you can talk and communicate deeply. Go for walks, or take time after dinner to connect. When you are together, make sure you build each other up with praise and compliments. Create a positive atmosphere in your home by the way you talk to each other. Taking time to talk is essential in building a strong and happy marriage.

You can practice strong communication in your marriage by doing the following:

- Say something positive and complimentary to your spouse each day. Be sincere when you do this.
- Practice asking your spouse questions and then listening in such a way that they cannot doubt your love for them.
- Find a time of day when you can talk to each other without any interruptions.
- Go for walks, and share your dreams and goals.
- Speak to each other kindly, positively, hopefully, and encouragingly.

7. Demonstrate empathy toward your spouse.

Nurturing marriage partners are empathetic. They understand the needs, concerns, and challenges of their spouse. Instead of being demanding, apathetic, or critical, a partner with empathy will listen and demonstrate to their spouse that they understand. Sympathy is when you feel sorry for someone; however, empathy means you can relate to them because you have been there and experienced what they have encountered. Ask yourself, "What is my spouse feeling right now?" Learn to put yourself in their shoes.

Years ago, I worked a late second job at a hospital where I was on call for psychiatric care. Often, after working a full day at my main job, I would then go work eight or nine hours at a hospital. I would leave for my first job at seven a.m. and not get home until after eleven p.m. three nights per week. The first thing I would do when I arrived home was look to see what the family had for dinner that night. Most of the time, Janie left me some great food on a plate, and I did the dumbest thing in the world—I sat down and ate a four-course meal at eleven thirty p.m.—just before going to bed. Yes, I did gain some weight at this time.

Occasionally, however, I would come home and there wouldn't be any food left out. Apparently Janie forgot, and I would often get upset about this. Rarely did I demonstrate empathy by realizing that Janie had six kids to manage by herself on those evenings when I was away working. She had lessons and activities to take them to, homework to help with, and then the herculean task of getting them all ready for bed—without my help. When I began thinking in those terms, I became much more forgiving and understanding. True empathy occurs when we can imagine what our partner is going through.

Learn to be positive, respectful, and patient towards your partner. Show your spouse that you understand them; demonstrate sensitivity. Men, if your wife is crying, don't roll your eyes and turn up the sound on the television. Hold her, and wipe away those tears. Ask her what you can do to help. Often, you will simply need to listen.

Wives, your husband may not ask to share his concerns, but create a safe atmosphere where he can do that without being judged. Be willing to share experiences to demonstrate that you understand where he is coming from. If you cannot do that, at least express your sorrow for what has happened. Seek for the Spirit so you can understand your spouse and know their needs. Pray for their successes and challenges.

Here are some ways to demonstrate empathy in a marriage:

- Practice the skill of imagining what your partner's day must be like.
- Learn to become interested in your spouse's point of view and in how they are feeling.
- Validate your partner's feelings, and show them that you truly understand.

The Apostle Paul said, "Rejoice with them that do rejoice, and weep with them that weep" (Romans 12:15). Dr. Carlfred Broderick further explained, "The principle of empathy is at the core of all satisfactory communication. Each of us hungers for a resonant soul that will affirm our joy and share our sorrow. Yet, in the hurly-burly of life, it is easy to miss our cues or find ourselves in a non-responsive mood. For myself, I have tried to make it a rule that nothing I am doing at the moment outranks my wife's claim upon me when she is joyous or despondent."[174]

8. Express admiration to your spouse.

Strong marriages are a mutual admiration society. It is not enough to admire a spouse from a distance; you must communicate your admiration. Expressions of admiration would inspire all of us to improve even more. If my wife tells me I can run fast, then I promise you I will try to run even faster. If I tell my wife she is the most amazing cook, then the next day we will have a meal that is even better than the night before. One marriage expert wrote, "Seeing the best in . . . your spouse is a priceless gift. . . . Recognizing the best in each other is one of the surest ways to encourage the goodness in each other. There is no better way to inspire people to be their best than recognizing the times when they are at their best."[175]

Expressing admiration to your spouse is a low-cost activity that yields high dividends. Try it! How difficult is it—what do you have to sacrifice—to tell your spouse, "I admire the way you handle yourself in front of a group," or, "I believe you have great leadership skills"? Too many people never express such kindnesses to the person they love the most.

You can practice admiration in your marriage by

- Writing a note to your spouse and sharing with them what you admire about them.
- Sending your spouse an e-mail or text and telling them why you look up to them.
- Sometimes, telling others about how you admire your spouse can be extremely important. Especially share these positive traits with your children.
- Express your admiration at least weekly.

Remember, love is like a flower, and it will only grow if it is fed, nourished, watered, and weeded!

9. **Demonstrate affection to your spouse in the way he or she would like to receive it.**

All of us want to be loved; we all want and need some kind of affection. The challenge is to show your spouse you love them in the manner they want to receive such love. Discover your spouse's love language, and speak that language to them. If your spouse needs physical affection, find out specifically what kind of affection they need and meet that need. If they need verbal expressions of love, then meet that need.

Hold hands with each other in public and private places; put your arms around each other when you walk. Don't be afraid to let your children catch you kissing each other in the kitchen. If your spouse's love language is acts of service, you can show affection by cleaning the house, fixing up the garage, pulling weeds in the yard, cooking, or taking care of the children. If your spouse's love language is time, you need to get on a date quickly!

Ways of showing affection include

- Physical gestures, such as holding hands, touching, and many other things.

- Giving gifts, spending time together, and saying wonderful things to each other.
- Making sure you go on weekly dates.
- Treating each other with the same kindness and courtesy you would have demonstrated on your first date.
- Writing love notes to each other.

President Spencer W. Kimball said, "I think [the Lord] smiles when he sees young husbands and wives, and older ones, with deep affection for each other, who continue their courtship as our prophet has said, who continue to love each other with all their souls until the day they die and then accentuate it through eternity."[176]

10. Strengthen the companionship in your marriage by being best friends.

The best marriage relationships are those in which the couple treasures their time together. They have developed a friendship where they enjoy each other's company. Simply put, married couples should be best friends. The Prophet Joseph Smith taught that husbands and wives "should be . . . companions, the nearest and dearest objects on earth in every sense of the word."[177]

Dear companions share their goals and dreams. They recognize each other's strengths and weaknesses, and they love each other unconditionally. They understand their roles. They can discuss anything. They miss each other when one of them is away. They would rather be with each other than anyone else.

The following practices will help you become better friends:
- Develop a hobby or an interest that you can both enjoy together.
- Find something that neither of you are good at; then, do it together. For example, build a model, assemble a puzzle, build a tree house, or make a gourmet meal.
- Get in the habit of talking every night before you go to bed—tell each other about your day, even if it's the most mundane thing in the world.
- Do fun things together as a couple, especially activities that will get you outdoors and away from your home base or comfort zone.

President James E. Faust taught, "We build our marriages with endless friendship, confidence, and integrity and also by ministering to and sustaining each other in our difficulties."[178] You married your best friend;

now continue to build that friendship into the greatest relationship life has to offer.

11. Learn how to deal with stress and crisis as a couple.

Just because you're happily married or married in the temple doesn't guarantee your life will be void of stress and challenges. Unfortunately, I have been a firsthand witness to many couples who have allowed their marriages to implode after a challenging or stressful event. Many couples pull away from each other instead of pulling together when a crisis comes.

Strong couples learn to rely on each other and the Lord when stresses occur. They recognize the resources in each other and learn to comfort and help each other. The ability to handle stress and crisis when they come is a mark of maturity. No marriage will be immune to hardships, disappointments, obstacles, or frustrations. If you want to be strong, you will need to learn to gain a proper perspective. Going through stress and trauma as a couple can bring you closer together—you will be able to empathize with each other. Moreover, surviving stress and trauma together has a way of binding people.

Here are some suggestions to deal with crisis and stress in your marriage:

- Fill your spiritual reservoirs by reading the scriptures, studying general conference talks, fasting, praying, attending the temple, and living the gospel. When difficult things occur, you will be prepared to face them head on.
- Identify the strengths you both have when stress occurs. Learn to rely on each other's strengths to pull you through.
- As a couple, create some down time. Just as important as playing and working together is learning how to relax together.

One of the greatest bonds that can be forged in marriage is when adversity strikes. This gives you an opportunity to pool your resources—your mental, emotional, and spiritual resources—and work together as a team. With the Lord's help, you will find that together the two of you can be stronger than you ever imagined.

12. Incorporate spirituality and values in your marriage and family.

The strongest marriage relationships in America are founded on religion and spirituality. Typically, when couples share the same religious convictions, their marriages will be stronger when compared to those who are not religious or have differing values. As Latter-day Saints, we understand that couples can be bonded emotionally and spiritually by studying and living the gospel together.

As we individually draw closer to the Savior, we will become more kind, more charitable, and more in tune to the needs of our spouse. The teachings of the Savior become the focal point for building a strong and successful marriage.

Couples should pray together, read scriptures as a team, attend the temple, discuss the gospel, help each other in callings, and teach the gospel to their children. President Spencer W. Kimball taught,

> If two people love the Lord more than their own lives and then love each other more than their own lives, working together in total harmony with the gospel program as their basic structure, they are sure to have this great happiness. When a husband and wife go together frequently to the holy temple, kneel in prayer together in their home with their family, go hand in hand to their religious meetings, keep their lives wholly chaste—mentally and physically—so that their whole thoughts and desires and loves are all centered in the one being, their companion, and both work together for the upbuilding of the kingdom of God, then happiness is at its pinnacle.[179]

Here are some practical ways to bring spirituality into your marriage:
- Attend firesides, conferences, and spiritual workshops together. Janie and I have enjoyed attending Education Week at Brigham Young University for years.
- When you read the scriptures together, discuss principles, and ask for each other's opinions.
- Pray together as a couple each night and morning. It is difficult to be mad at each other when you are praying for each other.
- Occasionally read each other's patriarchal blessings with the intent to treat your spouse as the Lord sees them.
- Worship in the temple together.
- Read good Church books together.
- Teach your children as a companionship.

In 1 Corinthians, Paul taught, "Neither is the man without the woman, neither the woman without the man, in the Lord" (11:11). Not only do we need each other as husbands and wives, but we need the Lord to be the centerpiece of the relationship. President James E. Faust taught,

"Having the companionship and enjoying the fruits of a Holy and Divine Presence is the kernel of a great happiness in marriage. Spiritual oneness is the anchor. Slow leaks in the sanctifying dimension of marriage often cause marriages to become flat tires."[180]

This is your great opportunity to build a celestial marriage and create a heaven on earth with your children. You do not have to do this alone. You have each other, and the Lord will help you every step of the way. Turn to Him for strength, peace, and knowledge.

Homework:
- Discuss which principles mentioned in this chapter could strengthen your marriage.
- Which of these principles do you feel you are successful in presently?
- Where do you need the most work?

Additional Readings:
- Douglas E. Brinley, "What Happily Married Couples Do," *Ensign*, January 2012.
- John M. Gottman, *The Seven Principles for Making Marriage Work* (New York: Three Rivers Press, 1999).
- Bruce C. Hafen, *Covenant Hearts: Why Marriage Matters and How to Make it Last* (Salt Lake City: Deseret Book, 2013).

References

167 Marvin J. Ashton, *Ye Are My Friends* (Salt Lake City: Deseret Book, 1972), 11–12.

168 "The Family: A Proclamation to the World," 1995.

169 Ibid.

170 Victor L. Cline, *How to Make a Good Marriage Great: Ten Keys to a Joyous Relationship*, (New York: Walker and Company, 1987), 193.

171 David O. McKay, *Gospel Ideals: Selections from the Discourses of David O. McKay* (Salt Lake City: Deseret Book, 1953), 187.

172 Spencer W. Kimball, "Oneness in Marriage," *Ensign*, March 1977.

173 Ibid.

174 Carlfred Broderick, *One Flesh, One Heart: Putting Celestial Love into Your Temple Marriage* (Salt Lake City: Deseret Book, 1986), 42.

175 Blain J. Fowers, PhD, *Beyond the Myth of Marital Happiness* (San Francisco: Jossey-Bass, Inc., 2000), 168.

176 Spencer W. Kimball, *I Know That My Redeemer Lives* (Salt Lake City: Deseret Book, 1990), 186.

177 Hyrum L. Andrus & Helen Mae Andrus, *They Knew the Prophet* (Salt Lake City: Bookcraft, 1974), 139.

178 James E. Faust, *In the Strength of the Lord: The Life and Teachings of James E. Faust* (Salt Lake City: Deseret Book, 1999), 365.

179 Spencer W. Kimball, "Oneness in Marriage," *Ensign*, March 1977.

180 James E. Faust, *In the Strength of the Lord: The Life and Teachings of James E. Faust* (Salt Lake City: Deseret Book, 1999), 369.

CONCLUSION

"Marriage can be more an exultant ecstasy than the human mind can
conceive. This is within the reach of every couple, every person."
-President Spencer W. Kimball[181]

THIS BOOK DOES NOT HAVE all of the answers to a happy and successful
marriage. The most important lessons in your life will be learned from
personal experience and from the Holy Ghost. What I have tried to
provide in this work are principles, doctrines, and tools that will help to
strengthen your marriage relationship.

I believe every marriage can be successful if couples are willing to go
to work. Successful marriages require time, energy, and commitment. If
you hope to have a happy marriage, you must be willing to understand
each other's needs and try to meet them. Our Heavenly Father wants your
marriage to be successful and happy. If you approach Him in prayer, He
will quietly provide you with answers and strength. Over time, you will
learn to develop Christlike attributes that will bless your spouse, your
children, and your grandchildren.

I conclude with a lesson from my high school days. My senior year, I
was on the track team—I ran the 800-meter race. At this particular meet,
I had qualified for the finals, which were held in the evening under the
stadium lights. I wanted to have a great performance since the track meet
was in my home stadium. Friends and family had come to watch me
compete, and I didn't want to disappoint any of them.

However, the excitement of my last race in front of the home crowd
caused my adrenaline to surge. When the gun sounded, I took off at a fast
pace; I was doing my best to stay with the top runners in our district. I
knew I was running faster than usual, and that was concerning. As you may
know, when running the 800, it's important to save some of your energy
and strength for the last few hundred meters. As we were completing the

first lap, my coach called out the "split" time, and I knew I was in trouble. I had just run 400 meters faster than I ever had in my life. The good news was that I was running right next to some of the best 800-meter runners in the Houston area. The bad news was I still had 400 more meters to go.

The second lap didn't go as well as the first. These excellent runners began to pull out ahead of me. On that last back stretch, I completely ran out of energy. I went from running to jogging. I was able to reach deep inside myself and sprint down the last 100 meters, but by then, it was too late. The first three finishers received medals and went on to compete in regionals. I finished fourth. No medal, no ribbon, no regional meet. Instead of the glory I had hoped for, I finished my high school track career as an average runner.

I learned from that experience that how you start is not as important as how you finish; great beginnings are not as important as strong endings.[182] Likewise, marriage is not a sprint; it's a marathon. It really doesn't matter how your marriage begins, so pace yourself. How your marriage ends is the most important thing. Don't worry if your relationship isn't perfect in the beginning. You have a lot of track ahead of you. Take your time, be patient, and pace yourself. Creating a happy marriage is a process that takes time. Many newlyweds get frustrated because their "marriage isn't all it's cracked up to be." Your marriage isn't supposed to be perfectly incredible and fulfilling from the start, just as the first time you rode a bike, shot a free throw, played the piano, or taught a missionary discussion wasn't masterful. The idea is to improve and get stronger.

During the course of life, all of us need to change and improve. With each lap we run, we become stronger. Remember, you're in this for the long haul. Marriage is a lifelong commitment. Don't give up. Keep trying, keep improving, and keep loving. Over time, with each passing year, your marriage will continue to grow and improve.

I have been married to Janie for thirty years now. Our love continues to grow, and our relationship is stronger and more durable than it was when we began our life together. Like all couples, we have had our share of challenges and storms. However, here is a great truth: for all of us who are willing to put our marriage at the top of our priority list, marriage will be enriching, happy, joyful, and the most fulfilling experience this life has to offer. Keep going. Keep reaching. Keep trying. Don't quit or give up!

The poet Robert Browning wrote:

Grow old along with me!
The best is yet to be.[183]

References

181 President Spencer W. Kimball, *Teachings of Spencer W. Kimball*, ed. Edward L. Kimball (Salt Lake City: Bookcraft, 1982), 305–306.

182 This concept was borrowed from James Dobson, *Love for a Lifetime* (Sisters, Oregon: Multnomah, 2003), 110.

183 Robert Browning, Rabbi Ben Ezra; http://www.poetryfoundation.org/poem/173031.

ABOUT THE AUTHOR

 Mark D. Ogletree served an LDS mission from 1982 to 1984 in Seattle, Washington. He earned a bachelor of arts degree in 1987 from Brigham Young University; a master of arts in 1990 in educational psychology from Northern Arizona University; a master of arts in mental health counseling in 1994 from Northern Arizona University; and a PhD in 2000 in family and human development from Utah State University.

Dr. Ogletree taught in the Church Educational System for twenty-one years. He worked as a seminary instructor and principal, an institute instructor, and finally as director of the Institute of Religion in Dallas, Texas. In 2010, Mark accepted a position at Brigham Young University as an associate professor in the Department of Church History and Doctrine. He teaches courses on preparing for marriage and teachings of the living prophets.

Mark has also worked in private practice for the past twenty years as a marriage and family therapist. Currently, he runs a part-time practice in Orem, Utah.

He has coauthored the following books: *First Comes Love*; *Then Comes Marriage*; *Courageous Parenting*; and *Raising an Army of Helaman's Warriors*.

In the Church, Mark has served most of his life in the young men's organization. He has also served on a stake high council and as a bishop in the McKinney Texas Stake. He was recently called as the bishop of the Sherwood Hills Ward in Provo, Utah.

Mark is married to the former Janie Cook, and they are the parents of eight children—all boys except for seven. Mark and Janie also enjoy five grandchildren. In addition to church activities, he enjoys playing racquetball, basketball, softball, and golf; writing; and remodeling his house.